CHARLES VIRION'S FRENCH COUNTRY COOKBOOK

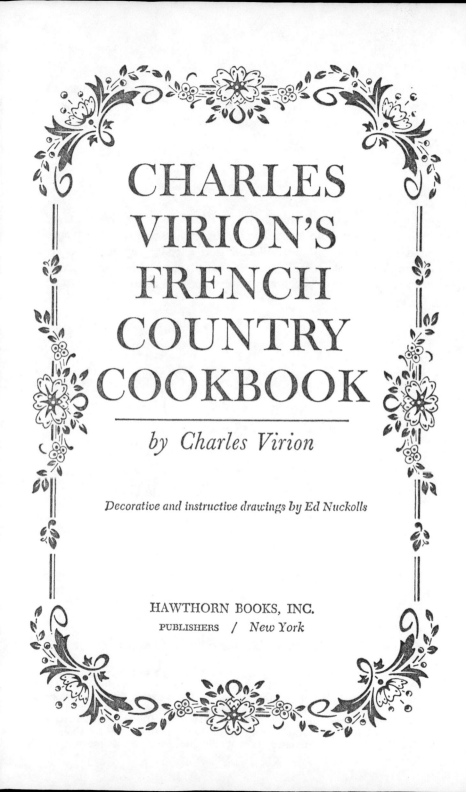

CHARLES VIRION'S FRENCH COUNTRY COOKBOOK

by Charles Virion

Decorative and instructive drawings by Ed Nuckolls

HAWTHORN BOOKS, INC.
PUBLISHERS / New York

I dedicate this book to my dear wife, Ethel, who has let me experiment in her kitchen for nearly four decades, who married me against her mother's advice: "Never should a girl marry a man who can cook," and who still has patience with me.

ACKNOWLEDGEMENTS

I owe this book to the many friends and former guests of Monblason Inn who wanted to try my recipes in their own homes and to Joan and Robert Bloom, who encouraged me to collect three decades of recipes. I owe special thanks to Joan Bloom, who has worked many long hours helping me test recipes and prepare the manuscript.

C. V.

CHARLES VIRION'S FRENCH COUNTRY COOKBOOK

Contents

Introduction

A FRENCH CHEF LOOKS BACKWARD
. . . AND FORWARD

Although the world is presently so concerned about air pollution, very few people seem to be alarmed about the degradation of their palates, or the dangers to their health due to the use of chemicals in preparing food. We have infringed on natural laws and have resorted to foods in which vitamins and minerals have been eliminated. Chemists, food processors, and packers have taken over and dictated what we can eat. The result has been a bland and unnutritious disaster.

In my youth, I spent many happy days at my grandparents' farm in the French province of Lorraine. It was in the era when a farm's products went directly to the consumer's table without being subjected to technical expediency. Baking every ten days was a great event. The brick oven was the baker's cathedral. From it came outstanding breads, quiches, tarts, and *pâtés en croute* with the delicious taste of yeast, organic butter and eggs, very fresh heavy cream, and unbleached flour. These natural ingredients made an excellent bread with a hearty crust— the necessary roughage so important to our health.

The farmers used only horse and cow manure for their crops. Pesticides were not used outside the vineyards. The chickens were fed only grain, and the calves drank only the milk of their mothers for many weeks. Pigs were fed skimmed milk mixed with boiled potatoes, grain, and green vegetables. Vegetables and fruits grown for the consumer's table had to be naturally ripened before they could be marketed.

No wonder La Grande Cuisine Française started in the farm country—look at the ingredients with which the French housewives were able to work.

Today, in this country, the goal of the general food industry has shifted away from quality and turned instead toward: unnatural, year-round availability of produce; unnatural quantity of produce, even if artificially induced; and unnatural physical appearance of produce, even if contrary to quality considerations. For example, living in the country as we do, we can easily find nice strawberries, juicy melons, fresh corn, and tasty ripe tomatoes in season. Off season, it is another story. Color may have been added, fruits may have been taken out of storage, or tomatoes may have been picked green. After sitting several days at the market, fruits and vegetables may still be for sale, but more often than not, they are unpalatable and unnutritional.

In addition, most eggs sold on the market are produced by inorganically fed chickens who are forced to lay eggs both day and night. The results of this unnatural schedule are eggs produced in greater quantities—but which are deficient in many other ways. I know; for years I used organic eggs in my kitchen at Monblason Inn in Pine Plains, New York. The chickens that laid these eggs were fed organic food, would rise with the sun, and go to sleep at sundown. The results were seen in my omelets, cakes, soufflés, and crêpes—our guests were really appreciative.

During my eleven years as owner-chef of Monblason Inn, I was amazed at the high percentage of guests who were sincerely worried about the conditions presently existing in the food industry, and the great deterioration in eating habits. These people are part of a growing number of Americans who, through education and travel, have developed a serious interest in eating well-prepared food. They are anxious to enlarge their knowledge of fine recipes, but they realize that the first step toward an excellent Tomatoes Provençales, for instance, is a first-class, fresh, ripe tomato, and the only way to produce a memorable Escalopes de Veau au Beurre is to use prime, milk-fed veal.

Unfortunately, these people receive very little encouragement when they go to the average market to buy ingredients. The market's employee knows nothing about food, cooking, or the relationship between the two. His work is to put the goods on the shelf, then mark the prices and wait at the cash register for the housewives to pay him. Thus it is quite an ordeal for the consumer to select the best-quality meat, vegetables, fish, fruits, and cheese for a healthful and tasty meal. Fortunately, there are some food producers who are still raising top-grade fruits, vegetables, and meats agreeable to the palates of the discriminating public. In most areas there are a few stores a cut above the general food market, where the owners do buy from top-grade producers.

Find a good butcher who handles milk-fed veal, prime beef, selected poultry, and pork. Certainly he will charge you more per unit than the supermarket, but the extra cost is returned to you in higher-quality meat—meat which cooks better, tastes better, has less waste, and is more nutritious. Explain what dish you want to prepare and for how many people, and your butcher will give you the most appropriate cut of meat. Always order meat in advance, with the understanding that you want the best. When it comes to vegetables, act in the same way. Be sure the produce comes to the store daily—the fresher, the better. In the off season, if good-quality, fresh vegetables are not available, buy frozen vegetables instead, and do not be ashamed to admit it. It is better to cook vegetables which are picked and frozen immediately, than to cook peas and string beans which are sold in the market when they are a week old. Once quality ingredients are gathered, there are no deep secrets to cooking.

For my friends I have adapted French country cooking to the availability of American products and ingredients, and I have incorporated methods that will not intimidate the average American who wants to improve his cuisine. In a few instances, I have gone somewhat beyond good, simple French rural cooking and included more elaborate, delicate recipes for fancy occasions. I have deliberately omitted some fine recipes which I believe should be demonstrated in cooking schools, such as Quenelles de Brochet, Canard Pressé, brioches, and croissants.

I began to appreciate good food early in my youth. This appreciation was based on the blessings of a good palate and membership in a family of excellent cooks. With these assets, I later became a self-made chef. My culinary career began because of the great depression following the 1929 Wall Street crash.

Beginning in the early 1930's, I cooked professionally for such employers as John Ringling North and Orson Welles. I retired in 1970 as chef-owner of Monblason Inn. I hope to explain here how homemakers and food lovers can learn to cook, as I did, without any professional training.

Remember, there are no great secrets or mysteries in creating good cuisine. Anyone with the proper approach and taste can become a good cook. I offer you some general guidelines.

Start slowly with simple recipes until you gain confidence in yourself. Experiment with recipes for dishes you have enjoyed in restaurants or in the homes of friends, which do not seem too complex or time-consuming. It is better to prepare an excellent stew than to make a poor Beef Wellington. If you are not satisfied with your preparation today, find out why and try again in a day or two. Confidence in yourself is primary. Even the greatest chefs have their failures.

One of the most vital elements in fine cooking is timing. No matter how good the ingredients are, they become useless without timing. Be sure to know how long it takes the dish to be done. Many meals are spoiled because they are overcooked. Remember that it is impossible to have complete standardization of timing and quantities except in baking. You will have to apply your own judgment and "taste" when you are in front of the stove. Perfection is hard to achieve. If you get the recipe right this time, do not relax the next time, or you won't get it right again!

Learn how to make your present kitchen equipment work nicely for you. I oppose the myths built up by leading manufacturers of kitchen equipment concerning the indispensable use of copper pots and pans, wire whisks, and soufflé dishes. Between the overly complex cookbooks and the manufacturers of "gourmet cookware," the willing cook often gets confused and discouraged. I have read and heard many times that the only way to make a good soufflé is to use a French wire whisk for beating egg whites stiff. I do not want you to get a nervous breakdown hunting for such a utensil. It is not necessary. I have made thousands of good soufflés with an electric mixer. And if you do not have a fancy soufflé dish, by all means use a Pyrex baking dish. I have tried both, and they both work well. As for copper utensils, they are excellent, but until you get your first star as a cook do not go and spend a small fortune to implement your kitchen. If you want to make a light omelet, do not buy an expensive French omelet pan—try a Teflon frying pan with a wooden spatula. You can't go wrong.

When you peruse food magazines and cookbooks, pick recipes which appeal to your sense of taste. Then buy the best ingredients available. Try such recipes on your family, or friends, and watch for their reactions. You will soon find out what is wrong with your cooking. Do not feel discouraged when you make mistakes. When I was ordered by my employers to prepare a dish I had never made before, I accepted the challenge. At first, I made unsatisfactory béarnaise sauce, hollandaise sauce which curdled under my fingers, and chocolate mousse that separated. Yet I was always determined to discover the reasons for my failures and correct them the next time.

When you visit a well-known restaurant, behave like a clever spy. Be nosy, inquisitive, and constantly on the alert. You can learn a great deal about cooking this way. Remember every detail when you start tasting the food: how it looks on the plate, what ingredients were used, the blending of flavors, whether it is overdone, or not done enough. Do not be impressed by a flamboyant name on the menu. You do not put a name in a casserole and make an excellent dish out of it. Some culinary writers, restaurant owners, and chefs make the public feel that their recipes are unique, unattainable, and only for professionals. For example, I had heard for years that Oysters Rockefeller as served at Antoine's in New Orleans was a culinary feat. Then one evening I tried them there. They were good but could have been duplicated easily by an amateur cook.

Novice cooks often take recipes too seriously. If they are short of a certain spice, or if their wine does not come from a certain section of the world as the recipe requires, they panic and feel like rushing to the nearest caterer. You must develop the confidence to make reasonable substitutions. In our own homes today, we do not all have the time to prepare stocks, a basic element of French country cooking. As a substitute, I discovered that there are some fairly good commercial consommés and stocks available, and that when some of our California cream sherries and port wines are added to them and simmered for two or three hours, the result is the base for excellent sauces.

In preparing this book, I have tried hard to eliminate unnecessary work and confusion in an effort to bring to your table excellent and substantial food. However, I cannot compromise with basic ingredients like butter, cream, and time. My book is not for those who diet, but for the majority of us who travel on our stomachs. If calories are important, eat less but not less well.

I sincerely hope that my attempt to bring a better understanding of meals impeccably cooked and served will give you great pleasure. As both a summary of this introduction and a starting point for the book, I offer to you:

Ten Commandments for Becoming a Good Cook

1. Cultivate a refined taste by exposure to as much good, varied food as possible.
2. Develop the determination to become a good cook.
3. Be prepared to spend the necessary time.
4. Buy the best available ingredients.
5. Do not undertake more than you can do well.
6. Choose good recipes and trust in them.
7. Have confidence in your ability to duplicate good dishes that others have made.
8. Use your imagination and make substitutions, if necessary.
9. Follow timing directions closely.
10. Do not be discouraged by failure. Try again!

Special Notes

On Canned Foods

You are taking too much of a risk if you buy badly dented or rusted cans of food. Do not rely on your sense of smell or taste to detect spoiled food. Botulism, that terrible poison, can be present without affecting odor or taste. Bring any cans you suspect to be seriously damaged to the attention of the store manager immediately. Someone not as careful as you may use the product and come to grief.

The danger signals are obvious:

1. The shape of the can is out of line; it bulges. The swell may give under pressure, but sometimes it is so hard it won't give even when considerable force is applied.

2. If you press on the top or bottom of the can and it indents with a pop, then let up and it pops out, something is wrong.

3. Watch out for leaks. Small dents in a can are no cause for alarm, but a large dent may have fractured the lining inside the can, bringing the food into contact with the bare metal. Sometimes a dent may open the seam of the can and cause a leak.

4. Rust is another danger sign and may be caused by liquid or water from outside the can or by a leak from inside the can. Even more serious, the contents may have become highly acidic and may have eaten right through the metal.

On Grated Cheeses

Imported Swiss Gruyère cheese and Norwegian Jarlsberg cheese are the best cheeses to use for grating and for "au gratin" dishes. I am not fond of using Parmesan, for too often the flavor is so strong that it detracts from the fundamental taste of the main ingredients, and sometimes the Parmesan cheese that is available already grated is old and stale and may spoil an otherwise delicious recipe.

CHARLES VIRION'S FRENCH COUNTRY COOKBOOK

CHAPTER 1

Stocks and Sauces

Fonds et Sauces

Fonds Brun
Demi-Glace
Fonds Blanc
Fonds de Poisson ou Fumet

Sauce Béchamel
Sauce Velouté
Sauce Suprême
Sauce Mornay
Sauce Blanche aux Champignons
Sauce de Tomates à la Provençale

Sauce Brune
Sauce Robert
Sauce Brune aux Champignons
Sauce au Madère
Sauce Bordelaise

Sauce Hollandaise
Sauce Mousseline
Sauce Béarnaise

Sauce Mayonnaise
Sauce Verte
Sauce Rémoulade
Sauce Vinaigrette
Sauce Salade
Sauce Ravigote

Beurre à la Maître d'Hôtel

❊

Crème Chantilly
Crème à la Vanille
Crème à l'Anglaise
Sauce au Chocolat

Fonds Brun
Brown Stock

I remember, alas too long ago, visions of the great French country kitchens where kettles of leftovers were simmering on the back of the stove. Into the kettles were thrown all available bones and scraps and out of it came the incomparable broth which gave delicious French country dishes their lift to perfection.

On the farm, my grandmother was not extravagant. Money was scarce and thrift was a necessity. When ordering a roast from the butcher, she would make certain that some raw beef and veal bones were added at no cost so that she could make a brown stock. You can do the same today. If you have the time and inclination, ask your butcher for veal and beef bones and try making your own brown stock.

You with little time for cooking can use the commercial varieties of canned stock. One or two large soup manufacturers have excellent canned beef stock, consommé, and bouillon. They are high in beef content, and when simmered with certain wines as indicated in the recipes which follow, they make a good base for sauces.

However, for those of you who want to use a homemade stock rather than a canned variety, here is my grandmother's recipe for French country-style brown stock.

MAKES 6 CUPS.

6 *pounds cracked veal and beef bones*
½ *pound suet or fat*
4 *large carrots, sliced*
4 *large onions, sliced*
4 *parsnips, sliced*
3 *quarts water*
2 *celery stalks, sliced*
1 *bay leaf*
3 *sprigs of parsley*
¼ *teaspoon thyme*
6 *peppercorns*
1 *teaspoon salt*

1. Place the bones and suet in a large roasting pan and roast them in a preheated 400° oven, stirring them often, for about 1 hour.

2. Then add 3 carrots, 3 onions, and 2 parsnips, all sliced. Reduce the heat to 350° and continue roasting until the bones and vegetables are well browned and the natural juices are caramelized. Do not allow the vegetables to burn, for this will completely spoil the taste of your broth. You want sweetness, not bitterness.

3. Remove the suet and place the bones in a large kettle, discarding the browned vegetables.

4. Pour a quart of water into the roasting pan to rinse it well, as some of the flavor of the stock will remain in the pan. Then pour the roasting-pan water into the kettle over the bones and add 2 more quarts of water.

5. Add the remaining sliced carrots, onions, and parsnips plus the celery, bay leaf, parsley, thyme, peppercorns, and salt.

6. Cover and simmer for 3 hours. Taste the stock. If it is not of the right flavor or consistency, uncover the kettle and cook it a little longer until the quality of a good soup or stock has been reached.

7. Strain the broth through cheesecloth. After it has been strained, let it cool for about 2 hours at room temperature and then refrigerate overnight. In the morning remove the congealed fat with a knife. Refrigerate the stock until it is ready to be used.

Demi-Glace
Meat Glaze

Meat glaze is made by reducing brown stock by a long, slow simmering process in an uncovered kettle to a thick concentrated gelatin. The glaze can be frozen and kept for many weeks. It has such an intense beef flavor that recipes that call for meat glaze usually require a very small quantity. Avoid using commercial meat glazes, such as bouillon cubes. They contain far too little beef and are exceedingly salty.

Fonds Blanc
White Stock

White stock is made by slowly simmering veal, cracked veal bones, chicken parts, nonstarchy vegetables, spices and herbs, and water. The slow simmering is very important—the stock must never be boiled rapidly.

White stock is used for braising meats, vegetables, stews, and fricassees. The longer the simmering, the stronger the flavor will be. After removing the bones, meats, and vegetables and straining the liquid, the stock can be simmered and reduced even more and used as a concentrated flavor-booster for white sauce, velouté sauce, and glazing.

MAKES 10 CUPS.

2 *to 3 pounds shoulder of veal*
3 *pounds veal knuckle*
4 *pounds chicken feet and wings, back and giblets*
2 *tablespoons salt*
5 *quarts water*
4 *medium-sized carrots, quartered*
4 *medium-sized white onions, peeled*
3 *ribs celery*
2 *leeks*
Bouquet garni: 5 sprigs parsley, 2 small bay leaves;
      tie together in a piece of cheesecloth

¼ *teaspoon thyme*
1 *5-pound roasting or stewing chicken (optional)* *

1. Bone the veal; crack the bones and place in a 10-quart sauce-pan, with the veal knuckle, chicken parts, salt, and water.
2. Bring to a boil; skim off the scum and discard.
3. Clean and peel the vegetables and add to the meat along with the bouquet garni and the thyme.
4. Bring again to a boil and cover partially with a lid.
5. Reduce the heat and simmer slowly 3½ hours or more. Do not let stock boil.
6. When the stock is ready, strain through fine cheesecloth and refrigerate until the fat has hardened on the surface and can be easily lifted off.

Fonds de Poisson ou Fumet
Fish Stock or Fumet

MAKES 2 CUPS.

Bouquet garni: 2 stalks celery, 5 sprigs parsley, 1 large bay leaf
Bones and 2 heads of any white-meat fish
1 *8-ounce bottle clam juice*
1 *cup clear White Stock (p. 6) or canned chicken consommé*
1 *cup dry white wine*
2 *cups water*
4 *carrots, sliced*
2 *onions, sliced*
¼ *teaspoon thyme*
12 *peppercorns*
1 *teaspoon salt*

1. Make a bouquet garni by tying the celery, parsley, and bay leaf together in a piece of cheesecloth.
2. Put the bouquet garni, fish bones and heads, clam juice, White Stock, white wine, water, carrots, onion, thyme, peppercorns, and salt in

* If you want a stronger chicken stock, you can add a chicken to the pot while stock is cooking. When the chicken is tender, set it aside for the Capon with Suprême Sauce (p. 225) or Chicken Fricassee with Suprême Sauce (p. 218). Then continue to simmer the stock until it is full flavored.

a large saucepan. Bring to a boil, and simmer uncovered for 45 minutes.

3. Strain stock through cheesecloth. Cool and keep it in the refrigerator, well covered, until you are ready to use it for poaching fish or as a base for sauces with fish dishes. The stock can also be frozen for future use.

Sauces

Sauces are of prime importance in French cuisine. A complete listing of French sauces would be voluminous, but when you look closely you will see that they all come from a few basic preparations. You will quickly learn how to use the same methods with different ingredients to produce a variety of sauces.

The use of high quality ingredients is extremely important. White or brown stocks are used frequently as a base for sauces. Homemade stocks always give excellent results, but there are also several brands of canned chicken and beef consommés and stocks which are quite good. However, keep away from the beef or chicken bouillon cubes.

Sauces can be classified in four categories:

1. Sauces that accompany hot main courses and are made with a stock, e.g., brown sauce, Bordelaise, or velouté.

2. Emulsion-type sauces that are made with egg yolks and oil or butter, e.g., hollandaise, mousseline, béarnaise, or mayonnaise.

3. Salad and cold-appetizer dressings, e.g., French dressing or vinaigrette.

4. Fruit and dessert sauces, e.g., English custard, chocolate sauce, caramel sauce, or vanilla sauce.

Many sauces can be made in advance and kept under refrigeration, but sauces made with cream, milk, or eggs deteriorate quickly and should not be made more than a day in advance, unless they are to be frozen.

Adding Wines to Sauces

The addition of red or white wine, port, sherry, vermouth, Madeira, calvados, or cognac will heighten the character of your sauces. Two rules of thumb: Do not add wine or spirits to your sauce at the last minute, for they will give a harsh taste to your sauce. The alcohol present in the wine or spirits must be evaporated during the cooking, and then the flavor remains. Also, remember that the wine or brandy you use should be of fine quality, because their flavor is of utmost importance in determining the taste. A wine that is unfit for drinking should never be used for cooking. It is better to omit the wine altogether if you do not have a good brand.

Making a Roux

The first step in preparing a white sauce—béchamel, velouté, or suprême—to be used with delicate ingredients like fish, eggs, or chicken is to make a roux (flour-butter mixture) and stir and cook it only until it is a light golden color. This operation eliminates the raw flour taste from the sauce and also prevents the formation of lumps. Gradually add liquid, usually milk or cream, sometimes combined with some light stock, stirring until you have a smooth thick sauce.

For heavier sauces like a French brown sauce or a demi-glace sauce, the roux should be cooked until it is a darker brown. Brown stock should be added as the liquid. The longer the flour is cooked with the butter, the less thickening power it will have, so recipes using brown sauces usually require about 50 percent more flour than those for white sauces.

Sauce Béchamel
Béchamel Sauce

MAKES 2 CUPS.

4 *tablespoons sweet butter*
4 *tablespoons flour*
2 *cups light cream, heated, or* 1 *cup milk and* 1 *cup*
    heavy cream, heated
½ *teaspoon salt*
Pinch freshly ground white pepper

1. Melt the butter in a heavy saucepan and blend in the flour.
2. Stir and cook over low heat for 2 minutes, until the roux is golden, but not brown.

3. Add the hot cream, a little at a time, stirring to make a smooth sauce. Cook 1 minute longer. Season with the salt and pepper.

Sauce Velouté
Velouté Sauce

___

MAKES 2 CUPS.

4 *tablespoons sweet butter*
4 *tablespoons flour*
2 *cups White Stock (p. 6) or canned chicken consommé*
½ *teaspoon salt*
Pinch freshly ground white pepper

1. Melt the butter in a heavy saucepan and blend in the flour.
2. Stir and cook over low heat for 2 minutes, until the roux is golden but not brown.
3. Add the White Stock or consommé slowly, stirring to make a smooth sauce. Cook 1 minute longer. Season with the salt and pepper.

Sauce Suprême
Suprême Sauce

___

This rich velouté sauce can be prepared in advance. It is usually served with chicken, veal, eggs, vegetables, or fish.

MAKES 6 TO 7 CUPS.

1 *cup sweet butter*
1 *cup flour*
4 *cups White Stock (p. 6) or canned chicken consommé,*
   heated
1 *cup heavy cream*
3 *egg yolks, beaten*
Salt and freshly ground white pepper to taste
Juice of ½ lemon

1. Melt ¾ cup of the butter in a heavy saucepan. Add the flour.

2. Stir and cook over low heat for 1 minute until the roux is golden, but not brown.

3. Add the hot White Stock or chicken consommé, a little at a time, to make a smooth sauce.

4. Add the cream and blend thoroughly.

5. Add the beaten egg yolks and blend. Simmer 2 minutes, stirring constantly. Do not let it boil.

6. Taste for seasoning, adding salt and pepper if necessary. Add lemon juice.

7. Just before serving, swirl in the extra 4 tablespoons of butter.

Sauce Mornay
Mornay Sauce

MAKES APPROXIMATELY 3 CUPS.

2 cups Béchamel Sauce (p. 9)
¾ to 1 cup White Stock (p. 6) or canned chicken consommé
¾ cup grated Swiss Gruyère cheese
Salt and freshly ground white pepper to taste

1. Prepare Béchamel Sauce as instructed.

2. Add the White Stock and grated cheese and stir until the cheese is melted and well blended. Add additional salt and pepper to taste.

Sauce Blanche aux Champignons
White Mushroom Sauce

MAKES 2 CUPS.

½ pound sliced mushrooms
1½ tablespoons sweet butter
1½ cups Béchamel Sauce (p. 9)

1. Sauté the mushrooms in the butter until tender, but not browned.

2. Strain the mushrooms and add them to the Béchamel Sauce. Heat and serve.

Sauce Tomates à la Provençale
Tomato Sauce Provençale

Serve this sauce with fish, eggs, chicken, or meat.

MAKES 3 CUPS.

6 *tablespoons olive oil*
4 *shallots, finely minced*
2 *cloves garlic, finely minced*
1 *quart canned tomatoes*
1½ *cups White Stock (p. 6) or canned chicken consommé*
1½ *teaspoons sugar*
½ *cup chopped fresh parsley*
Salt and freshly ground black pepper to taste

1. Heat the oil in a heavy saucepan and sauté the shallots and garlic in it until they are tender, but not browned.
2. Add the tomatoes, White Stock or consommé, sugar, and parsley and simmer slowly for 1 hour, or until the sauce has thickened. Season with some salt and pepper and strain through a sieve.

Sauce Brune
Brown Sauce

MAKES 2 CUPS.

1 *carrot, minced*
1 *stalk celery, minced*
2 *small white onions, minced*
5 *tablespoons sweet butter*
1 *bay leaf*
¼ *teaspoon thyme*
1 *tablespoon chopped fresh parsley*
1 *clove garlic, mashed*

4 *tablespoons flour*
4 *cups Brown Stock (p. 4) or canned beef consommé, heated*
2 *tablespoons tomato paste*
Salt and freshly ground black pepper

1. Sauté the carrot, celery, and onions in 1 tablespoon of the butter until slightly browned. Add the bay leaf, thyme, parsley, and garlic and cook 1 minute longer. Set aside.

2. In a saucepan over moderate heat, melt the remaining 4 tablespoons butter and add the flour. Stir and cook until the roux is golden, but not brown.

3. Gradually stir in the hot Brown Stock or consommé. Blend well.

4. Add the vegetables and tomato paste and simmer gently for 2 hours, covered.

5. If the sauce is too thin, continue to simmer, uncovered, until it becomes the right consistency. If the sauce is too thick, add a bit more stock. Taste for seasoning. Strain and discard vegetables.

Sauce Robert
Sauce Robert

Serve this sauce with pork chops or sautéed calf's liver.

MAKES 2¼ CUPS.

3 *white onions, finely minced*
2 *tablespoons sweet butter*
¾ *cup dry white wine*
1½ *tablespoons wine vinegar*
1 *cup Brown Sauce (p. 12) or canned beef consommé*
2 *tablespoons tomato puree*
1 *tablespoon Dijon mustard*
2 *tablespoons finely chopped fresh parsley*
1 *tablespoon finely chopped sour pickles*
Salt and freshly ground black pepper to taste

1. Sauté the onions in the butter until slightly browned.

2. Add the wine and vinegar and simmer, uncovered, until reduced to ½ cup.

3. Stir in the Brown Sauce or consommé and tomato puree. Simmer for another 15 minutes.

4. Add the mustard, parsley, and pickles. Season with the salt and pepper.

Sauce Brune aux Champignons
Brown Mushroom Sauce

MAKES 2 CUPS.

½ *pound sliced fresh mushrooms*
1½ *tablespoons sweet butter*
1½ *cups Brown Sauce* (*p.* 12)

1. Sauté the mushrooms in the butter until tender, but not browned.

2. Strain the mushrooms and add them to the Brown Sauce. Heat and serve.

Sauce au Madère
Madeira Sauce

Serve with fillet of beef.

MAKES 3 CUPS.

End pieces cut from the fillet of beef
8 *tablespoons sweet butter*
5 *shallots, minced*
2 *cups Brown Stock* (*p.* 4) *or canned beef consommé*
½ *cup Madeira wine*
6 *sprigs parsley*
1 *bay leaf*
¼ *teaspoon thyme*
2 *tablespoons flour*

1 *pound fresh mushrooms, sliced and sautéed in butter*
1 *truffle, sliced*

1. Cut the two ends of the fillet in small pieces and sauté them in 6 tablespoons butter until the meat is cooked and nicely browned.

2. Add the minced shallots and sauté them until slightly browned.

3. Add the Brown Stock or consommé, Madeira wine, parsley sprigs, bay leaf, and thyme. Bring to a boil. Reduce heat and simmer for 1 hour. Strain the liquid.

4. Melt 2 tablespoons butter; add 2 tablespoons flour; stir and cook together slowly until golden. Add the strained Madeira-stock mixture slowly to make a smooth sauce. Simmer for ½ hour, then add the sliced, sautéed mushrooms and the sliced truffle.

Sauce Bordelaise
Bordelaise Sauce

MAKES ¾ CUP.

4 *shallots, minced*
3 *tablespoons sweet butter*
¾ *cup red wine*
Pinch of thyme
Pinch of marjoram
¾ *cup Brown Stock (p. 4) or canned beef consommé*
Few drops lemon juice
1 *tablespoon chopped fresh parsley*
Salt and freshly ground black pepper

1. Sauté the shallots in 2 tablespoons of the butter until they are transparent. Do not brown them.

2. Add the wine, thyme, and marjoram and simmer rapidly until reduced to ½ its quantity.

3. Add the Brown Stock or consommé and reduce again by half.

4. Add the lemon juice and parsley and simmer for 5 minutes. Strain and add the remaining tablespoon of butter. Season to taste with salt and pepper.

Sauce Hollandaise
Hollandaise Sauce

MAKES 1½ CUPS.

1 *cup sweet butter, softened*
4 *large egg yolks, beaten*
2 *tablespoons lemon juice*
Salt and freshly ground black pepper
Dash cayenne pepper

HOLLANDAISE
SAUCE.

1. Put ¼ cup of the butter into the top of a double boiler over hot, but not boiling, water.

2. Add the egg yolks and lemon juice.

3. Beat constantly with a wire whisk until the butter is melted.

4. Add another ¼ cup butter and stir. When the sauce thickens, add another ¼ cup butter. Continue stirring until the butter is absorbed. Add the last ¼ cup butter; stir and cook until the sauce has thickened even more. Immediately remove from the heat. Season to taste and stir.

NOTE: Should the sauce curdle, add 2 tablespoons boiling water, beating constantly to remake the emulsion.

Sauce Mousseline
Mousseline Sauce

MAKES 2 CUPS.

1½ cups Hollandaise Sauce (p. 16)
½ cup heavy cream, whipped

1. As soon as you have completed the Hollandaise Sauce and the last bit of butter is added, keep the sauce over the hot but not boiling water and add the whipped cream.
2. Stir 1 minute until well blended. Serve over poached fish.

Sauce Béarnaise
Béarnaise Sauce

MAKES 1½ CUPS.

4 shallots, minced
½ cup tarragon vinegar
4 egg yolks
¾ cup sweet butter, melted
3 teaspoons lemon juice
½ teaspoon minced fresh or ¼ teaspoon dried parsley
½ teaspoon minced fresh or ¼ teaspoon dried tarragon
½ teaspoon minced fresh or ¼ teaspoon dried chervil
½ teaspoon salt
½ teaspoon freshly ground black pepper

1. Add the shallots to the tarragon vinegar and reduce to ¼ cup by simmering. Strain and set aside.
2. Place egg yolks in the top of a double boiler and with a wire whisk, over hot but not boiling water, start beating the yolks until they are fluffy. Make sure the water does not boil, or the eggs will curdle.
3. Add ¼ cup of the melted butter and beat constantly until the butter is completely absorbed by the yolks and the sauce begins to thicken. Continue to add the rest of the butter, 2 tablespoons at a time, stirring constantly.
4. Add the lemon juice and the reduced shallot-vinegar mixture.

Your sauce will be thin at first, but continue to stir it with a wire whisk for several minutes until it develops a nice consistency. Taste and add the fresh herbs, salt, and pepper.

NOTE: Should the sauce curdle, add 1 tablespoon of boiling water and beat continually to rebuild the smoothness.

Sauce Mayonnaise
Mayonnaise Sauce

MAKES 1½ CUPS.

3 *egg yolks*
1 *tablespoon tarragon vinegar*
1 *cup olive oil*
1 *tablespoon Dijon mustard*
1 *teaspoon anchovy paste*
½ *teaspoon salt*
¼ *teaspoon freshly ground black pepper*

1. Place the egg yolks in a mixing bowl and beat with a wire whisk.

MAYONNAISE
SAUCE.

2. Add ½ the vinegar and beat until blended with the yolks.

3. Gradually add the oil a little at a time, beating constantly. The oil must be incorporated a few drops at a time until about ½ cup of it has been used.

4. Beat in the mustard and the anchovy paste.

5. Add the rest of the oil, 1 tablespoon at a time.

6. Add the rest of the vinegar; and the salt and pepper. If your mayonnaise curdles, put another yolk into a bowl and slowly pour the mixed mayonnaise into it, while stirring or beating constantly.

Sauce Verte
Green Sauce

MAKES 1¾ CUPS.

1½ *tablespoons fresh parsley*
1 *tablespoon fresh chervil*
1 *tablespoon fresh tarragon*
1 *tablespoon fresh watercress*
1½ *cups Mayonnaise Sauce* (*p.* 18)
Few leaves fresh spinach, pureed in the blender (*optional*)
Salt and freshly ground black pepper to taste
Few drops lemon juice (*optional*)

1. Mince the fresh herbs. They must be chopped *very* finely.

2. Add them to the Mayonnaise Sauce along with the pureed spinach if you are using it. Blend well.

3. Add salt and black pepper to taste. Add a few drops of lemon juice if you wish. Serve with cold fish.

Sauce Rémoulade
Remoulade Sauce

MAKES 2 CUPS.

1 *cup Mayonnaise Sauce* (*p.* 18)
2 *tablespoons Dijon mustard*
1 *tablespoon chopped fresh parsley*

1 *tablespoon chopped fresh chervil*
1 *tablespoon chopped fresh chives*
1 *teaspoon fresh tarragon*
2 *gherkin pickles, chopped fine*
2 *tablespoons capers*
1 *teaspoon anchovy paste*
½ *teaspoon salt*
¼ *to* ½ *teaspoon freshly ground black pepper*

1. Combine with the Mayonnaise Sauce: mustard, parsley, chervil, chives, tarragon, pickles, capers, and anchovy paste. Add the salt and pepper; taste for additional seasoning.

Sauce Vinaigrette
Vinegar Dressing

This is a basic salad dressing to which many different ingredients can be added. I have deliberately omitted garlic, onions, or shallots as their strong flavor overpowers some of the vegetables used in cold salads, such as green beans, asparagus, leeks, Belgian endive, etc.

When preparing vegetables like leeks, asparagus, or string beans for cold salads, cook them in boiling salted water, then cool them and pour the Vinaigrette over. If you are using string beans, add some thinly sliced white onions.

MAKES 1½ CUPS.

3 *tablespoons wine vinegar*
9 *tablespoons light olive oil*
1 *teaspoon Dijon mustard*
½ *teaspoon salt*
½ *teaspoon freshly ground black pepper*
½ *teaspoon sugar* (*optional*)
½ *teaspoon fresh or* ¼ *teaspoon dried parsley*
½ *teaspoon fresh or* ¼ *teaspoon dried tarragon*
½ *teaspoon fresh or* ¼ *teaspoon dried chives*
½ *teaspoon fresh or* ¼ *teaspoon dried chervil*

1. Place all the ingredients in a small mixing bowl and beat vigorously with a wire whisk until well mixed.

2. If you use dried herbs, add them before mixing the salad dressing ingredients together. If you are using fresh herbs, add them just before pouring the dressing over the vegetables.

Sauce Salade
French Dressing

MAKES 4 TO 5 CUPS.

6 *or* 7 *shallots, peeled*
6 *cloves garlic, peeled*
1½ *tablespoons salt*
¾ *tablespoon freshly ground black pepper*
2 *tablespoons sugar*
1 *tablespoon Dijon mustard*
1 *tablespoon water*
¾ *cup tarragon vinegar*
3 *to* 4 *cups corn oil, olive oil, or a combination of both,*
    to taste

1. Place the shallots, garlic, salt, pepper, sugar, mustard, water, and vinegar in the container of a blender. Blend for about 1 minute.
2. Add 3 to 4 cups of the oil, depending on the strength dressing you desire. This dressing can be stored in a jar in the refrigerator. If the amount seems too great, you can cut the recipe in half.

Sauce Ravigote
Ravigote Sauce

MAKES 1½ CUPS.

1 *cup Mayonnaise Sauce (p. 18)*
1 *tablespoon capers, drained of all liquid*
2 *shallots, minced*
1 *tablespoon fresh tarragon*
1 *tablespoon chopped fresh chervil*
1 *tablespoon chopped fresh chives*
1 *tablespoon chopped fresh parsley*

¼ *teaspoon salt*
¼ *teaspoon freshly ground black pepper*
2 *hard-cooked eggs, chopped* (*optional*)

1. Mix together the Mayonnaise Sauce, capers, shallots, tarragon, chervil, chives, parsley, salt, and pepper.
2. Taste for seasoning. The saltiness of the capers may make additional salt unnecessary. If the capers have made the sauce too salty, add the eggs.

Beurre à la Maître d'Hôtel
Maître d'Hôtel Butter

MAKES ½ CUP.

½ *cup sweet butter, softened*
½ *cup finely minced parsley*
1 *tablespoon lemon juice*
¼ *teaspoon salt*
¼ *teaspoon freshly ground black pepper*

1. Mix the soft, but not melted, butter with the parsley and lemon juice.
2. Add the salt and pepper; taste for additional seasoning.

Crème Chantilly
Crème Chantilly

MAKES 2 CUPS.

1 *teaspoon superfine sugar*
¼ *teaspoon vanilla extract*
1 *cup heavy cream, cold*

1. Add the sugar and vanilla to the cream.

2. Whip together with a rotary beater until cream is stiff enough to hold its shape.

3. Refrigerate until ready to serve.

Crème à la Vanille
Vanilla Sauce

MAKES 1¾ CUPS.

4 *egg yolks*
¼ *cup superfine sugar*
1 *cup light cream, scalded*
1 *teaspoon vanilla extract or a ¼-inch piece of vanilla*
    bean, split

1. Beat the egg yolks in the top of a double boiler. Add the sugar and beat again.

2. Place the double boiler over moderate heat until the mixture is barely boiling. Mix the cream with the yolks.

3. Cook the mixture very slowly, stirring with a wire whisk. When the custard begins to thicken, remove from the stove.

4. When cool, add the vanilla to taste.

Crème à l'Anglaise
Soft Custard Sauce

MAKES 2½ CUPS.

8 *egg yolks*
½ *cup superfine sugar*
2 *cups milk, scalded*
1 *tablespoon vanilla extract or a 1-inch piece of vanilla*
    bean, split

1. Beat the egg yolks with the sugar in the top of a double boiler.

2. Gradually add the scalded milk to the egg yolks and sugar, stirring constantly.

3. Cook the mixture over hot water, stirring constantly, until it thickens and coats the spoon.

4. Add the vanilla and cool the mixture.

Sauce au Chocolat
Chocolate Sauce

This sauce can be kept for weeks in the refrigerator. It is excellent as a topping for ice creams, puddings, and cakes.

MAKES 3½ CUPS.

3 *squares unsweetened chocolate*
4 *tablespoons sweet butter*
1 *cup boiling water*
1½ *cups superfine sugar*
6 *tablespoons light corn syrup*
¼ *teaspoon salt*
2 *teaspoons vanilla extract or a ½-inch piece of vanilla bean,*
   split

1. Melt the chocolate over hot water in the top of a double boiler.
2. Add the butter and blend.
3. Pour in the boiling water and mix well.
4. Bring to a boil and stir in the sugar and corn syrup. Cook for 10 minutes. Let the mixture cool.
5. Add the salt and vanilla.
6. When completely cold, pour the sauce into a container or glass jar. Cover and keep in the refrigerator.
7. To reheat the sauce, which thickens under refrigeration, put the jar into a saucepan with hot water and heat until the sauce is hot enough to be poured.

CHAPTER 2

Hors
d'Oeuvres

Hors-d'oeuvres

Quiche Lorraine
Quiche au Bacon
Quiche aux Saucisses
Quiche de Campagne à la Crème
Quiche aux Fruits de Mer
Quiche à l'Oignon
Quiche aux Anchois à la Provençale

Soufflé au Fromage

Pâté de Foie de Poulet
Pâté de Campagne

Profiteroles Variées

Fonds d'Artichauts Farcis Mirepoix
Avocats Farcis avec Crabe à la Rémoulade
Champignons Farcis

Escargots en Coquilles
Escargots sur Croûtons à la Provençale

Homard Froid à la Mayonnaise
Homard Chaud à la Beurre
Huîtres Monblason
Fruits de Mer Froids à la Ravigote

Coquilles de Crabe Monblason
Coquilles de Crevettes Monblason
Coquilles de Homard Monblason
Coquilles de Fruits de Mer Monblason
Coquilles de Volaille au Gratin

A meal should be planned somewhat like a book, with a foreword or introduction to begin it. An appetizer should stimulate but never be so substantial as to dull the appetite for what is to come. Too many canapés, together with too many cocktails, can bring disaster to an otherwise well-planned meal. Here is a tasty selection of appetizers and hors d'oeuvres which can be served either at the dinner table as a first course, or in some cases, in the living room before dinner is served. Just be sure to make your portions moderate so your guests can look forward to dinner with hearty appetites.

Quiches

So often during my vacations on the farm I used to watch my sweet grandmother and aunts preparing quiches in the *four* (oven) on bread-baking day. Their classic yet simple way of making quiches in those days was to use the same yeast dough for the quiche crusts as they used for the bread.

I recommend that all pastry shells be partially baked ahead of time. The filling can also be prepared in advance. Preheat your oven to 400° and 35 minutes before serving your guests place the filled pastry shell in the oven. If you have some leftover quiche it can be reheated. It will be as tasty as ever but will not puff up the second time.

Combination, variation, and imagination can all play a great role in making quiches. Although my Lorraine ancestors introduced us to a great line of appetizing entrées, I know they never used lobster, shrimp, and crabmeat in their quiches—the ocean was too far away. Here is the original Quiche Lorraine and a few tasty variations.

Quiche Lorraine
Quiche Lorraine

SERVES 8.

Pastry:
1 *cup sifted flour*
¼ *teaspoon salt*
5 *tablespoons sweet butter*
1 *tablespoon vegetable shortening*
Approximately 3 *tablespoons cold water*

Filling:
1½ *cups grated Swiss Gruyère cheese*
½ *pound boiled Polish ham, diced*
2 *eggs*
3 *egg yolks*
1 *cup heavy cream*
½ *teaspoon salt*
½ *teaspoon freshly ground black pepper*
¼ *teaspoon ground or freshly grated nutmeg*
2 *tablespoons sweet butter*

1. Sift the flour and salt into a mixing bowl. Add the butter and vegetable shortening, cutting these ingredients in with a pastry cutter until the mixture resembles coarse meal.

2. Add the cold water and blend with a fork. Gather dough into a ball and refrigerate for at least 3 hours (preferably overnight).

3. Roll dough out on a floured pastry board and place it in a well-buttered 9-inch pie plate. Place an 8-inch pie plate on top. This will prevent the crust from puffing up and buckling while it is baking.

4. Bake in a preheated 400° oven for about 5 minutes. Lower the heat to 350°, and bake until the crust is golden brown, about 10 min-

utes longer. Watch the crust carefully, so that it does not get too well done. Remove from oven and let it cool off.

5. When crust is cool, put a thin layer of the grated cheese on the bottom of the crust, then a layer of the ham, then another layer each of the cheese and ham, and finally, a little more of the cheese on top.

6. Beat together thoroughly the whole eggs, egg yolks, cream, salt, pepper, and nutmeg and pour gently over the ham and cheese. Dot the top with little pieces of butter.

7. Bake in a preheated 400° oven for 10 minutes. Reduce the heat to 300° and bake for another 25 to 30 minutes, or until cheese custard is set and golden brown on top. Serve hot.

Variations for Quiche Lorraine: You can vary Quiche Lorraine by using bacon, thin slices of cooked sausages, or other cured meats.

Quiche au Bacon
Quiche with Bacon

SERVES 8.

1 *9-inch pastry shell, partially baked* (*p.* 29)
8 *slices of lean bacon, medium thickness*
Ingredients for Filling of Quiche Lorraine (*p.* 29), *omitting ham*

1. Prepare pastry shell as directed on p. 29.

2. Cut the slices of bacon into strips about ⅓ inch wide. Blanch the pieces in boiling water for 6 minutes to get rid of the strong smoky taste. Drain the bacon pieces and dry them well. Sauté the bacon in a skillet until slightly browned.

3. Proceed exactly as for Quiche Lorraine, substituting the blanched bacon for the ham.

4. Bake in a preheated 400° oven for 10 minutes. Reduce the heat to 300° and bake for another 25 minutes, or until cheese custard is set and golden brown on top. Serve hot.

Quiche aux Saucisses
Quiche with Sausage

SERVES 8.

1 *9-inch pastry shell, partially baked* (*p.* 29)
½ *pound hot Italian sausage*
Ingredients for Filling of Quiche Lorraine (*p.* 29), *omitting ham*

1. Prepare pastry shell as directed on p. 29.
2. Sauté the sausage for 5 to 10 minutes. Drain and cool. Slice the sausage into ½-inch-thick pieces.
3. Proceed exactly as for Quiche Lorraine, substituting the precooked sausage for the ham.
4. Bake in a preheated 400° oven for 10 minutes. Reduce the heat to 300° and bake for another 25 minutes, or until cheese custard is set and golden brown on top. Serve hot.

Quiche de Campagne à la Crème
Country Quiche with Cream

SERVES 8.

1 *9-inch pastry shell, partially baked* (*p.* 29)
Ingredients for Filling of Quiche Lorraine (*p.* 29), *omitting*
    cheese and increasing the heavy cream from 1 to 1½ cups

1. Prepare pastry shell as directed on p. 29.
2. Proceed exactly as for Quiche Lorraine (p. 29), omitting the cheese and increasing the cream to 1½ cups.
3. Bake in a preheated 400° oven for 10 minutes. Reduce the heat to 300° and bake for another 25 minutes, or until custard is set and golden brown on top. Serve hot.

Quiche aux Fruits de Mer
Quiche with Seafood

SERVES 8.

3 *shallots, finely minced*
5 *tablespoons sweet butter*
3 *tablespoons cream sherry*
6 *ounces cooked shrimp or cooked lobster, diced; or cooked*
    crab meat, shredded; or fresh or canned salmon or tuna,
    flaked
2 *eggs*
2 *egg yolks*
1 *cup heavy cream*
¼ *teaspoon salt*
¼ *teaspoon freshly ground black pepper*
½ *cup Swiss Gruyère cheese, grated*
1 *9-inch pastry shell, partially baked* (*p.* 29)

1. Sauté the minced shallots in 3 tablespoons of the butter until tender, but not browned.

2. Add the sherry and simmer, covered, for 2 minutes.

3. Add the fish or seafood you have selected. Taste for seasoning.

4. Beat together the whole eggs, egg yolks, cream, salt, pepper, and ¼ cup cheese.

5. Blend in the fish mixture.

6. Correct seasoning and pour the mixture into the partially baked pastry shell. Sprinkle another ¼ cup cheese on top, dot with 2 tablespoons butter, and bake in a preheated 400° oven for 10 minutes.

7. Reduce the heat to 325° and continue baking for 20 minutes or until done. The quiche will have puffed up and the top should be browned. A knife inserted into the center of the quiche should come out clean. Serve immediately.

Quiche à l'Oignon
Quiche with Onion

SERVES 8.

1 9-*inch pastry shell, partially baked* (*p.* 29)
1½ *cups sliced onions*
3 *tablespoons sweet butter*
¾ *cup grated Swiss Gruyère cheese*
2 *eggs*
3 *egg yolks*
1 *cup light cream*
Pinch of ground or freshly grated nutmeg
½ *teaspoon salt*
¼ *teaspoon freshly ground black pepper*

1. Prepare the pastry shell as directed in recipe for Quiche Lorraine (p. 29). Cool the baked pastry shell.

2. Sauté the onions in 2 tablespoons of the butter until tender and transparent but not browned.

3. Spread ½ of the cheese over the bottom of the pastry shell and add the onions so that they cover the cheese completely.

4. Beat the whole eggs, egg yolks, cream, nutmeg, salt, and pepper together. Pour the mixture over the onions. Spread the rest of the cheese on top. Dot with 1 tablespoon of the butter.

5. Bake in a preheated 400° oven for 10 minutes. Reduce the heat to 300° and bake for another 25 to 30 minutes, or until the mixture is set and slightly browned. Serve hot.

Quiche aux Anchois à la Provençale
Quiche with Anchovies and Tomato Sauce

SERVES 8.

2 *white onions, finely chopped*
2 *tablespoons olive oil*
6 *medium-sized tomatoes*
2 *cloves garlic, finely minced*

½ teaspoon oregano
½ teaspoon salt
¼ teaspoon freshly ground black pepper
2 eggs
2 egg yolks
10 filets of anchovies, with oil
2 tablespoons virgin olive oil
2 tablespoons tomato paste
4 tablespoons chopped fresh parsley
⅛ teaspoon cayenne pepper
1 teaspoon paprika
1 9-inch pastry shell, partially baked (p. 29)
16 pitted ripe black olives (Mediterranean type), halved
⅓ cup grated Swiss Gruyère cheese
1 tablespoon sweet butter

1. Sauté the onions in the olive oil over moderate heat until tender, but not browned.

2. Peel the tomatoes by dropping them into boiling water for a couple of minutes and then slipping off the skins. Cut them in quarters and remove the seeds.

3. Add the tomatoes to the onions, along with the garlic, oregano, salt, and pepper. Simmer until the tomatoes are cooked and all their juice has evaporated.

4. In a mixing bowl, beat the whole eggs, egg yolks, anchovies with oil, olive oil, tomato paste, parsley, cayenne pepper, and paprika and then stir in the cooked tomato mixture. Correct seasoning, taking into account the saltiness of the anchovies.

5. Spread the tomato mixture evenly in the partially baked pastry shell. Place the olive halves on top, equally spaced. Spread the cheese on top and dot with butter.

6. Bake in a preheated 350° oven until the quiche has puffed up and is nicely browned on top, approximately 30 minutes. Serve hot.

Soufflé au Fromage
Cheese Soufflé

A cheese soufflé makes a nice first course at dinner to replace soup or an appetizer. Just be sure your guests are all seated and ready to eat when the soufflé is about to be served (see my notes on soufflés on pp. 350–351). It is better to have the guests waiting for the soufflé than to have the soufflé waiting for the guests.

SERVES 6.

4 *tablespoons sweet butter*
4 *tablespoons flour*
1¼ *cups milk, scalded*
Pinch of ground or freshly grated nutmeg
½ *teaspoon salt*
¼ *teaspoon freshly ground black pepper*
⅛ *teaspoon cayenne pepper*
1 *cup grated Swiss Gruyère or Norwegian Jarlsberg cheese*
4 *egg yolks*
6 *egg whites, at room temperature*

1. Melt the butter in the top of a double boiler and blend in the flour.

2. Stir for 2 minutes and add the milk, little by little, stirring constantly until you have a thick, smooth white sauce.

3. Add nutmeg, salt, black pepper, cayenne pepper, and ¾ cup of the cheese.

4. Remove from stove; cool slightly and stir in the egg yolks. Set aside until ready.

5. About 40 minutes before you want to serve the soufflé, beat the egg whites until they form stiff but not dry peaks. Fold beaten egg whites gently into the cheese mixture. Pour into either a 2-quart well-buttered soufflé dish or a buttered Pyrex baking dish of the same capacity. Be certain not to fill it higher than 1 inch below the rim of the dish. Sprinkle the rest of the cheese on top.

6. Bake in a preheated 350° oven for 10 minutes. Reduce the heat to 300° and continue to bake for another 15 minutes for a soft French-style soufflé. Bake longer if you want your soufflé to be firm.

For Ham and Cheese Soufflé: Proceed as for Cheese Soufflé above, but omit the nutmeg. Add ½ cup of finely ground boiled Polish ham to the cheese sauce before folding in the egg whites.

Pâté de Foie de Poulet
Chicken Liver Pâté

SERVES 6 TO 8.

3 *tablespoons finely minced shallots*
1 *clove garlic, minced*
4 *tablespoons sweet butter*
½ *pound chicken livers*
3 *tablespoons cognac*
¾ *cup diced boiled Polish ham*
½ *teaspoon salt*
¼ *teaspoon freshly ground black pepper*
¼ *to ⅓ cup heavy cream*

1. In a skillet, sauté the shallots and garlic in the butter until they are tender but not browned.
2. Add the chicken livers and brown them thoroughly.
3. Add the cognac and ignite.
4. When the flames die out, add the ham and salt and pepper and cook for 2 more minutes. Cool the mixture.
5. Put the entire mixture through a meat grinder and mash it into a smooth paste.
6. The pâté will be very thick. Add the heavy cream, a little at a time, until the pâté is of a nice spreading consistency. Serve on crackers or with crusty French bread.

Pâté de Campagne
Country Pâté

SERVES 20.

1½ *pounds fresh pork fat*
1¼ *pounds lean pork*
1¼ *pounds lean veal*
1¼ *pounds lean boiled Polish ham*
¾ *pound chicken livers*
4 *eggs*

⅓ cup heavy cream
½ cup cognac
6 cloves garlic
½ teaspoon cinnamon
½ teaspoon allspice
1 tablespoon freshly ground white pepper
1 tablespoon salt
4 tablespoons flour

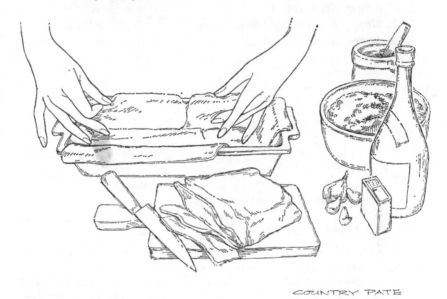

COUNTRY PATE

1. Take ½ pound of the pork fat and slice it very thin.

2. Line 2 1½-quart oblong molds or baking dishes with the thin slices of pork fat, letting the long ends of the fat hang outside the molds.

3. Take another ½ pound of the pork fat and grind it with the lean pork and veal.

4. Grind the remaining ½ pound of the pork fat with the ham, using the coarse blade of the meat grinder. Or, if you wish, dice the ham and the fat. The pieces should be coarser than the veal and pork.

5. Puree the chicken livers in a blender with the eggs, cream, cognac, and garlic. Then add ½ of the veal and pork mixture.

6. Combine all the meats with the cinnamon, allspice, pepper, salt, and flour in a large mixing bowl. Mix all the ingredients thoroughly.

7. Fill the molds with the mixture and fold the overhanging slices of pork fat over the top. Cover with heavy-duty aluminum foil.

8. Set the molds in a flat roasting pan with 1 inch hot water (or

enough water to reach halfway up the side of the roasting pan) and place the pan in a preheated 400° oven. Bake for 3½ hours. Replenish water if it evaporates.

9. Remove the aluminum foil and bake for another 20 minutes, or until the top gets nicely browned.

10. Remove the molds from the oven. Place a smaller mold or pan on top of the pâté. Fill it with something heavy like a weight or a brick, allowing the pâté to compress and get completely cold before you remove it from the mold. This weighting process makes the pâté easier to slice. Now you can either use the pâté molds or freeze them for future use. Leave the fat on the pâté, and it will keep under refrigeration for 1 to 2 weeks.

Profiteroles Variées
Cream Puff Hors d'Oeuvres

MAKES 50 SMALL CREAM PUFFS.

Cream Puffs:
1 *cup water*
½ *cup sweet butter*
¼ *teaspoon salt*
1 *cup flour*
4 *large eggs*

Fillings:
2 *cups ground boiled ham; or salmon, fresh or smoked; or tuna;*
    or lobster; or shrimp; or mushrooms; or sardines; or
    3 *to* 3½ *cups foie gras*
1 *to* 1½ *cups Mayonnaise Sauce* (p. 18), *to bind fillings*

1. Put the water, butter, and salt in a saucepan and bring to a boil. Remove from heat.

2. Add all the flour at once and stir. Return to the stove and stir and cook until the mixture leaves the sides of the pan and forms a stiff ball. Remove again from the heat.

3. Beat in the eggs, 1 at a time, incorporating each egg before adding the next. Do not overbeat; it will reduce the rising of the puffs.

4. Fill a pastry bag with the mixture or use a teaspoon and put drops of the paste on a lightly buttered baking sheet, 1½ inches apart. For hors d'oeuvres, I suggest you make the drops fairly small, as they do swell in baking, and you will want them to be easy to pick up and eat.

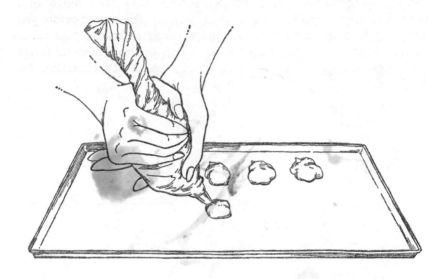

PROFITEROLES HORS D'OEUVRES.

5. Bake in a preheated 375° oven for 20 to 25 minutes or until well puffed and golden brown. Do not underbake. Turn off the heat and make a small slit with a sharp pointed knife in the side of each puff to let the steam escape. Leave the baking sheets in the oven for another 10 minutes to let the centers of the puffs dry out. Remove from oven and cool on a wire rack.

6. When cool, cut a little piece off the bottom of each puff.

7. Blend 2 cups of any of the above fillings, except the foie gras, with 1 to 1½ cups Mayonnaise Sauce to make a smooth filling. The foie gras should be used as is, since it is already a smooth mixture.

8. Insert the filling into the puff and replace the bottom of the puff to hold the filling.

Fonds d'Artichauts Farcis Mirepoix
Artichoke Bottoms Stuffed with a Mirepoix

I strongly recommend that you buy the imported canned artichoke bottoms if you intend to use them as a garnish. You will save considerable time and money. Each can contains approximately 8 to 10 artichoke bottoms. If you wish to prepare them as a vegetable, just rinse them in lukewarm water. Drain them and sauté them in butter. Serve them with a béchamel sauce, a mushroom sauce, or just butter and lemon juice. Artichoke bottoms can be served cold as an appetizer stuffed with cooked shrimps, lobster, crab meat, salmon, or tuna mixed with a mayonnaise sauce. Here is a recipe for serving hot artichoke bottoms with a mirepoix stuffing.

SERVES 5.

4 *shallots, minced*
2 *tablespoons sweet butter*
8 *medium-sized fresh mushrooms, sliced*
⅓ *cup Béchamel Sauce (p. 9)*
⅓ *cup grated Swiss Gruyère cheese*
Salt and freshly ground black pepper to taste
10 *artichoke bottoms*

1. Sauté the minced shallots in the butter until transparent, but not browned.
2. Add the mushrooms and simmer until their liquid has evaporated.
3. In a blender, puree the shallots and mushrooms, Béchamel Sauce, and ½ of the grated cheese. Taste for seasoning and add some salt and pepper if necessary.
4. Fill the artichoke bottoms with the stuffing and sprinkle the rest of the cheese on top. Cook, under the broiler, until hot and slightly browned. Serve as an appetizer or as a garnish with broiled meats, such as steak, lamb chops, or chicken.

Avocats Farcis avec Crabe à la Rémoulade
Avocados Stuffed with Crab Meat in Remoulade Sauce

SERVES 6.

3 *avocados*
1 *cup Mayonnaise Sauce (p. 18)*
2 *tablespoons Dijon mustard*
1 *tablespoon chopped fresh parsley*
1 *tablespoon chopped fresh chervil*
1 *tablespoon chopped fresh chives*
1 *teaspoon chopped fresh tarragon*
2 *gherkin pickles, chopped fine*
2 *tablespoons capers*
1 *teaspoon anchovy paste*
2 *cups fresh crab meat or canned Japanese crab meat*
Garnishes: Boston or Bibb lettuce leaves, 3 teaspoons
chopped fresh parsley

1. The avocados should be fully ripe but firm. Slice them in half lengthwise and remove the stones. Peel the avocado halves.

2. In a mixing bowl combine the Mayonnaise Sauce with the mustard, parsley, chervil, chives, tarragon, pickles, capers, and anchovy paste. Mix well.

3. Stir in the crab meat. Taste for seasoning.

4. Fill the avocado halves with the crab-meat mixture. Place the filled avocados on a bed of lettuce leaves and sprinkle the top of each with ½ teaspoon parsley.

5. Refrigerate and serve chilled.

Champignons Farcis
Stuffed Mushrooms

This makes a very nice first course served at the table. You can prepare everything ahead of time and just put the pan into the oven ½ hour before serving time. A nice variation is the use of artichoke bottoms instead of mushrooms, particularly when mushrooms are out of season. See p. 40 for the preparation of artichoke bottoms.

SERVES 6.

24 *large fresh mushroom caps, with their stems minced*
8 *tablespoons sweet butter, melted*
Salt and freshly ground black pepper
½ *cup minced white onions*
½ *cup minced shallots*
½ *cup cream sherry*
¾ *cup dry bread crumbs*
2 *cups grated Swiss Gruyère or Norwegian Jarlsberg cheese*
½ *cup minced fresh parsley*
Few leaves of fresh tarragon, chopped, or pinch of dried
    tarragon
½ *cup heavy cream*
4 *tablespoons sweet butter for topping*

1. Clean the mushroom caps and brush them with 4 tablespoons of the butter. Season lightly with some salt and pepper and place caps side by side, rounded-side down, in a roasting pan.

2. Sauté the onions and shallots in 4 tablespoons of the butter until cooked but not browned.

3. Add the mushroom stems and simmer gently until all their juice has evaporated. Do not brown the stems, or they will impart a bitter taste.

4. Add the sherry and boil it down until almost evaporated.

5. Remove the mushroom-onion-shallot mixture from the stove and add the bread crumbs, 1½ cups of the grated cheese, parsley, tarragon, and more salt and pepper.

6. Then blend in the cream, 1 spoonful at a time, adding just enough for the mixture to hold its shape.

7. Fill the mushroom caps with the stuffing, and top with the remaining ½ cup of cheese and 4 tablespoons butter.

8. About ½ hour before serving, bake in a preheated 350° oven for 25 minutes, until the caps are cooked and browned lightly on top.

Escargots en Coquilles
Snails in Their Shells

SERVES 4.

24 *canned imported snails*
10 *tablespoons sweet butter*
4 *shallots, finely minced*
3 *cloves garlic, finely minced*
⅓ *cup chopped fresh parsley*
⅛ *teaspoon ground or freshly grated nutmeg*
⅛ *teaspoon thyme*
1 *teaspoon salt*
½ *teaspoon freshly ground black pepper*
24 *snail shells (coquilles)*

1. Drain the snails of their liquid.

2. Cream the butter. Add the shallots, garlic, parsley, nutmeg, thyme, salt, and pepper to the butter and mix well.

3. Put a dot of the butter into each shell, slide a snail into the shell, and cover each snail with additional butter, so that the opening to the shell is covered.

4. Place the shells side by side and close together in a shallow baking dish so they won't slide around. Place dish in a preheated 450° oven.

5. When the butter starts bubbling, in approximately 7 to 10 minutes, wait 1 more minute and then take the shells out of the oven. Serve piping hot.

NOTE: If you fear your guests may be overly sensitive to the strong garlic flavor, you can use less than the 3 cloves recommended.

NOTE ON SHELLS: Porcelain, ceramic snail shells are now available in gourmet specialty stores. It is easier to wash and handle the porcelain shells than the natural ones.

Escargots sur Croûtons à la Provençale
Snails on Toast with Tomato Sauce

SERVES 6.

2 *cans large-sized imported snails* (48 *snails*)
1 *cup dry white wine*
4 *medium-sized tomatoes*
10 *tablespoons sweet butter*
3 *cloves garlic, finely minced*
6 *shallots, finely minced*
Salt and freshly ground black pepper
6 *pieces buttered toast* (*preferably French bread*)
2 *tablespoons chopped fresh parsley*

1. Drain the snails.
2. Simmer the wine, uncovered, in a saucepan until reduced to ⅔ of a cup.
3. Add the snails to the wine. Cover, bring to a boil, and simmer for 8 minutes. Drain the snails and reserve the wine for the sauce.
4. Remove the tomato skins by dropping the tomatoes in boiling water for a few seconds. Remove and drain. Now you can peel them easily and cut them in quarters.
5. Melt 6 tablespoons of the butter in a saucepan and add the tomatoes. Simmer for 15 minutes.
6. Add the reserved wine and let the sauce simmer until reduced by half.
7. Add the garlic and shallots and simmer for 5 minutes longer.
8. Melt the remaining 4 tablespoons of the butter in a skillet and sauté the snails, stirring frequently, for 4 minutes.
9. Add the sauce; stir and taste for the addition of some salt and pepper. Serve immediately on buttered toast. Sprinkle with parsley.

Homard Froid à la Mayonnaise
Cold Boiled Lobster with Mayonnaise Sauce

SERVES 6.

3 *live lobsters, 1½ pounds each*
Salt
1½ *cups Mayonnaise Sauce (p.* 18)
Garnishes: 1 *head Bibb or Boston lettuce,* 3 *tablespoons*
     capers, ¼ *cup chopped fresh parsley*

1. Plunge the lobsters head first into a kettle of rapidly boiling salted water, and bring the water back to a boil. Cook for 18 to 20 minutes. Remove the lobsters and let them cool.
2. When cold, split the lobsters in halves lengthwise; clean the insides; crack the claws and set them in the refrigerator until ready to be used.
3. Prepare the Mayonnaise Sauce.
4. When ready to serve, put some of the Mayonnaise Sauce in the empty spaces in the lobster shells. Place the lobsters on a bed of lettuce; sprinkle some capers and chopped parsley on top and serve.

Homard Chaud à la Beurre
Hot Lobster with Butter Sauce

If you with to serve the lobsters hot with a butter sauce, boil them the same way. When they come out of the boiling water, split and clean them immediately, then crack the claws and serve them with hot melted butter in a sauceboat. Hot Lobster with Butter Sauce may be served as an entrée if you increase the amount of lobster to 1 to 2 lobsters per person.

Huîtres Monblason
Oysters Monblason

On one of my visits to New Orleans many years ago, I had dinner at Antoine's. On that particular evening, I wanted to taste their famous

Oysters Rockefeller. The oysters were good, but how they were able to build the reputation of a restaurant with just one recipe is beyond my comprehension.

It has been said that the culinary success of Oysters Rockefeller depends on a few drops of absinthe. I would suggest that you first prepare a couple of oysters with the absinthe or anisette, and then a couple without, and then be the judge yourself. I am prejudiced against the licorice taste in food, but each to his own taste.

Here is a recipe for baked oysters which I feel challenges Oysters Rockefeller. You can vary this recipe if you wish by substituting watercress or sorrel for the spinach.

SERVES 6 OR MORE.

8 *shallots, minced*
⅓ *cup minced celery*
1 *tablespoon minced chervil*
1½ *teaspoons fresh tarragon leaves*
4 *sprigs fresh parsley*
1 *cup chopped and washed fresh young spinach leaves*
½ *cup soft bread crumbs*
1 *cup sweet butter, softened*
1 *teaspoon anchovy paste*
1 *tablespoon Worcestershire sauce*
½ *teaspoon salt*
¼ *teaspoon freshly ground black pepper*
1 *tablespoon absinthe or anisette* (*optional*)
3 *dozen fresh oysters on the half shell*
¾ *cup grated Swiss Gruyère cheese*

1. Blend the shallots, celery, chervil, tarragon, parsley, and spinach, in a blender until chopped. Transfer the mixture to a bowl.

2. Combine with the bread crumbs and softened butter. Mix well and add the anchovy paste, Worcestershire sauce, salt, pepper, and a little of the absinthe, if you choose to use it. Taste and adjust the seasonings to your own palate.

3. The best way to handle and serve the oysters is to use tin pie plates and fill them with rock salt. Set the oysters on top of the rock salt, 6 to a plate. Place 1 tablespoon of the spinach and bread-crumb mixture to cover each oyster and sprinkle lightly with the cheese.

4. Bake the oysters in a preheated 425° oven until the sauce bub-

bles, approximately 5 to 6 minutes, then under a hot broiler for 2 more minutes to slightly brown the cheese.

Fruits de Mer Froids à la Ravigote
Cold Seafood with Ravigote Sauce

1 *cup Mayonnaise Sauce* (*p.* 18)
1 *tablespoon capers, drained of all liquid*
2 *shallots, finely minced*
1 *tablespoon chopped fresh tarragon*
1 *tablespoon chopped fresh chervil*
1 *tablespoon chopped fresh chives*
1 *tablespoon chopped fresh parsley*
¼ *teaspoon salt* (*optional*)
¼ *teaspoon freshly ground black pepper*
2 *hard-boiled eggs, finely chopped* (*optional*)
2 *cups cold seafood: tuna, salmon, crab meat, lobster, shrimp,*
    fillet, or mackerel
Boston or Bibb lettuce leaves

1. Mix together the Mayonnaise Sauce, capers, shallots, tarragon, chervil, chives, and parsley.
2. Taste for seasoning. The saltiness of the capers may make additional salt unnecessary. If the capers have given too much salt to the sauce, you can add the chopped hard-boiled eggs.
3. Combine the sauce with the seafood and serve on lettuce leaves.

Coquilles de Crabe Monblason
Crab Coquilles Monblason

SERVES 6.

1½ *cups fresh or* 1 *7-ounce can Alaskan king or Japanese*
    crab meat
3 *shallots, minced*
5 *tablespoons sweet butter*

½ cup cream sherry
3 tablespoons flour
1¼ cups light cream, heated
1 cup grated Swiss Gruyère cheese
1 teaspoon Worcestershire sauce
1 pound mushrooms, sliced and sautéed in butter
½ teaspoon salt
¼ teaspoon freshly ground black pepper
6 scallop shells (coquilles)

1. Pick through the crab meat to remove the membranes, then place the crab meat in the refrigerator until you are ready to use it.

2. Sauté the shallots in 2 tablespoons of the butter until transparent and tender but not browned.

3. Add the cream sherry and simmer for 5 minutes.

4. Melt the remaining 3 tablespoons of the butter in another sauce-pan and blend in the flour. Stir over low heat until golden and then mix with the shallots and cream sherry.

5. Gradually add the hot cream, stirring until you have a smooth sauce.

6. Add ½ cup cheese, Worcestershire sauce, and the mushrooms. Then add the crab meat and the salt and pepper. Taste for seasoning.

7. Fill 6 empty scallop shells or any individual bake-and-serve

COQUILLES·

dishes with the mixture and top with the remaining grated cheese. When ready to serve, place the shells or dishes under the broiler until they are piping hot and the cheese is nicely browned.

Coquilles de Crevettes Monblason
Shrimp Coquilles Monblason

SERVES 8.

1 cup clam juice
1 cup White Stock (p. 6) or canned chicken consommé
40 large fresh or frozen shrimp, peeled and deveined
3 shallots, finely minced
6 tablespoons sweet butter
½ cup cream sherry
3 tablespoons flour
1 clove garlic, minced
1 cup light cream, scalded
1½ cups grated Swiss Gruyère cheese
½ teaspoon salt
¼ teaspoon freshly ground black pepper
8 scallop shells or ramekins

1. In a saucepan bring the clam juice and White Stock or consommé to a boil.

2. Add the shrimp. When the liquid starts to boil again, remove the saucepan from the heat and let the shrimp stand in the liquid for 1 minute. Drain the shrimp, reserving ⅓ cup of the liquid.

3. Sauté the shallots in 1 tablespoon of the butter. When transparent, add the sherry. Simmer and reduce to ¼ cup. Set aside.

4. Melt 3 tablespoons of the butter in a saucepan and blend in the flour, cooking for about 3 minutes over moderate heat until a light golden color.

5. Add the shallots-sherry mixture and blend.

6. Add the ⅓ cup reserved White Stock and clam juice mixture and the garlic; stir.

7. Add the cream and stir to make a smooth sauce.

8. Stir in ¾ cup of the grated cheese and blend, but do not boil.

9. Add the cooked shrimp and simmer for 2 minutes. Correct the seasoning with the salt and pepper.

10. Place 5 shrimp in each of the scallop shells. Spoon the shallot-sherry mixture over them and sprinkle the rest of the cheese evenly over the tops. Dot with little pieces of the remaining 2 tablespoons of the butter and place the shells on a cookie sheet or baking pan.

11. Bake in a preheated 350° oven for about 15 to 20 minutes, or until the tops are browned and crisp. You can turn on the broiler for the last few minutes to hasten the browning.

Coquilles de Homard Monblason
Lobster Coquilles Monblason

SERVES 8.

¾ pound fresh mushrooms, sliced
9 tablespoons sweet butter
2 shallots, minced
⅓ cup cream sherry
3 tablespoons flour
1 tablespoon brandy
1 cup light cream, scalded
1 teaspoon Worcestershire sauce
1 cup grated Swiss Gruyère cheese
2 cups cooked lobster meat
½ teaspoon salt
¼ teaspoon freshly ground black pepper
8 scallop shells or ramekins

1. Sauté the mushrooms in 2 tablespoons of the butter until the liquid evaporates. Set aside.

2. Sauté the shallots in 1 tablespoon of the butter until transparent but not browned.

3. Add the sherry to the shallots and simmer until the liquid is reduced to ¼ cup. Set aside.

4. Melt 4 tablespoons of the butter and stir in the flour, cooking over moderate heat for a few minutes until the mixture takes on a light yellow color.

5. Add the brandy and stir for 1 minute.

6. Add the sherry and shallots and the scalded cream, then the mushrooms, Worcestershire sauce, ½ of the cheese, and the lobster

meat. If the sauce is too thick, add a little more cream. Add the salt and pepper.

7. Spoon the mixture into individual scallop shells or ramekins. Sprinkle the rest of the cheese evenly over the tops. Dot with little pieces of the remaining 2 tablespoons of the butter.

8. Place the shells on a cookie sheet or baking pan and bake in a preheated 350° oven for about 15 to 20 minutes, or until the tops are browned and crisp. The broiler can be turned on for a few minutes before serving to hasten the browning of the tops.

Coquilles de Fruits de Mer Monblason
Seafood Coquilles Monblason

This recipe can be made a day in advance. It should be served in scallop shells (coquilles), which are available in almost any gourmet shop. The filled shells can be frozen for use at a later time.

SERVES 12.

¾ *pound fresh or frozen shrimp*
1 *pound fresh or frozen scallops*
4 *shallots, minced*
8 *tablespoons sweet butter*
1 *cup dry white wine*
6 *sprigs parsley*
¼ *teaspoon thyme*
1 *bay leaf*
¾ *pound fresh mushrooms, sliced*
1 *8-ounce bottle clam juice*
1½ *cups fresh or 1 7-ounce can Alaskan king or Japanese
    crab meat*
4 *tablespoons flour*
2 *tablespoons cognac*
½ *cup sherry*
2 *cups grated Swiss Gruyère or Norwegian Jarlsberg cheese*
1 *cup heavy cream*
Salt and freshly ground black pepper

1. If you are using frozen shrimp and scallops, defrost them, approximately 2 to 3 hours.

2. Sauté the shallots in 2 tablespoons of the butter until tender and transparent, but not browned.

3. Add the wine, parsley, thyme, and bay leaf and simmer, covered, for 5 minutes. Remove the parsley and bay leaf and continue to simmer the wine until it is reduced to ½ cup.

4. Sauté the mushrooms in 2 tablespoons of the butter until all the liquid has evaporated. Set aside.

5. Pour the clam juice into a saucepan and bring to a boil. Drop in the shrimp. When the liquid starts to boil again, remove the pan from the stove and let it stand for 1 minute. Shrimp get hard and dry if overcooked, so be sure not to leave them on the stove too long. If you have used fresh shrimp, shell them and remove the veins. Split them in half lengthwise.

6. Drain the clam juice into another saucepan. Bring the liquid to a boil again and drop in the scallops. When the juice starts to boil again, cook for just 2 minutes. Drain the juice from the scallops and set aside with the shrimp.

7. Remove all the bones from the crab meat. Set aside.

8. Melt the remaining 4 tablespoons of the butter in a saucepan. Stir in the flour. Blend and cook until slightly brown. Add the cognac and stir for 1 minute. Add the sherry and cook for 2 minutes.

9. Combine the clam juice and the reduced wine and gradually add this liquid to the butter-flour mixture. Stir and cook slowly until you have a smooth sauce.

10. Add 1 cup of the cheese. Mix well and pour in the cream and the sautéed mushrooms. Taste for seasoning.

11. Fold in the crab meat, scallops, and shrimp. Mix well and fill the scallop shells with this mixture. Sprinkle the balance of the cheese on top.

12. When almost ready to serve, put the shells in a shallow roasting pan, side by side, and bake in a preheated 400° oven for 10 minutes. When the sauce starts to bubble on the side of the scallop shells, place under a hot broiler until the tops are nicely browned.

Coquilles de Volaille au Gratin
Chicken Coquilles au Gratin

SERVES 8.

4 cups diced, cooked chicken
2½ cups Mornay Sauce (p. 11)

Salt and freshly ground black pepper to taste
½ *pound fresh mushrooms, sliced and sautéed in butter*
     (*optional*)
8 *scallop shells or ramekins*
¾ *cup grated Swiss Gruyère or Norwegian Jarlsberg cheese*
2 *to 3 tablespoons sweet butter*

1. Combine the chicken with the Mornay Sauce. Correct the seasoning with some salt and pepper if necessary and simmer over low heat for 2 to 3 minutes.

2. Add the mushrooms if you are using them.

3. Spoon the mixture into individual scallop shells or ramekins. Sprinkle the cheese evenly over the chicken; dot with little pieces of butter and arrange the shells on a cookie sheet or baking pan.

4. Bake in a preheated 375° oven for about 15 minutes, until the tops are browned and crisp. You can turn on the broiler for the last few minutes to hasten the browning.

CHAPTER 3

Soups

Potages

Soupe à l'Oignon Gratinée
Soupe Fermière aux Saucisses à la Vosgienne

Bouillabaisse Simple
Cotriade, ou Bouillabaisse Bretonne

Poule-au-Pot
Soupe aux Gombos à la Créole
Soupe Fermière aux Haricots Blancs Secs

Potage Crème de Carottes
Potage Crème de Champignons
Potage Crème de Cresson
Potage Crème d'Oignons
Potage Crème d'Oseille
Potage Crème de Poireaux et Pommes de Terre, ou "Vichyssoise"
Potage Crème de Potiron
Potage Crème de Romaine Paysanne

Potage Purée de Crevettes
Potage Purée de Crabes
Potage Purée de Homards

Potage Purée de Volaille à la Reine

Potage Purée de Haricots Noirs à l'Américaine
Potage Purée de Haricots Rouges à la Virion
Potage Purée de Lentilles
Potage Purée de Marrons
Potage Purée de Pois Frais, ou "Saint-Germain"
Potage Purée de Potiron au Lait

The aristocratic word for soup in French is *potage*. The word *potage* was originally used to describe great dishes of meat or fish boiled with vegetables. Many people avoid eating these heavy, peasant-style soups as appetizers for dinner because they leave hardly any room for the rest of the meal. But for lunch, a good bowl of hearty soup and French bread, followed with some nice cheese, is perfect. Even today in our diet-conscious world, an excellent *potage* has an important place as part of a formal dinner. Just eat it slowly and take a breathing spell after each course.

A good way to learn cooking is to prepare soups. Any vegetable or salad green will make a nice soup if it is given a good base. White stock is by far the best base for most soups, for it does not conflict with the taste of the various ingredients used. When you have leftovers from the day before, such as peas, carrots, asparagus, or cauliflower, try using them for soups. Heat the vegetables in some white stock and then puree the mixture in a blender. Put the mixture back on the stove, adding more stock if necessary. You can also add some milk or a combination of egg yolks and heavy cream just before serving. Taste for seasoning.

You will notice that nearly all my cream soups are made without the use of flour. Instead, I use potatoes, heavy cream, tapioca, or egg yolks. These give the soups a quality that flour cannot.

Soupe à l'Oignon Gratinée
Onion Soup

The central market of Paris, Les Halles, was always an attraction to American tourists. All the food delicacies were on hand and the all-night restaurants specialized in onion soup. It was quite fashionable to go there after attending the theater or the opera and then eat an earthy soup in the early morning hours. Some say the soup was an antidote for the heavy drinking done the evening before.

My recipe for onion soup depends largely on the quality of the brown stock you use. I use a good clear beef bouillon, much like the one from the Boiled Beef with Vegetables (p. 122). I can hear the critics: Why no Parmesan cheese? Why croutons, not toast? The Swiss Gruyère cheese lends a smoother, more subtle flavor than the Parmesan. The croutons sautéed in butter add greatly to the soup. The chervil used in small quantity brings the final touch to my recipe.

Do not worry if you do not have special onion soup casseroles. I have always felt that the browning of a half dozen individual bowls of soup in the oven was a difficult, if not dangerous, task for the harried housewife with only two hands. Regular deep soup bowls will be fine.

SERVES 6.

6 *white onions, sliced*
4 *tablespoons sweet butter*
6 *cups strong beef bouillon*
24 *small pieces of bread (1 inch x 1 inch), sautéed in ½ cup*
       sweet butter until crisp
1 *cup grated Swiss Gruyère cheese*
1 *tablespoon chopped fresh chervil or parsley*

1. Sauté the onions in 4 tablespoons butter until tender and cooked to a light tan color. Be sure not to burn them.

2. Add the onions to the beef bouillon. Simmer for 20 minutes and set aside.

3. Have your soup bowls ready. Place 4 of the croutons in each of the 6 bowls. Divide the cheese among the bowls along with a sprinkle of chervil or parsley. Now pour the piping hot onion soup into each bowl.

Soupe Fermière aux Saucisses à la Vosgienne
Country Vegetable Soup with Smoked Sausage

SERVES 6 TO 8.

2 *pounds smoked sausage*
½ *pound salt pork*
2½ *quarts water*
3 *medium-sized turnips, cleaned, peeled, and cubed*
3 *large carrots, cleaned, peeled, and quartered*
2 *leeks, cleaned and sliced*
2 *medium-sized onions, cleaned, peeled, and chopped*
6 *medium-sized potatoes, cleaned, peeled, and diced*
1 *small head cabbage, cleaned, peeled, and quartered*
1 *to 1½ teaspoons salt*
½ *to 1 teaspoon freshly ground black pepper*
2 *tablespoons chopped fresh chervil or parsley*

1. In a large pot, place the smoked sausage, salt pork, and water and bring to a boil. Reduce the heat and simmer for 1 hour.

2. Add the turnips, carrots, leeks, onions, and potatoes. Bring again to a boil. Reduce the heat and simmer for 30 minutes.

3. Add the cabbage. Simmer until all the vegetables are tender.

4. Season with the salt and pepper. Slice the meat and put some in each soup serving. Sprinkle chervil or parsley on top and serve hot.

Bouillabaisse Simple
Simple Bouillabaisse

SERVES 6 TO 8.

4 *medium-sized yellow onions*
5 *tablespoons sweet butter*
3 *small green peppers, sliced*
3 *medium-sized potatoes, peeled and sliced*
1 *clove garlic, minced*

1 *bay leaf*
1 *teaspoon salt*
4 *cups boiling water*
4 *tablespoons tomato paste*
1 *pound fish fillets (sole, flounder, or cod)*
16 *large shrimp, peeled and deveined*
1 *6½-ounce can Alaskan king crab meat*
1 *tablespoon chopped fresh parsley*

1. In a large kettle simmer the onions in butter until slightly browned. Be careful not to burn them.
2. Add the peppers, potatoes, garlic, bay leaf, and salt. Cook for a few minutes longer.
3. Add boiling water. Cover and simmer gently for 25 minutes, until the peppers and potatoes are tender.
4. Add the tomato paste and blend.
5. Add the fish fillets and simmer for 5 minutes.
6. Add the shrimp and cook for an additional 5 minutes.
7. Add the crab meat and cook the entire mixture for another 5 minutes.
8. Taste for additional seasoning. Sprinkle parsley on top and serve in deep soup bowls.

Cotriade, ou Bouillabaisse Bretonne
Cotriade, or Brittany Bouillabaisse

The Cotriade is the Brittany fisherman's favorite soup. As a kid, I used to see the fishermen using fresh sardines, mackerel, Daurade, red mullet, and conger eel for the Cotriade. The secret of a good fish soup like Bouillabaisse or Cotriade is the use of good fresh fish and plenty of them. I prefer the Cotriade to the Mediterranean Bouillabaisse, because I love the fish from the cold waters of the Atlantic Ocean or the North Sea. There is no substitute for fresh fish just out of the ocean, trout just caught from a brook, or salmon recently pulled from a roaring river.

It is great fun to cook this recipe outdoors in the authentic way, over a wood fire. Of course, you can also make the same recipe on the top of your kitchen stove.

In place of the traditional fish used in Brittany, you can use cod, red snapper, mackerel, lobster, mussels, or clams. Just be sure the fish is absolutely fresh.

SERVES 6 TO 8.

6 *tablespoons sweet butter*
6 *large yellow onions, sliced*
3 *quarts water*
6 *large potatoes, peeled and cut in quarters*
¼ *teaspoon thyme*
1 *clove garlic, minced*
2 *bay leaves*
4 *sprigs fresh parsley*
Fish of your choice (5 to 6 pounds, cut in large chunks)
Salt and freshly ground black pepper
French bread, sliced and toasted

1. Heat butter in a large kettle over a wood fire and in it sauté the onions. When the onions begin to turn a pale gold, add the water.

2. Add the potatoes, thyme, garlic, bay leaves, and parsley.

3. Bring the mixture to a boil and cook until the potatoes are nearly cooked.

4. Add the fish and boil rapidly for 5 to 10 minutes or until just done. Do not overcook. Season to taste.

5. To serve, put all the liquid in a tureen with the slices of toasted French bread and place the fish on a large platter surrounded by the potatoes.

Poule-au-Pot
Chicken Soup with Julienne Vegetables

This is a full-flavored chicken broth served with assorted julienne vegetables. The chicken used in the broth should be reserved for other recipes, such as Chicken Fricassee with Suprême Sauce (p. 218). Any leftover strained broth can be served as a Consommé de Volaille. It can also be used as the base for the sauce in the fricassee.

Poule-au-Pot makes a lovely first course before an elegant dinner.

SERVES 8.

1 *5-pound stewing chicken*
3 *quarts White Stock* (*p. 6*) *or canned chicken consommé*
2 *carrots, finely cut into matchstick slices*
2 *white onions, finely shredded*
2 *stalks celery, finely cut into matchstick slices*
¼ *pound string beans, sliced*
1 *cup small peas*
2 *to 3 tablespoons sweet butter*
1 *tablespoon chopped fresh chervil or parsley*
Salt and freshly ground black pepper to taste

1. Place the chicken in the broth and bring it to a boil. Simmer until tender, approximately 2 hours. Do not overcook, or your bird will fall apart.

2. Remove the chicken from the broth and reserve it for use in another recipe. Strain the broth through cheesecloth or a finely woven towel. Cool and refrigerate overnight. Now you have a Consommé de Volaille.

3. Cook all of the vegetables very slowly in the butter until they are just tender.

4. Remove the jellied broth or Consommé de Volaille from the refrigerator and skim off the top layer of congealed fat. Reheat the broth and the vegetables together just before dinner.

5. Add the chervil or parsley, and seasonings. Serve piping hot.

Soupe aux Gombos à la Créole
Chicken Gumbo Soup

SERVES 10.

4 *tablespoons sweet butter*
1 *3-pound chicken, cooked, boned, with chicken meat cut into*
    small pieces
2 *small white onions, sliced*
3 *cups sliced okra, fresh or frozen*

3½ *cups canned tomatoes, or 6 large tomatoes, peeled and chopped*
6 *cups White Stock (p. 6) or canned chicken consommé*
2 *sprigs fresh parsley*
1 *bay leaf*
¼ *teaspoon thyme*
½ *teaspoon salt*
¼ *teaspoon freshly ground black pepper or dash cayenne pepper*
1½ *cups cooked rice*

1. Melt the butter in a large skillet and sauté the chicken pieces for about 10 minutes, or until lightly browned. Remove the chicken.
2. In the same skillet, sauté the onions and okra until slightly tender.
3. Add the tomatoes and simmer for 10 minutes.
4. In a large saucepan, place the chicken, onions, okra, tomatoes, White Stock or consommé, parsley, bay leaf, and thyme and simmer, covered, for about 1 hour.
5. Add the salt and pepper and the cooked rice and serve.

Soupe Fermière aux Haricots Blancs Secs
Country Vegetable Soup with Dried White Beans

SERVES 8 TO 10.

3 *to 4 tablespoons sweet butter*
4 *carrots, sliced*
2 *turnips, diced*
2 *large yellow onions, chopped*
1 *leek, chopped*
2 *stalks celery, sliced*
8 *cups White Stock (p. 6) or canned chicken consommé*
1 *cup cooked dried white beans*
Salt and freshly ground black pepper
8 *to 10 thin slices of French bread, toasted*
2 *to 3 tablespoons chopped fresh chervil or parsley*

1. Melt the butter and sauté the carrots, turnips, onions, leek, and celery in a covered pan for 6 to 8 minutes. Do not scorch any of the vegetables.

2. Add the White Stock or consommé and cook slowly until the vegetables are tender, approximately 40 minutes.

3. Add the cooked beans and simmer for 5 minutes longer.

4. Taste for seasoning. Serve over the French bread. Sprinkle parsley or chervil over each serving.

Potage Crème de Carottes
Cream of Carrot Soup

This soup can also be served cold.

SERVES 8.

8 *medium-sized carrots, sliced*
2 *small white onions, sliced*
2 *stalks celery, sliced*
3 *cups White Stock (p. 6) or canned chicken consommé*
1 *teaspoon salt*
½ *teaspoon freshly ground black pepper*
3 *egg yolks*
1 *cup heavy cream*
Pinch of cayenne pepper
½ *cup chopped fresh parsley*

1. In a covered saucepan, slowly simmer the carrots, onions, and celery in the White Stock or consommé until they are tender. Season with the salt and pepper.

2. Place the cooked mixture in the blender on high speed until you have a smooth puree. You may have to do this in 2 operations so as not to overload the blender.

3. When ready to serve, beat the egg yolks and cream together and add them to the hot soup. Do not allow the soup to boil. Add the cayenne pepper.

4. Sprinkle parsley on top and serve hot.

Potage Crème de Champignons
Cream of Mushroom Soup

SERVES 8.

5 cups White Stock (p. 6) or canned chicken consommé
1 small bay leaf
4 sprigs fresh parsley
¼ teaspoon thyme
1½ pounds fresh mushrooms
6 tablespoons sweet butter
2 small white onions, chopped fine
3 tablespoons flour
3 egg yolks
¾ cup heavy cream
½ teaspoon salt
½ teaspoon freshly ground black pepper
1 teaspoon lemon juice or 1 teaspoon Madeira wine (optional)
1 tablespoon chopped fresh parsley

1. Simmer the White Stock or consommé with the bay leaf, parsley, and thyme for 10 minutes. Remove the herbs. Set aside.

2. Wash the mushrooms and drain. Cut the mushrooms in fine pieces and sauté in 2 tablespoons of the butter until the mushroom liquid evaporates. Do not scorch the mushrooms, or the taste will be bitter. Remove from the heat and set aside.

3. Over moderately high heat sauté the onions in the remaining 4 tablespoons of butter.

4. When onions are tender and transparent, add the flour and stir constantly so that the butter is well blended with the flour.

5. Cook the mixture slowly for 3 or 4 minutes, then start adding the stock, a little at a time, until you have a smooth white sauce. Add the mushrooms and cool. If you think the mixture is too thick, add a little bit more of the stock.

6. Put the entire mixture through the blender until smooth.

7. Beat together the egg yolks and cream. When soup is ready to be served, reheat it gently. When very hot, but not boiling, add the egg yolk-cream mixture, stirring until well blended. Season with the salt and pepper.

8. You can now add the optional lemon juice or Madeira, if you wish. Sprinkle with parsley and serve.

Potage Crème de Cresson
Cream of Watercress Soup

SERVES 6.

1 *bunch fresh watercress*
3 *tablespoons sweet butter*
4 *medium-sized potatoes, peeled and quartered*
2 *cups White Stock (p. 6) or canned chicken consommé*
1 *cup boiling milk*
3 *egg yolks*
½ *cup heavy cream*
¾ *teaspoon salt*
½ *teaspoon freshly ground black pepper*

1. Wash the watercress well. Cut stems and leaves in ¼-inch pieces. Drain.
2. Put the pieces in a saucepan with the butter. Cover and cook for approximately 15 minutes, or until tender.
3. In another saucepan, boil the potatoes until tender. Add the cooked potatoes to the watercress along with the White Stock or consommé.
4. Put the entire mixture through the blender to make a smooth puree.
5. Transfer to a saucepan and add boiling milk.
6. In a bowl, beat together the egg yolks and cream. When ready to serve, heat the watercress soup until almost ready to boil. Remove from the stove and stir in the egg yolk and cream mixture. Season with the salt and pepper. Mix well and serve immediately.

Potage Crème d'Oignons
Cream of Onion Soup

SERVES 6 TO 8.

4 *tablespoons sweet butter*
6 *medium-sized white onions, finely chopped*

½ *green pepper, finely chopped*
5 *cups White Stock (p. 6) or canned chicken consommé*
3 *egg yolks*
1 *cup light cream*
Salt and freshly ground black pepper
2 *tablespoons chopped fresh parsley*

1. Melt the butter and sauté the onions and green pepper in it until transparent and slightly tender, but not browned.

2. Add the White Stock or consommé and simmer gently for 45 minutes, covered.

3. Beat the egg yolks and the cream together and stir into the soup. Reheat the soup but do not let it boil.

4. Season to taste. Sprinkle some parsley on top and serve hot.

NOTE: If you wish to have a smooth-textured soup, you can puree the soup in the blender just before adding the egg yolks and cream.

Potage Crème d'Oseille
Cream of Sorrel Soup

SERVES 6.

20 *sorrel leaves*
3 *tablespoons sweet butter*
1 *quart White Stock (p. 6) or canned chicken consommé*
3 *tablespoons instant tapioca*
1½ *cups scalded milk*
1 *teaspoon salt*
½ *teaspoon freshly ground black pepper*
3 *egg yolks*
½ *cup heavy cream*

1. Cut the sorrel leaves into fine shreds and sauté them in the butter for 5 minutes.

2. Add the White Stock or consommé and bring to a boil.

3. Stir in the tapioca, cooking for 2 minutes, stirring constantly.

4. Add the milk and season the soup with the salt and pepper.

5. Just before serving, reheat the soup not quite to a boil. Remove from the stove.

6. Beat together the egg yolks and cream and add them to the hot soup, stirring until well blended. Serve immediately.

Potage Crème de Poireaux et Pommes de Terre, ou "Vichyssoise"
Cream of Leek and Potato Soup

SERVES 6 TO 8.

5 *or* 6 *leeks*
½ *cup water*
4 *large potatoes, peeled and quartered*
3 *cups White Stock* (*p.* 6) *or canned chicken consommé*
6 *tablespoons sweet butter*
½ *teaspoon freshly ground black pepper*
½ *cup minced fresh parsley*
1 *cup boiling milk*
3 *egg yolks*
1 *cup heavy cream*
1 *teaspoon salt*

1. Clean the leeks very well. Discard the outside by trimming part of the green leaves and the root end of the leeks. Split the remainder and wash thoroughly. Be certain to remove all the sand. Drain well and chop the leeks into small pieces.

2. Cook the leeks in a large saucepan with the water. Bring to a boil. Cover and let simmer slowly until the leeks are tender. Set aside.

3. In another pot, cook the potatoes in boiling water.

4. When the potatoes are tender, approximately 25 minutes, drain them. Combine the potatoes, leeks, White Stock or consommé, butter, and black pepper and cook together for a few minutes.

5. When the mixture is well blended, cool it thoroughly. Put it through a blender until it is all pureed. You may have to do this in 2 operations so as not to overload the blender.

6. Put the puree in a saucepan. Add the parsley and the milk.

7. In a little bowl, beat together the egg yolks and the cream.

8. When ready to serve the soup, reheat it not quite to a boil and add the egg yolk and cream mixture. Season with the salt and extra pepper if necessary. Serve hot.

Potage Crème de Potiron
Cream of Pumpkin Soup

SERVES 6 TO 8.

5 *tablespoons sweet butter*
2 *small white onions, minced*
1 *1-pound fresh pumpkin, peeled and diced*
4 *cups White Stock* (*p. 6*) *or canned chicken consommé*
Dash of ginger
Dash of mace
3 *egg yolks*
1 *cup heavy cream*
½ *teaspoon salt* (*optional*)
1 *tablespoon chopped fresh parsley*
½ *cup croutons, sautéed in butter* (*optional*)

1. Melt 2 tablespoons of the butter and sauté the chopped onions in it until tender but not browned.
2. Add the pumpkin and the White Stock or consommé and simmer until the pumpkin is tender.
3. Add the ginger and mace and puree the mixture in the blender.
4. Return the pumpkin puree to the pan and reheat. Beat together the egg yolks and cream and add to the pumpkin mixture. Do not let the soup come to the boil. Correct seasoning by adding the salt if necessary.
5. Swirl in the remaining 3 tablespoons of butter and serve sprinkled with parsley and croutons if you wish.

Potage Crème de Romaine Paysanne
Cream of Romaine Lettuce Soup

This soup can be varied by using Boston lettuce, spinach, or escarole instead of the Romaine, if you like. Since it is a soup with a chicken-stock base, you must take into account the saltiness of the stock before seasoning the soup. Always taste your food before adding any seasoning and then add just a little at a time.

SERVES 6.

2 *small white onions, chopped*
3 *tablespoons sweet butter*
3 *cups White Stock (p. 6) or canned chicken consommé*
10 *leaves of Romaine lettuce, chopped fine*
2 *tablespoons instant tapioca*
1 *cup milk, boiled*
3 *egg yolks*
½ *cup heavy cream*
1 *teaspoon salt*
½ *teaspoon freshly ground black pepper*
1 *tablespoon chopped fresh parsley*

1. Sauté the chopped onions in the butter until tender and transparent, but not browned.

2. Add the White Stock or consommé and bring to a boil.

3. Add the Romaine lettuce and cook slowly for about 15 minutes, or until the Romaine is wilted. Cool slightly.

4. Put the mixture through a blender until it is a smooth puree.

5. Pour once again into a saucepan and bring to a boil. Add the tapioca and stir over the heat for just 1 minute, no more. Remove from the stove.

6. Just before serving, add the milk and stir well. Bring slowly to a boil and remove from the heat.

7. Beat the egg yolks and cream together. Stir them into the soup until the mixture is well blended. Be sure not to let the soup boil after the egg yolk and cream mixture is added, or it will curdle.

8. Season with the salt and pepper. Sprinkle a little parsley on top and serve.

Potage Purée de Crevettes
Cream of Shrimp Soup

SERVES 6 TO 8.

1 8-ounce bottle clam juice
½ cup dry white wine
3 sprigs fresh parsley
1 large bay leaf
¼ teaspoon thyme
1½ pounds frozen shrimp, peeled and deveined, or
    fresh shrimp, in the shells
5 tablespoons sweet butter
2 small white onions, chopped
2 stalks celery, chopped
2 small carrots, sliced
4 cups White Stock (p. 6) or canned chicken consommé
3 egg yolks
½ cup heavy cream
Salt and freshly ground black pepper to taste
2 tablespoons chopped fresh parsley

1. Put the clam juice, wine, parsley, bay leaf, and thyme into a saucepan and bring to a boil.

2. Add the frozen shrimp. When the liquid begins to boil again, remove the pan from the stove. Let it stand, covered, for 1 minute and then remove the shrimp and reserve the juice. If you use fresh shrimp, add them to the boiling liquid with the shells on. When the liquid comes back to a boil, reduce the heat and simmer 2 to 5 minutes, depending on the size of the shrimp. Then remove the shrimp and shell and devein them. Reserve the juice.

3. In another saucepan, melt 3 tablespoons of the butter and sauté the onions, celery, and carrots in it until tender, being careful not to let them brown.

4. Add the White Stock or consommé and the reserved shrimp liquid. Bring to a boil and simmer gently until all the vegetables are cooked. Remove the parsley and bay leaf and discard.

5. Cut the shrimp in little pieces. Add to the vegetables and stock and puree the entire mixture in a blender.

6. Return the pureed shrimp soup to the pan and slowly reheat.

Beat the egg yolks and cream together and add the mixture to the soup, being careful not to let the soup boil.

7. Correct seasoning with some salt and pepper if necessary. Swirl in the remaining 2 tablespoons of butter and serve with parsley on top.

Potage Purée de Crabes
Cream of Crab Meat Soup

SERVES 6 TO 8.

1 8-*ounce bottle clam juice*
½ *cup dry white wine*
3 *sprigs fresh parsley*
1 *large bay leaf*
¼ *teaspoon thyme*
2 8-*ounce cans Japanese crab meat or 1 pound fresh crab meat, cartilage removed*
5 *tablespoons sweet butter*
2 *small white onions, chopped*
2 *stalks celery, chopped*
2 *small carrots, sliced*
4 *cups White Stock* (*p. 6*) *or canned chicken consommé*
3 *egg yolks*
½ *cup heavy cream*
Salt and freshly ground black pepper to taste
2 *tablespoons chopped fresh parsley*

1. Put the clam juice, wine, parsley, bay leaf, and thyme into a saucepan and bring to a boil.

2. Add the crab meat. When the liquid begins to boil again, remove the pan from the stove. Let it stand, covered, for 1 minute and then remove the crab meat and reserve the juice.

3. In another saucepan melt 3 tablespoons of the butter and sauté the onions, celery, and carrots in it until tender, being careful not to let them brown.

4. Add the White Stock or consommé and the reserved crab-meat liquid. Bring to a boil and simmer gently until all the vegetables are cooked. Remove the parsley and bay leaf and discard.

5. Cut the crab meat into little pieces. Add to the vegetables and stock and puree the entire mixture in a blender.

6. Return the pureed crab-meat soup to the pan and slowly reheat. Beat the egg yolks and cream together and add the mixture to the soup, being careful not to let the soup boil.

7. Correct seasoning with salt and pepper if necessary. Swirl in the remaining 2 tablespoons of butter and serve with parsley on top.

Potage Purée de Homards
Cream of Lobster Soup

SERVES 6 TO 8.

1 8-ounce bottle clam juice
½ cup dry white wine
3 sprigs fresh parsley
1 large bay leaf
¼ teaspoon thyme
1 pound fresh or frozen lobster meat
5 tablespoons sweet butter
2 small white onions, chopped
2 stalks celery, chopped
2 small carrots, sliced
4 cups White Stock (p. 6) or canned chicken consommé
3 egg yolks
½ cup heavy cream
Salt and freshly ground black pepper to taste
2 tablespoons chopped fresh parsley

1. Put the clam juice, wine, parsley, bay leaf, and thyme into a saucepan and bring to a boil.

2. Add the lobster meat. When the liquid begins to boil again, remove the pan from the stove. Let it stand, covered, for 1 minute and then remove the lobster and reserve the juice.

3. In another saucepan, melt 3 tablespoons of the butter and sauté the onions, celery, and carrots in it until tender, being careful not to let them brown.

4. Add the White Stock or consommé and the reserved lobster liquid. Bring to a boil and simmer gently until all the vegetables are cooked. Remove the parsley and bay leaf and discard.

5. Cut the lobster into little pieces. Add to the vegetables and stock, and puree the entire mixture in a blender.

6. Return the pureed lobster soup to the pan and slowly reheat. Beat the egg yolks and cream together and add the mixture to the soup, being careful not to let the soup boil.

7. Correct seasoning with salt and pepper if necessary. Swirl in the remaining 2 tablespoons of butter and serve with parsley on top.

Potage Purée de Volaille à la Reine
Puree of Chicken Soup à la Reine

SERVES 8 TO 10.

1 *large whole broiling chicken* (*approximately* 3 *pounds*)
1 *leek, diced*
1 *heart of celery, diced*
3 *small white onions, diced*
5 *cups White Stock* (*p.* 6) *or canned chicken consommé*
⅓ *cup uncooked long-grain rice*
1 *teaspoon salt*
½ *teaspoon freshly ground black pepper*
3 *egg yolks*
⅔ *cup heavy cream*
4 *tablespoons sweet butter*
¼ *cup chopped fresh parsley*

1. In a large pot put the chicken, leek, celery, onions, and White Stock or consommé. Bring to a boil.

2. Add the rice. Cover and simmer gently until the chicken and rice are cooked.

3. Bone the chicken and cut the meat into small pieces. Return the meat to the stock and the vegetables and put the entire mixture through a blender to make a puree. You may have to do this in several operations because of the quantity of the ingredients.

4. Return the puree to the pan. If too thick, add more White Stock or consommé. Season with the salt and pepper.

5. Just before serving, beat together the egg yolks and cream. Add to the chicken-vegetable puree. Then swirl in the butter. Heat the

soup but do not let it boil. Correct the seasoning. Serve with parsley sprinkled on top.

Potage Purée de Haricots Noirs à l'Américaine
Puree of Black Bean Soup à l'Américaine

SERVES 12.

1¾ *cups dried black beans*
2 *small white onions, minced*
2 *tablespoons rendered salt pork fat*
1 *ham bone*
2 *small carrots, minced*
2 *stalks celery, minced*
5 *sprigs fresh parsley*
1 *large bay leaf*
3 *cloves*
2 *whole allspice or pinch ground allspice*
7 *cups water*
1 *teaspoon salt*
¼ *teaspoon freshly ground black pepper*
1 *tablespoon flour* (*optional*)
1 *tablespoon butter* (*optional*)
¼ *teaspoon cayenne pepper*
¾ *cup cream sherry*
Garnishes: 3 or 4 hard-boiled eggs, coarsely chopped;
*   2 tablespoons chopped fresh parsley; 1 lemon, thinly*
*   sliced*

1. Soak the beans overnight in cold water to cover.

2. The next day, in a large pot, sauté the onions in the pork fat until slightly browned, but not burned.

3. Add the drained black beans, ham bone, carrots, celery, parsley, bay leaf, cloves, allspice, water, salt, and black pepper.

4. Bring the soup to a boil and then let it simmer slowly, covered, for 2 hours, or until the beans are tender. If the soup seems too thick during the cooking, add a little more water.

5. Remove the parsley, bay leaf, cloves, allspice, and ham bone and strain the soup through a fine sieve or food mill. If the soup is too thin, thicken it with 1 tablespoon of the flour mixed together with 1 tablespoon of the butter.

6. Add the cayenne pepper and bring the soup to a boil.

7. Just before serving, add the sherry and taste for additional seasoning.

8. Ladle the soup into each bowl and garnish each portion with some of the chopped eggs, parsley, and a thin slice of lemon.

Potage Purée de Haricots Rouges à la Virion
Puree of Kidney Bean Soup à la Virion

This recipe is faster to make than Puree of Black Bean Soup à l'Américaine (p. 75). It is made with dark-red kidney beans, which are more readily available and don't need to be soaked.

SERVES 12.

2 *small white onions, minced*
2 *tablespoons sweet butter*
2 *small carrots, minced*
3 *stalks celery, minced*
5 *sprigs fresh parsley*
3 *cloves*
2 *whole allspice, or pinch of ground allspice*
1 *2-pound smoked cured butt of pork shoulder*
2 *cups Brown Stock (p. 4) or canned beef consommé*
3 *cups water*
2 *15½-ounce cans dark red kidney beans*
¼ *teaspoon cayenne pepper*
¾ *cup cream sherry*
Salt and freshly ground black pepper
Garnishes: 3 *or* 4 *hard-boiled eggs, coarsely chopped;*
       chopped fresh parsley; 1 *lemon, thinly sliced*

1. Sauté the onions in the butter in a large saucepan until slightly browned, but not burned.

2. Add the carrots, celery, parsley, cloves, allspice, and the pork butt.

3. Cover with the Brown Stock or consommé and water. Bring the mixture to a boil and let it simmer until the pork is tender, about 1½ hours.

4. Remove the meat, parsley, and spices.

5. Add the beans and cayenne pepper to the soup and simmer, covered, for 10 minutes.

6. Put the whole mixture through a blender, in several operations.

7. When ready to serve, add the sherry and some salt, black pepper, and extra cayenne pepper if necessary.

8. Ladle the soup into each bowl and garnish each portion with some of the chopped eggs, parsley, and a thin slice of lemon.

NOTE: The smoked pork butt is excellent served sliced, hot or cold, with cold potato salad.

Potage Purée de Lentilles
Puree of Lentil Soup

SERVES 6.

1 *cup dried lentils*
½ *cup chopped celery*
½ *cup diced carrots*
4 *small white onions, sliced*
4 *cups Brown Stock (p. 4) or canned beef consommé*
6 *sprigs fresh parsley, chopped*
¼ *teaspoon thyme*
¼ *teaspoon rosemary*
2 *small bay leaves*
3 *egg yolks*
½ *cup heavy cream*
1 *teaspoon salt*
½ *teaspoon freshly ground black pepper*

1. Soak the lentils in cold water for 1 hour, no more.

2. Add the lentils, celery, carrots, and onions to the Brown Stock or consommé in a covered saucepan and season with the parsley, thyme, rosemary, and bay leaves. Simmer slowly until all the vegetables are tender, approximately 2 hours. Add more stock if necessary, since the lentils absorb it.

3. Remove the bay leaves and put the mixture through a blender until you have a smooth, thick puree.

4. When ready to serve, reheat the mixture. Beat together the egg yolks and the cream. Add the egg yolk and cream mixture to the hot soup, stirring until well blended. Season with the salt and pepper and serve immediately.

Potage Purée de Marrons
Puree of Chestnut Soup

SERVES 6.

3 *tablespoons sweet butter*
4 *stalks celery, chopped*
2 *small white onions, chopped*
4 *cups White Stock (p. 6) or canned chicken consommé*
1 *15-ounce can unsweetened chestnut puree imported from France; or 1 pound fresh chestnuts in season, shelled, peeled, and cooked in broth until tender; or 1 1-pound can whole chestnuts*
2 *egg yolks (optional)*
½ *cup heavy cream*
½ *teaspoon salt*
½ *teaspoon freshly ground black pepper*
24 *croutons, sautéed in butter*

1. Melt the butter in a saucepan and sauté the celery and onions in it until tender.

2. Add the White Stock or consommé and either the chestnut puree or cooked fresh or canned whole chestnuts. Puree the mixture in a blender.

3. Just before serving, beat together the egg yolks and cream and add to the soup. You can omit the egg yolks if desired and just add the cream. If the soup seems a bit too thick, you can add a little more stock or consommé.

4. Season with the salt and pepper and serve hot with croutons sprinkled on top.

Potage Purée de Pois Frais, ou "Saint-Germain"
Puree of Fresh Pea Soup

The original Potage Saint-Germain was made with dried split peas, which have to be soaked overnight, and with ham bones. My version uses fresh or frozen peas and boiled ham and is faster and easier to prepare as well as very tasty.

SERVES 6 TO 8.

4 *cups fresh or frozen peas*
2 *stalks celery, diced*
2 *small carrots, diced*
2 *small white onions, diced*
1 *cup boiling water*
3 *cups White Stock (p. 6) or canned chicken consommé*
⅓ *pound Polish boiled ham, diced*
1 *teaspoon salt*
½ *teaspoon freshly ground black pepper*
3 *tablespoons sweet butter*
¾ *cup heavy cream*
2 *tablespoons chopped fresh parsley*
¼ *cup croutons, sautéed in butter (optional)*

1. Simmer the peas, celery, carrots, and onions together in the boiling water until tender, approximately 45 minutes.

2. Add the White Stock or consommé and the ham and simmer for 5 minutes.

3. Puree all the ingredients in a blender. Return to the pan and season with the salt and pepper.

4. Stir in the butter and cream just before serving. Sprinkle some parsley and some croutons on top, if you wish.

Potage Purée de Potiron au Lait
Puree of Pumpkin Soup with Milk

SERVES 6 TO 8.

1 1-*pound fresh pumpkin, peeled and diced*
⅓ *cup water*
3 *tablespoons sweet butter*
3 *to 4 cups boiling milk*
1 *to 1½ tablespoons superfine sugar*
¼ *teaspoon salt (optional)*
¼ *teaspoon freshly ground black pepper (optional)*
¼ *cup croutons, sautéed in butter*

1. Cook the diced pumpkin in the water and butter in a covered saucepan until very soft, approximately 30 minutes.

2. Using a wire whisk, stir vigorously until the pumpkin becomes pureed, or puree the mixture in a blender.

3. Add the milk and sugar, according to taste. Add the salt and pepper if necessary. Serve with croutons sprinkled on top.

CHAPTER 4

Eggs

Oeufs

Omelette à la Française
Omelette aux Fines Herbes Monblason
Omelette à la Chasseur
Omelette à la Parmentier

❈

Oeufs Pochés
Oeufs Pochés au Gratin
Oeufs Pochés à la Florentine
Oeufs Pochés à la "Benedict"

❈

Oeufs en Cocotte à l'Aspic

❈

Oeufs Moulés

❈

Oeufs Brouillés

❈

Oeufs au Beurre Noir

❈

Pain Perdu Monblason

I have met quite a few people who, although they have tried for years, have not been successful in cooking a simple omelet. To make a good omelet, you have to work fast. It is just the opposite for scrambled eggs; they must be cooked slowly.

I had heard so often that the best omelet in the entire world was made at Mont St. Michel on the west coast of France. A special omelet recipe had been created by a French lady, Mme. Poulard, and it was the specialty of her restaurant there.

In the spring of 1970, I had the pleasure of visiting that beautiful spot and eating at Mme. Poulard's famous restaurant. At lunchtime we ordered a splendid meal, beginning with, of course, the omelet. When the platter came to our table, the omelet looked simply beautiful, nicely browned and quite light and high. It was a delight to the eye. I never should have touched it. As soon as I took the first bite, all my wonderful dreams evaporated. I was greatly disappointed. It was more like a soufflé than an omelet. I could hardly taste the eggs. Instead I tasted a noticeable trace of flour and too many egg whites, which overpowered the taste of the yolks.

You have to understand eggs. They have a sensibility of their own. Do not push them too far. Eggs will take only so much cooking and then no more. For a cook, the secret is to know just how much cooking is needed. Handle eggs with care, and they will react magnificently in your cakes, soufflés, mousses, sauces, and omelets.

Omelette à la Française
French Omelet

Often guests have insisted on watching me make an omelet and were amazed to see how simple it is. It really is easy to make a good omelet. Use a Teflon frying pan and a wooden spatula. Forget about iron or copper pans or about not washing the pan as you probably have been told for so many years.

What you must bear in mind is that the longer you cook eggs, the harder they get. An omelet should be cooked, but still soft in the center when you put it on the hot serving dish. I believe in using the same number of yolks and whites, more pepper than salt, good fresh heavy cream, and sweet butter.

SERVES 2.

4 *eggs*
¼ *teaspoon salt*
At least ¼ teaspoon freshly ground black pepper (more at your discretion)
2 *tablespoons heavy cream*
2 *to 3 tablespoons sweet butter*

1. Beat the eggs moderately with a wire whisk.
2. Add the salt, pepper, and cream and mix together.

3. Melt the butter in the Teflon frying pan. Do not let it burn. When the butter has melted and begins to sizzle, beat the eggs again briskly and pour them in on top of the sizzling butter.

4. Here is the trick with the wooden spatula. As soon as the omelet starts cooking and sets to the pan, move the mixture with the spatula so that the liquid egg mixture on top rolls to the edges to take the place of the mixture already done. Repeat this process until the entire egg mixture is cooked, but still creamy in the center.

5. Quickly, fold half of the omelet over onto the other half. Wait just a couple of seconds for the bottom to brown and slip the omelet out, upside down, onto a hot dish.

Omelette aux Fines Herbes Monblason
Omelet with Fresh Herbs Monblason

This omelet is typically French and was a great success at Monblason, where I almost always served it for breakfast. It is essential that all the herbs be freshly cut in season. I used to go out to the garden early in the morning and get what I needed a few minutes before preparing the omelets.

SERVES 2.

Ingredients for French Omelet (p. 84)
1 *teaspoon to 1 tablespoon each of finely chopped fresh parsley, chervil, chives, and tarragon*

1. Add to the egg mixture a combination of chopped parsley, chervil, chives, and tarragon, or whichever of these herbs are in season.
2. Cook the omelet as described on p. 84.

Omelette à la Chasseur
Omelet with Mushrooms and Chicken Livers

SERVES 2.

½ *pound chicken livers*
6 *large fresh mushrooms, sliced*

4 *tablespoons sweet butter*
3 *small white onions or shallots, minced*
¼ *cup Meat Glaze (p. 6) or Brown Sauce (p. 12)*
¼ *cup dry white wine*
¼ *teaspoon salt*
¼ *teaspoon freshly ground black pepper*
Ingredients for French Omelet (p. 84)
2 *tablespoons chopped fresh parsley*

1. Sauté the chicken livers and the mushrooms in the butter until the livers lose their pinkish color. Remove them.
2. Sauté the onions or shallots in the same skillet until tender and transparent.
3. Add the Meat Glaze or Brown Sauce, livers, mushrooms, and wine and simmer for 2 minutes. Season with the salt and pepper and set aside. Keep warm.
4. Prepare the omelet according to the recipe on p. 84.
5. Just before the omelet is ready to be folded over, spread half the chicken-liver mixture on one half and fold the other half over it. Slide the omelet onto a hot serving platter and top with the remaining chicken-liver mixture. Sprinkle with parsley and serve immediately.

Omelette à la Parmentier
Potato Omelet

SERVES 2 TO 3.

4 *tablespoons sweet butter*
2 *cups sliced or diced potatoes*
½ *teaspoon salt*
¼ *teaspoon freshly ground black pepper*
Ingredients for French Omelet (p. 84)
Garnishes: crisp bacon, cooked ham, or browned sausage;
    1 *tablespoon chopped fresh parsley*

1. Melt the butter in a skillet. Add the potatoes and cook over moderate heat until the potatoes are cooked through and nicely browned. Season with the salt and pepper.
2. Prepare the omelet mixture according to the recipe on p. 84.
3. Pour the omelet over the potatoes and cook as indicated.

4. Fold the omelet onto a hot platter. Garnish with the bacon, ham, or sausage and sprinkle the parsley on top.

Oeufs Pochés
Poached Eggs

There are two basic ways to poach an egg—with an egg poacher or without one. Of course, it is easier to do it with a regular poacher, but if you don't have one, you can improvise.

THE POACHER METHOD

1. Put 1 teaspoon of butter into each cup of the egg poacher. Then break an egg into each.

2. Bring the water in the pan to a gentle boil and cover the pan. The steam will cook a film of white over the yolk.

3. Cook until egg is nearly firm—just the center of the yolk should be soft. Lift the eggs out of the water and drain.

POACHED EGGS.

THE SKILLET METHOD

1. Put enough water in a large skillet to cover the eggs when they are put in the pan. Add 1 tablespoon of vinegar for 1 quart of water.

2. Without the eggs, bring the water to a boil, then reduce the heat. Just at the moment the water stops boiling, break the eggs 1 at a time into a saucer and slip each egg into the water.

3. When all the eggs are in, reheat the water to the simmering point. Cover the pan and remove it from the heat.

4. Let the eggs stand 4 to 5 minutes and test for the right firmness. The yolks should be soft in the center.

5. Lift the eggs out of the water, and drain them well. Trim the uneven edges of the whites and put the eggs aside to use in the following recipes.

Oeufs Pochés au Gratin
Poached Eggs au Gratin

This is a nice luncheon dish. It can be served with cooked fresh spinach or asparagus.

SERVES 3.

6 *eggs*
1 *cup grated Swiss Gruyère cheese*
2 *cups Béchamel Sauce (p. 9)*
Salt and freshly ground black pepper to taste

1. Poach the eggs according to the directions on pp. 87–88.

2. Add ½ cup of the grated cheese to the White Sauce and blend well. Season with some salt and pepper.

3. Pour ½ of the cheese sauce into a shallow baking dish. Place the eggs on the sauce and pour the balance of the sauce on top of each egg. Sprinkle the remaining ½ cup of cheese evenly on top.

4. Bake in a preheated 350° oven for 5 minutes. Broil to let the top get slightly browned. Do not overcook, or the eggs will get too hard. It is important that the center of the yolks stays soft.

Oeufs Pochés à la Florentine
Poached Eggs à la Florentine

SERVES 6.

2 *pounds fresh spinach*
5 *tablespoons sweet butter*

¼ teaspoon freshly ground or grated nutmeg
Salt and freshly ground black pepper
12 eggs
2 cups Mornay Sauce (p. 11), heated
1 cup grated Swiss Gruyère or Norwegian Jarlsberg cheese

1. Wash the spinach thoroughly to remove all the grit. Drain it thoroughly and chop it fine.
2. Place the spinach in a saucepan with the butter. Cover and cook very slowly until tender.
3. Season to taste with nutmeg, salt, and pepper. Drain excess liquid if any.
4. Place spinach in a shallow baking dish and keep warm in a preheated 250° oven.
5. Poach the eggs according to the directions on pp. 87–88 and place them on top of the spinach.
6. Cover the eggs with the hot Mornay Sauce and sprinkle the cheese evenly over the top.
7. Turn on the broiler and brown the top lightly. Serve hot.

Oeufs Pochés à la "Benedict"
Poached Eggs à la Benedict

SERVES 3.

6 eggs
6 slices boiled Polish ham
2 tablespoons sweet butter
6 slices white bread, toasted, or 3 English muffins, halved
    and toasted
1½ cups Hollandaise Sauce (p. 16)
Garnish: hot asparagus

1. Poach the eggs according to the directions on pp. 87–88. Remove the eggs from the pan; drain them well and trim the edges.
2. Sauté the slices of ham in the butter.
3. Place each slice of ham on a slice of toast or English-muffin half and top each with a poached egg.
4. Cover with Hollandaise Sauce. For lunch, you may garnish with hot asparagus.

Oeufs en Cocotte à l'Aspic
Eggs en Cocotte in Aspic

When something is served à l'aspic, it means that the food is coated with or molded in jelly. A quick and effective way to do this is to use commercial gelatin and canned consommé. The flavor of the aspic is sometimes enhanced by the addition of wine.

The French do not usually use commercial gelatin for their aspics. Their consommé contains sufficient gelatin derived from the beef, veal, or chicken bones that are cooked with it. If you wish to make a homemade light stock with enough bones to make it jell, then you can omit the commercial gelatin used in this recipe. Otherwise, use the canned consommé and commercial gelatin. You will have a lovely aspic with a minimum of time and effort.

Eggs en Cocotte in Aspic is a very good-looking dish. If it is done properly, the aspic should be transparent and completely cover the eggs.

SERVES 3.

1½ envelopes unflavored gelatin
⅓ cup cold water
2½ cups canned chicken consommé or White Stock (p. 6)
½ cup dry white wine
6 eggs
6 leaves fresh tarragon or 2 teaspoons chopped fresh parsley
6 small, thin slices boiled Polish ham
Lettuce leaves
Garnishes: string beans, asparagus vinaigrette

1. Put the gelatin into a small bowl and pour the cold water over it. Let it soften for about 5 minutes.

2. Bring the consommé and wine to a boil and add to the softened gelatin. Stir until the gelatin is completely dissolved. Cool.

3. Pour a ½-inch layer of cooled aspic into 6 individual ramekins or custard cups. Be sure that the cups are large enough so that the trimmed poached eggs will not touch the sides. Set the dishes in the refrigerator until the aspic is firm.

4. Poach the eggs by either of the methods indicated on pp. 87–88. Refrigerate eggs for 15 to 20 minutes.

EGGS EN COCOTTE IN ASPIC.

5. Place leaf of tarragon or cluster of parsley on top of gelatin. Then put a chilled egg in and a slice of ham on top.

6. Pour in some more aspic, cool but still liquid, until it covers the eggs by ¼ inch. The gelatin should completely surround the eggs and coat the sides of the dish. Set in the refrigerator again and when completely set, unmold the eggs onto a platter over a bed of lettuce. You can garnish the platter with string beans or asparagus vinaigrette.

Oeufs Moulés
Molded Eggs

SERVES 3.

2 tablespoons sweet butter
2 tablespoons herbs, finely chopped (parsley, chervil, chives,
   and/or tarragon)
2 tablespoons chopped boiled ham or diced cooked bacon
   or chopped sautéed mushrooms
6 eggs
½ teaspoon salt
½ teaspoon freshly ground black pepper

6 *slices buttered toast, or* 3 *English muffins, halved and*
   toasted
Tomato Sauce Provençale (*p.* 12) (*optional*)

1. Set a roasting pan, partially filled with hot water, into a 325°
oven. Have ready 6 individual ramekins or custard cups which will be
set into the pan. Be sure the water level comes about ¾ up the sides of
the cups.
2. Butter the insides of the custard cups generously and spread
the herbs and the ham, bacon, or mushrooms on the bottom and sides
of each. Break an egg into each cup. Sprinkle with the salt and pepper.
3. Place the cups in the pan of hot water and bake until the whites
of the eggs are set firmly enough to be unmolded and to retain their
shape, approximately 15 minutes. The yolks should be soft as in poached
eggs. Remove from the oven.
4. Unmold the eggs on buttered toast or toasted English muffins.
If desired, serve with Tomato Sauce Provençale.

Oeufs Brouillés
Scrambled Eggs

I have seen many cooks break eggs into a skillet and stir them
until they become stiff with some particles of white showing here and
there. They call them scrambled eggs. My method for making scrambled eggs is to beat the eggs in a bowl first, then mix in heavy cream
and seasoning and cook and stir them gently over moderate heat until
they are slightly firm.

SERVES 2.

4 *eggs*
¼ *teaspoon salt*
¼ *teaspoon freshly ground black pepper, or more according*
   to taste
4 *tablespoons heavy cream*
2 *tablespoons sweet butter*

1. In a bowl combine the eggs, salt, pepper, and cream. Beat moderately with a whisk until the yolks and whites of eggs are well blended.

2. Melt the butter in a skillet and when sizzling, add the egg mixture. Lower the heat. Stir gently and continuously until slightly firm. Some people prefer their eggs softer while others like them well cooked. The time to remove them from the heat is when they look smooth and creamy.

Oeufs au Beurre Noir
Eggs with Burned Butter

This is strictly a French specialty. Heat butter in a skillet and cook until it is black. Break eggs into the black butter and fry them. After the eggs are done and transferred to a platter, add some more butter to the frying pan along with a few drops of vinegar for each egg. Heat; pour this mixture over the eggs. Garnish with chopped parsley and/or some capers.

Pain Perdu Monblason
French Toast Monblason

Pain perdu translated means "lost bread." It really means stale bread, too dry to be used as such at the table. In the French tradition of letting nothing go to waste, the stale bread was soaked overnight in a mixture of eggs, milk, sugar, and vanilla extract, and became a French dessert.

Later on, it was adopted by the United States, and served here as a breakfast dish. Unfortunately, in this country, the bread is often dipped in the egg mixture just before cooking, and what you get is a dry piece of fried bread with some syrup on top. When serving French toast for breakfast at Monblason, we never could make enough to satisfy our customers. The reason is quite simple: We soaked the bread overnight so it completely absorbed the egg mixture, and our guests loved it.

SERVES 6.

6 *eggs*
2 *tablespoons granulated sugar*

1½ *cups milk or heavy cream*
1 *teaspoon vanilla extract or a ½-inch piece of vanilla bean*
12 *slices of white or French bread, stale or not*
8 *tablespoons sweet butter*
Garnishes: 1½ *to* 2 *pounds ham, bacon, or sausages; maple*
    syrup

1. Beat the eggs and sugar together in an electric mixer until well blended.

2. Add the milk or cream and continue beating at low speed for 2 minutes more.

3. Add the vanilla extract or vanilla bean.

4. In a shallow baking dish place the slices of bread side by side. Do not let them overlap. Pour the egg mixture on top of each slice. Place in the refrigerator the night before using. In the morning the liquid will be completely absorbed by the bread.

5. In a large skillet melt some butter and sauté the French toast until firm and nicely browned on both sides. Repeat the operation until the 12 slices are done. Serve with ham, bacon, or sausages, and a jar of maple syrup.

CHAPTER 5

Fish and
Seafood

Poissons et Fruits de Mer

Bar Farci

❋

Grand Flétan Grillé au Beurre Maître d'Hôtel

❋

Homard Thermidor Monblason

❋

Filets de Maquereau au Beurre Maître d'Hôtel
Filets de Maquereau au Gratin

❋

Moules à la Crème à Ma Façon

❋

Ouefs d'Alose Sautés à la Hollandaise
Oeufs d'Alose à l'Oseille

Côtelettes de Saumon au Beurre Maître d'Hôtel
Darne de Saumon Pochée (Chaud) à la Mousseline
Darne de Saumon Pochée (Froid) à la Mayonnaise
Soufflé de Saumon

❋

Filets de Sole au Vin Blanc
Filets de Sole au Crabe Monblason
Mousse de Sole

Thon aux Tomates

❋

Truites de Rivière Monblason
Truites de Rivière Sautées aux Amandes
Truites de Rivière en Matelote à la Bourguignonne
Truites de Rivière à la Crème

The world has been eating freshwater fish for thousands of years, and today commercial fishing boats are sailing thousands of miles to look for saltwater fish. Fish is a life staple, and thanks to modern freezing, refrigeration, and canning equipment on board fishing vessels, fish has become an important diet item in many sections of the world that are far from the sea. The process of drying, salting, and smoking for preserving saltwater fish was started a long time ago. French, Portuguese, and Scandinavian sailors sailed across the Atlantic Ocean to catch cod on the banks not far from Canada. The cod was pickled in salt, then dried and kept for many weeks before reaching its final destination—the consumer in Europe and Africa.

Fish has approximately the same high quality of protein as meat, and yet is not as fatty. Only the darker-fleshed fish such as mackerel, tuna, and salmon are heavy in oil. Also, fish is one of our few sources of iodine and carries additional types of vitamins and nutrients which are beneficial to our health.

Since fish does not keep very long, even when refrigerated, you have to be very careful in selecting fish which is fresh. My recommendation is to find a reliable fish market—one which receives its shipments daily, straight from the fishing piers. In selecting fish, look for clear, bright eyes. The scales should be bright colored, the gills reddish in color, the flesh firm and elastic to the touch, and the odor should be fresh, not objectionable.

Frozen fish can never replace fresh fish. In culinary work, even an amateur cook will notice the difference, for the frozen fish loses much of its goodness in defrosting and becomes flabby. Bear in mind, however, that it is better to eat a fresh, quick-frozen fish when defrosted than to eat a supposedly fresh fish that has been waiting for two days at the market for your purchase.

Always remember that fish deteriorates quickly and should be well covered in the refrigerator. If it is not tightly covered, its odor may contaminate the other food.

Bar Farci
Baked Stuffed Striped Bass

SERVES 4 TO 6.

1   2½- to 3½-pound striped bass
Salt and freshly ground black pepper
1   recipe Stuffing (see below)
6   tablespoons sweet butter
¾   cup dry white wine
2   tablespoons lemon juice
4   sprigs fresh parsley

BAKED STUFFED
STRIPED BASS.

1. Season the fish lightly with salt and pepper, and stuff it loosely with the Stuffing and close the opening by sewing with a large needle and strong thread.

2. Place some heavy-duty aluminum foil in the bottom of a baking pan and place the fish on top. This foil will help you to lift the fish without breaking it.

3. Melt 4 tablespoons of the butter in a saucepan, and add the wine, lemon juice, and parsley. Pour over the bass and bake in a pre-heated 400° oven for about 35 minutes, or until the fish flakes easily when tested with a fork.

4. Place the fish on a warm platter and remove the foil and thread.

5. Strain the sauce into a saucepan and swirl another 2 tablespoons of the butter into it. Pour the warm sauce over the fish and serve.

Stuffing

1 *cup finely chopped small white onions or shallots*
4 *tablespoons sweet butter*
1 *cup finely chopped fresh mushrooms*
1 *egg*
½ *cup milk*
2 *cups bread crumbs*
½ *cup finely chopped fresh parsley*
1 *teaspoon salt*
½ *teaspoon freshly ground black pepper*
Dash of freshly grated or ground nutmeg

1. Sauté the onions or shallots in 2 tablespoons of the butter until transparent and soft but not browned.

2. In another saucepan sauté the mushrooms in the remaining 2 tablespoons of butter until their liquid is evaporated.

3. Beat the egg and milk together.

4. Combine onions, mushrooms, and egg-milk mixture in a large bowl. Add bread crumbs, parsley, salt, pepper, and nutmeg and mix well. Taste for seasoning.

NOTE: This stuffing can be used not only for the striped bass but also for other fish like salmon or large trout.

Grand Flétan Grillé au Beurre Maître d'Hôtel
Grilled Halibut with Maître d'Hôtel Butter

SERVES 6.

½ cup Maître d'Hôtel Butter (p. 22)
2½ pounds halibut, cut into serving pieces
Salt and freshly ground black pepper
Flour
4 tablespoons vegetable oil

1. Prepare the Maître d'Hôtel Butter as directed on p. 22. Set aside until the fish is ready to serve.
2. Sprinkle the fish lightly with some salt and pepper and dip the pieces into some flour. Shake to remove any excess flour.
3. Put the vegetable oil into a broiler pan and place pan in a preheated 500° oven to heat the pan and the oil. When the pan is moderately hot, place the fish in it and baste the top with a little of the oil.
4. Broil the fish quickly on 1 side, approximately 6 minutes. Turn the pieces over carefully and baste again with oil. Broil again for 6 minutes, or until the fish flakes easily when pierced with a fork.
5. Place the fish on a platter and top each piece with the Maître d'Hôtel Butter. Serve.

Homard Thermidor Monblason
Lobster Thermidor Monblason

When I started to make my living as a cook, I used to follow to the letter all the original recipes I found in the books of *haute cuisine*. In the lobster recipes, they usually called for the splitting and cutting of live lobsters. (This should be called to the attention of the A.S.P.C.A.!) In a recipe for Lobster Thermidor, for example, they would instruct the cook to split the lobster alive and then to flame it in a hot oven with brandy. I can well imagine the average housewife's reaction on reading these instructions. Perhaps one out of a hundred would have the courage to do it.

Some may possibly notice the difference in taste between such recipes and mine. But is it worth it to make both the lobster and the cook suffer during the preparation of the recipe? Here I give you my modern and more humane version of Lobster Thermidor.

SERVES 3.

3 *live lobsters, 1½ pounds each*
4 *shallots, minced*
6 *tablespoons sweet butter*
½ *cup cream sherry, or white wine*
1 *pound fresh mushrooms, sliced*
3 *tablespoons flour*
2 *tablespoons cognac*
½ *teaspoon dry English mustard*
1 *cup heavy cream*
1 *cup grated Swiss Gruyère or Norwegian Jarlsberg cheese*
1¼ *cups milk (optional)*
Salt and freshly ground black pepper

1. Plunge the lobsters, head first, into a kettle of boiling water to which you have added some salt. Cook for 15 minutes. Remove the lobsters and let them cool.

2. Sauté the shallots in 1 tablespoon of the butter until they are tender and transparent, but not browned.

3. Add the sherry or wine and simmer until reduced to ¼ cup. Set aside.

4. Sauté the mushrooms in 2 tablespoons of the butter until all their liquid has evaporated. Do not brown. Set aside.

5. In a saucepan, melt the remaining 3 tablespoons of the butter and stir in the flour. Blend and cook slowly until slightly brown. Add the cognac and stir for 1 minute.

6. Add the mustard and then pour in the sherry or wine and shallots.

7. Continue to stir; pour in the cream, a little at a time, without stopping the stirring. You should have a smooth sauce.

8. Add the sautéed mushrooms and ½ cup of the grated cheese. If the sauce seems too thick, add a little milk. Set aside.

9. Now split the lobsters lengthwise. Crack the claws and legs and remove the meat. Wash the shells and turn them over to drain.

10. Cut the lobster meat into cubes and mix with the sauce. Taste for seasoning.

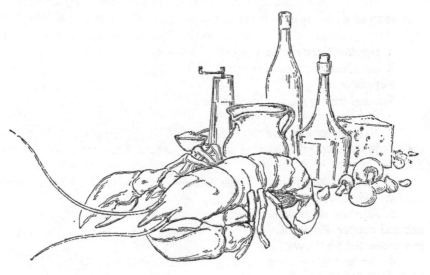

LOBSTER THERMIDOR.

11. Fill the shells with the mixture and sprinkle the rest of the cheese on top of each lobster. Place in a shallow baking pan and bake in a preheated 400° oven for 10 minutes, then under the broiler for 5 more minutes, or until nicely browned and crusty.

NOTE: This recipe can be prepared a day in advance up until the final baking and broiling operation. Just cover the filled lobster shells tightly with aluminum foil and refrigerate. Take them out of the refrigerator a while before you are ready to bake them. If you have more Lobster Thermidor than can fit into the shells, keep the leftovers for tomorrow's lunch. You can fill scallop shells with the mixture. Sprinkle some cheese on top and bake or broil them when ready to use.

Filets de Maquereau au Beurre Maître d'Hôtel
Fillets of Mackerel with Maître d'Hôtel Butter

There are many species of mackerel. This fish has a rich and delicious flavor, but should be prepared only when fresh, since it acquires a stronger flavor as it ages. Be careful when buying it. Patronize only the fish market that receives a fresh supply of fish daily.

SERVES 4.

2 1-*pound fresh mackerel, cut into 4 fillets*
2 *cups Maître d'Hôtel Butter* (*p.* 22)
Vegetable oil
Salt and freshly ground black pepper

1. Ask the man in the fish market to clean each mackerel; cut off the head; slit each fish along the back; remove the bone and cut it into 2 fillets.
2. Prepare the Maître d'Hôtel Butter as directed on p. 22. Reserve until the fish is ready to serve.
3. Rub the fillets with the oil. Sprinkle the fillets lightly with some salt and pepper. Place them in a flat, shallow baking dish and broil them in a preheated 500° oven for 5 minutes on each side.
4. Set the fillets on a platter and spread each with some of the Maître d'Hôtel Butter. Serve hot.

Filets de Maquereau au Gratin
Fillets of Mackerel au Gratin

SERVES 4.

2 1-*pound fresh mackerel, cut into 4 fillets*
Salt and freshly ground black pepper
4 *tablespoons sweet butter*
1 *tablespoon lemon juice*
6 *tablespoons dry white wine*
4 *shallots, minced*
½ *pound fresh mushrooms, sliced*
1 *tablespoon tomato puree*
½ *cup bread crumbs*

1. Ask the man in your fish market to clean each mackerel; cut off the head; slit each fish along the back; remove the bone, and cut it into two fillets.
2. Season the mackerel lightly with some salt and pepper.

3. Lightly butter a shallow Pyrex baking dish and put the fillets in it. Pour the lemon juice and white wine over them.

4. Melt 2 tablespoons of the butter in a skillet and sauté the shallots and the mushrooms until tender, but not browned. Add the tomato puree and set aside.

5. Bake the fish in a preheated 375° oven for 6 minutes.

6. Drain the liquid from the baking pan and simmer it until reduced by half. Add it to the shallots and mushrooms. Mix well and taste for seasoning.

7. Pour the sauce over the fillets. Sprinkle on the bread crumbs and the remaining 2 tablespoons of melted butter. Brown under a hot broiler and serve.

Moules à la Crème à Ma Façon
Mussels with Cream

SERVES 6.

6 *dozen mussels*
6 *shallots, minced*
4 *tablespoons sweet butter*
2 *cups Chablis or other dry white wine*
2 *cloves garlic, chopped*
1 *bay leaf*
½ *cup finely chopped fresh parsley*
½ *teaspoon freshly ground black pepper*
¼ *teaspoon salt*
2 *egg yolks*
1 *cup heavy cream*

1. Rinse the mussels thoroughly, so that no sand remains.

2. Sauté the minced shallots in the butter. Do not brown them, just cook them until they are tender.

3. Add the wine. Simmer gently for 1 hour until reduced by half.

4. Add the cleaned mussels, garlic, bay leaf, all but 2 tablespoons of the parsley, pepper, and a little salt. Do not add too much salt at this time, as the mussels will release a little salty sea water when they open. Cook, covered, for about 10 minutes.

5. When the mussels start to open, shake them well. Cook another 2 minutes and remove them from the pot.

6. Strain the liquid and bring to a boil.

7. Beat the egg yolks and the cream together and add the mixture to the sauce. Heat the sauce but do not let it boil. Taste for additional salt. Pour the sauce over the mussels. Sprinkle with parsley and serve in deep soup dishes. The sauce makes this dish a kind of mussel soup.

Oeufs d'Alose Sautés à la Hollandaise
Sautéed Shad Roe with Hollandaise Sauce

Shad roe must be poached before it can be sautéed. When you select the roe, be sure that its membrane is intact. Handle it very carefully during the poaching and sautéeing, as it is quite delicate.

SERVES 4.

2 *quarts water*
2 *tablespoons lemon juice, or vinegar*
1 *tablespoon salt*
4 *shad roe, medium to large size*
Flour
4 *tablespoons sweet butter*
2 *cups Hollandaise Sauce (p. 16)*

1. Put the water, the lemon juice or vinegar, and the salt into a pan and bring to a boil.

2. Gently place the roe into the water; reduce the heat and simmer, covered, for 10 to 15 minutes, depending on the size of the roe.

3. Drain and let the poached roe stand in cold water until they are cool. You may remove the membrane or not, as you wish.

4. Dry the roe thoroughly. Sprinkle with some flour and shake off the excess.

5. In a skillet melt the butter and when it starts bubbling, sauté the shad roe in it gently for about 5 minutes on each side.

6. Set the roe on a warm platter and serve with a sauceboat of Hollandaise Sauce on the side.

Broiled Shad Roe with Hollandaise Sauce

You may want to broil the roe instead of sautéeing it. Preheat the broiler until it is very hot and place the poached roe in the broiler 2 to 3 inches from the heat. Broil for 4 to 5 minutes on each side. Serve with a sauceboat of Hollandaise Sauce on the side.

Oeufs d'Alose à l'Oseille
Shad Roe with Sorrel

SERVES 4.

3 *tablespoons sweet butter*
4 *shallots, minced*
12 *leaves fresh sorrel, chopped fine, or ⅓ cup canned sorrel*
1 *cup dry white wine*
¼ *cup dry vermouth*
4 *poached shad roe (p. 105)*
1¼ *cups heavy cream*
Salt and freshly ground black pepper (optional)

1. Melt the butter in a skillet over low heat and sauté the shallots until tender and transparent, but not scorched or burned.

2. Add the chopped sorrel, wine, and vermouth. Bring to a boil. Reduce heat and simmer, covered, for 10 minutes.

3. Add the shad roe and continue the simmering for another 20 minutes. Remove the roe to a warm platter and keep warm in a preheated 250° oven.

4. Add the cream to the sorrel sauce. With the skillet uncovered, bring the sauce almost to a boil. Simmer and reduce the sauce to the consistency of a medium white sauce.

5. Taste for seasoning and correct with some salt and pepper if necessary. Pour over the shad roe and serve hot.

Côtelettes de Saumon au Beurre Maître d'Hôtel
Salmon Cutlets with Maître d'Hôtel Butter

SERVES 6.

6 ¾-inch-thick salmon slices (cut crosswise from fillets)
Vegetable oil
Salt and freshly ground black pepper
½ cup Maître d'Hôtel Butter (p. 22)

1. Dry salmon slices between paper towels. Brush lightly with oil and sprinkle each side with some salt and pepper and let stand for 15 minutes.
2. Set the salmon in a broiler pan. Place the pan under preheated 500° broiler and broil for 3 to 4 minutes on each side. The fish, when ready, should flake when tested with a fork and separate from the bones. Do not overcook the salmon, or it will get dry.
3. Pour some of the Maître d'Hôtel Butter over each slice of salmon. Serve immediately.

Darne de Saumon Pochée (Chaud) à la Mousseline
Poached Salmon Steak (Hot) with Mousseline Sauce

SERVES 6.

1 3½-pound salmon steak
2 cups Fish Stock (p. 7)
Garnishes: parslied potatoes and lemon wedges
1 cup Mousseline Sauce (p. 17)

1. Place the salmon in a saucepan or skillet and cover with the Fish Stock. Bring the liquid to a boil.
2. Lower the heat. Cover and simmer gently until the fish flakes when tested with a fork. It takes approximately 7 to 8 minutes cooking time per pound.
3. Remove the salmon from the pan and carefully remove the skin and bones.
4. Set on a platter. Surround with some small boiled parslied pota-

toes and lemon wedges. Serve some Mousseline Sauce in a sauceboat as an accompaniment.

Darne de Saumon Pochée (Froid) à la Mayonnaise Poached Salmon Steak (Cold) with Mayonnaise Sauce

SERVES 6.

1 3½-*pound salmon steak*
2 *cups Fish Stock (p. 7)*
Garnishes: lemon wedges, tomato wedges, and cucumber slices
1 *cup Mayonnaise Sauce (p. 18) or Green Sauce (p. 19)*

1. If you want to serve the salmon cold, poach it in the same manner as for Poached Salmon Steak (Hot) with Mousseline Sauce (p. 107) but cook just 6 minutes per pound.
2. Remove from the stove and let the fish cool off in the Fish Stock.
3. When it is at room temperature, remove the salmon from the cooking liquid and remove the skin and bones.
4. Set on a platter and surround with lemon wedges and salad vegetables such as tomatoes and cucumbers. Refrigerate. When ready to serve, pass a sauceboat of Mayonnaise Sauce or Green Sauce along with the cold salmon.

Soufflé de Saumon Salmon Soufflé

SERVES 6.

3 *tablespoons sweet butter*
4 *shallots, minced*
3 *tablespoons flour*
½ *cup Fish Stock (p. 7)*
½ *cup light cream*
1 *tablespoon tomato puree*
½ *teaspoon oregano*
1 *teaspoon salt*
½ *teaspoon freshly ground black pepper*

½ *cup grated Swiss Gruyère cheese*
4 *egg yolks*
1 *cup finely shredded salmon (fresh-cooked or canned)*
6 *egg whites*
¼ *teaspoon cream of tartar*

1. Melt the butter in a saucepan and sauté the shallots until tender and transparent, but not browned.

2. Add the flour and blend. Cook for 2 or 3 minutes more, being careful not to scorch the flour.

3. Heat the Fish Stock and the cream together. Gradually add this mixture to the flour, stirring until it is smooth and thickened.

4. Add the tomato puree, oregano, and the salt and pepper. Stir over the heat for 1 minute.

5. Remove from the stove, and add all but 2 tablespoons of cheese.

6. Add the egg yolks, 1 at a time, beating well after adding each.

7. Stir in the shredded salmon.

8. Beat the egg whites with the cream of tartar until stiff but not dry.

9. Fold them carefully into the soufflé mixture and transfer to a well-buttered 2-quart soufflé dish or Pyrex baking dish. Sprinkle the top with the remaining cheese.

10. Place the dish in the center of a preheated 375° oven and bake for 5 minutes. Reduce the heat to 325° and bake for another 20 to 25 minutes, or until done.

Filets de Sole Au Vin Blanc
Fillets of Sole with White Wine

SERVES 6.

2 *pounds fillets of gray sole*
3 *shallots, minced*
4 *tablespoons sweet butter*
⅓ *cup Chablis or other dry white wine*
⅓ *cup Fish Stock (p. 7)*
½ *cup chopped fresh parsley*
½ *to 1 teaspoon salt*

½ *to* 1 *teaspoon freshly ground black pepper*
1 *tablespoon lemon juice*
½ *cup heavy cream*
Garnish: lemon wedges

1. Wash and clean sole and set aside.
2. Sauté the shallots in 2 tablespoons of the butter until tender and transparent, but not browned.
3. Add the wine and Fish Stock. Simmer for 5 minutes and set aside.
4. In a shallow baking dish large enough to hold the fillets side by side, place the wine mixture and some of the parsley.
5. Sprinkle the fillets on both sides with the salt and pepper and place them in the liquid in the baking dish. Dot with the remaining butter and sprinkle with the lemon juice.
6. Bake, uncovered, in a preheated 375° oven for 15 minutes, basting often with the wine sauce.
7. Pour the cream over the fillets and brown under a hot broiler.
8. Remove the fillets from the baking dish and arrange on a warm platter.
9. Stir the sauce in the baking dish and pour over the fish on the platter. Sprinkle with the balance of the parsley. Decorate with lemon wedges and serve.

Filets de Sole au Crabe Monblason
Fillets of Sole with Crab Meat Monblason

SERVES 4 TO 6.

2 *cups dry white wine*
1 *8-ounce bottle clam juice*
3 *sprigs fresh parsley*
1 *bay leaf*
¼ *teaspoon thyme*
½ *pound sliced fresh mushrooms*
5 *tablespoons sweet butter*
3 *tablespoons flour*
2 *tablespoons brandy*
1 *cup grated Swiss Gruyère cheese*
¼ *cup cream sherry*

½ *pound crab meat, fresh or canned*
½ *cup heavy cream*
Salt and freshly ground black pepper to taste
1½ *pounds fillets of gray sole*

1. Simmer the wine until reduced by half.
2. Add the clam juice, parsley, bay leaf, and thyme to wine. Simmer for 15 minutes and then strain the liquid.
3. Sauté the sliced mushrooms in 2 tablespoons of the butter until all the moisture has evaporated.
4. Melt the remaining 3 tablespoons of the butter; stir in the flour and cook gently until slightly browned.
5. Stir in the brandy.
6. Gradually add the wine and clam juice to make a smooth, slightly thickened sauce.
7. Add the sautéed mushrooms, ½ cup of the grated cheese, cream sherry, crab meat, and cream. Mix well and season with the salt and pepper.
8. Spread ½ of the sauce in the bottom of a large, flat Pyrex dish, or in 2 smaller ones. Place the fillets over the sauce and cover with the balance of the sauce. Cover evenly with the remaining ½ cup of grated cheese.
9. Bake in a preheated 400° oven for 15 minutes and glaze under the broiler until a golden crust is formed. Do not overcook.

Mousse de Sole
Sole Mousse

The fillets of sole must be ground very fine through a meat grinder in order to get the smooth texture necessary for a mousse. Do not use a blender, since there is not enough liquid within the sole to make a smooth puree.

If you wish, you can make other kinds of fish mousses, such as salmon, shrimp, and lobster.

SERVES 8.

2 *pounds fillets of sole* (6 *to* 10 *fillets*)
5 *egg whites*
1½ *tablespoons dried dill weed, ground, or minced fresh dill*

2½ to 3 teaspoons salt
¼ teaspoon white pepper
¼ teaspoon cayenne pepper
½ cup bread crumbs
1½ cups heavy cream, well chilled
2 cups Velouté Sauce (p. 10), substituting 1 cup heavy cream
    and 1 cup Fish Stock (p. 7) for the 2 cups White Stock
Garnishes: 1 envelope unflavored gelatin, if serving cold;
    ¼ pound cooked, medium-sized shrimp; 2 large
    tomatoes, sliced; 1 head Bibb or Boston lettuce

1. Be sure all the bones in the fillets have been removed. Cut the fillets into 1-inch cubes and pass them through a meat grinder.

2. Beat the egg whites for 1 minute with an electric mixer and add the ground fish.

3. Season the mixture with the dill weed, salt, and pepper and add the bread crumbs, which will give the mousse a smoother texture.

4. Cover the bowl and set it in the refrigerator for about 2 hours.

5. Using the electric mixer, add the cream to the cold fish mixture, 1 spoonful at a time, until all the cream is well absorbed.

6. Transfer the mixture to a well-buttered 9-inch x 5-inch x 3-inch loaf pan. Set this into a roasting pan with boiling water coming ½ way up the loaf pan. Cover with wax paper and bake in a preheated 350° oven for 40 to 50 minutes, or until set.

TO SERVE HOT: Unmold onto a heated platter, draining off any excess liquid. Serve with a sauceboat of Velouté Sauce made with cream and Fish Stock.

TO SERVE COLD: This dish can be prepared a day in advance. Cool the mousse in the pan and then chill in the refrigerator. When cold, unmold onto a chilled platter. Prepare 2 cups of Velouté Sauce made from cream and Fish Stock. Soften 1 envelope gelatin in a few tablespoons of Fish Stock or white wine. Then dissolve the gelatin in the hot sauce. Refrigerate the sauce, and when just on the point of setting, but still liquid, spoon it over the chilled mousse and refrigerate until set. Garnish with cooked shrimp and sliced tomatoes on a bed of lettuce.

Thon aux Tomates
Tuna with Tomato Sauce

Tuna is related to the mackerel family. Its flesh is firm and savory. Unfortunately, it is seldom found in the average fish market, as most of it is canned in oil for salads and sandwiches. However, if you are near a fishing center on either the Atlantic or Pacific coasts of the United States, you will probably find restaurants which prepare and serve fresh tuna or albacore, and fish markets in those areas will be able to get it for you.

SERVES 6.

6 *tomatoes, sliced*
4 *shallots, minced*
4 *small white onions, minced*
½ *cup white wine*
½ *cup White Stock* (p. 6) *or canned chicken consommé*
1 *pound fresh mushrooms, thinly sliced*
½ *cup sweet butter*
2 *pounds fresh tuna steaks* (*sliced no more than* 1½ *inches*
     thick)
Salt and freshly ground black pepper
½ *cup chopped fresh parsley*

1. In an uncovered saucepan, simmer the tomatoes with the shallots and onions until ¾ of their juice has evaporated.

2. Add the wine and White Stock or consommé and simmer together for another 20 minutes. Strain the sauce and set aside.

3. Sauté the mushrooms in ½ the butter until all their juice has evaporated. Add the mushrooms to the tomatoes.

4. Sprinkle the tuna slices with some salt and pepper and brown on both sides in remaining butter in a large frying pan. Do not overcook.

5. Add the sauce to the fish and cover the skillet. Simmer until the fish flakes when pierced with a fork, approximately 15 to 20 minutes. Place the fish on a platter, keeping it warm until serving time.

6. Simmer the sauce until it is reduced to a nice consistency. Pour over the tuna. Sprinkle with parsley and serve.

Truites de Rivière Monblason
Broiled Brook Trout Monblason

Fresh trout caught in the cold water of a mountain brook, if not sabotaged by a careless cook, can be delicious. It is one of my favorite fishes.

I remember vividly when traveling with the Ringling Bros. and Barnum & Bailey Circus as chef to John Ringling North that during our stopovers in Denver, the ringmaster, my friend, the late Fred Bradna, would often go early in the morning to fish for trout in the mountain streams of the Rockies.

On one occasion, Fred came back just in time for lunch and gave me half a dozen freshly caught trout. I like fish, especially trout, so I decided to have a couple for lunch. I browned them delicately in butter and made a Maître d'Hôtel sauce to accompany them. They were so tasty and tender that I cooked two more and then still another to make a grand total of five for lunch that day. They were so fresh and the meat so delicate—I had cooked them just enough so that the flesh fell easily from the bones.

Very rarely does one have the opportunity to cook trout just out of the water. Still, the only secret I know to enjoy fish at its best is to cook it when it is still fresh.

SERVES 6.

6 *¾-pound brook trout*
Salt and freshly ground black pepper
½ cup sweet butter
2 *tablespoons lemon juice*
½ cup chopped fresh parsley

1. Sprinkle the trout lightly with some salt and pepper inside and out.

2. In a baking dish large enough to hold the 6 trout, place 4 tablespoons of the butter. Set the pan in a preheated 450° oven.

3. When the butter starts bubbling, place the trout side by side in the pan and bake for 3 minutes.

4. Turn the trout over and immediately turn the broiler on. Keep the door ajar. When the skin starts to brown, turn the trout and broil the other side until the skin is crisp. Cooking time is about 10 minutes altogether.

5. Remove the trout from the pan and arrange them on a hot platter. Reserve pan juices.

6. Melt the other 4 tablespoons of the butter in a saucepan and add the lemon juice, parsley, and pan juices. Stir and heat the sauce and pour over the trout. Serve immediately.

Truites de Rivière Sautées aux Amandes
Fried Brook Trout with Almonds

SERVES 6.

1 *teaspoon salt*
1 *cup milk*
6 *¾-pound fresh brook trout*
Flour
½ *cup sweet butter*
Freshly ground black pepper
½ *cup blanched, sliced almonds*

1. Add the salt to the milk and dip the trout into it. Roll each fish in flour and shake off the excess.

2. Melt 5 tablespoons of the butter in a large frying pan, and fry the trout on both sides until browned, about 5 minutes on each side. Remove the trout to a warm platter and sprinkle a little pepper on each. Keep warm in a 250° oven.

3. Add 3 more tablespoons butter to the pan and add the almonds. Cook and stir until the almonds are slightly browned. Pour over the trout and serve.

Truites de Rivière en Matelote à la Bourguignonne
Brook Trout Baked in Burgundy Wine Sauce

SERVES 6.

2 *cups Burgundy wine*
1 *cup Brown Stock (p. 4) or canned beef consommé*
½ *cup sweet butter*
18 *small white onions*

¼ *cup granulated sugar*
1 *pound small, firm, fresh white mushrooms*
6 *¾-pound brook trout*
½ *teaspoon salt*
½ *teaspoon freshly ground black pepper*
1½ *tablespoons flour*
¼ *cup chopped fresh parsley*

1. Simmer the wine and ½ cup of the Brown Stock or comsommé in an uncovered saucepan until reduced to 1½ cups. Set aside.

2. Melt 3 tablespoons of the butter in a skillet and sauté the white onions until tender and browned. Add the remaining ½ cup of the Brown Stock and the sugar and continue to simmer until the liquid has evaporated and the onions are glazed. Set aside.

3. Sauté the mushrooms in 3 tablespoons of the butter until their juices have evaporated. Do not scorch. Set aside.

4. Place the trout in a shallow Pyrex baking dish. Add the reduced wine-stock mixture. Bake in a preheated 375° oven for 20 minutes, or until the fish flakes when pierced with a fork. Set the trout on a warm serving platter and keep warm.

5. Pour ½ of the liquid from the baking dish into the saucepan with the onions, and the other ½ of the liquid into the pan with the mushrooms. Simmer both mixtures in the 2 covered pans for 5 minutes. Strain the liquid from each; combine the liquids and add the salt and pepper.

6. Melt 2 tablespoons of the butter in a saucepan and stir in the flour. Blend over a moderate heat for 2 minutes and stir in the wine-stock liquid to make a smooth sauce.

7. Pour over the trout on the serving platter. Arrange the mushrooms on one end, the onions on the other end of the platter. Sprinkle some parsley on top and serve.

Truites de Rivière à la Crème
Brook Trout with Cream Sauce

SERVES 6.

6 *¾-pound brook trout*
Salt and freshly ground black pepper
6 *tablespoons sweet butter*
1 *cup Fish Stock (p. 7)*

1 *cup heavy cream*
2 *tablespoons chopped fresh parsley*
Garnish: Duchess Potatoes (*p.* 304) (*optional*)

1. Sprinkle the trout lightly with some salt and pepper inside and out.

2. Put the butter into a shallow Pyrex baking dish large enough to hold the trout side by side, and set the baking dish under a hot broiler. When the butter starts to sizzle, add the trout.

3. Broil the trout for 4 minutes on each side.

4. Add the hot Fish Stock and broil for 2 more minutes on each side, basting 2 or 3 times during the process.

5. Transfer the trout to a warm platter and keep warm in the oven while you make the sauce.

6. Pour the liquid from the baking dish into a saucepan. Bring to a boil, add the cream, and boil until mixture is reduced to 1 cup. Taste for seasoning and add more salt and pepper if necessary.

7. Pour sauce over the trout and sprinkle some parsley on top.

8. If you wish to use Duchess Potatoes, prepare them as directed on p. 304 before you cook the trout. When the trout are ready to serve, place the potatoes around the platter and glaze under a hot broiler until they are lightly browned. Serve immediately.

ALTERNATE METHOD: This recipe can also be prepared by sautéing the trout in butter in a large frying pan or skillet. Prepare the sauce right in the same skillet, after removing the fish.

CHAPTER 6

Beef

Boeuf

Pot-au-Feu de Boeuf aux Légumes

Boeuf à la Mode
Boeuf à la Bourguignonne
Daube de Boeuf

Filet de Boeuf Stroganoff

Chateaubriand à la Béarnaise
Tournedos Rossini
Bifteck à la Bordelaise
Steak Sauté au Beurre Maître d'Hôtel

Contre-filet Rôti au Porto
Filet de Boeuf Wellington

Hamburgers à la Orson Welles
Meat Loaf Monblason
Hachis à la Parmentier

We in the United States can purchase the best beef in the entire world. Here are some hints for getting the best beef for your special purposes:

1. *Select a butcher in whom you have confidence.* He should take time to listen to you and to answer your questions honestly. If you find him disinterested or evasive, find another butcher.

2. *Know the differences among the grades of beef.* Approximately one-fourth of a beef carcass contains the tender and therefore most expensive cuts. The five grades of beef are Prime, Choice, Good, Commercial, and Utility. Top grade, U.S. Prime, is easily recognized by the large amount of fat covering the meat. Since you pay for the fat, it makes the meat quite expensive. Second grade, U.S. Choice, is not so heavy in fat, but is also of excellent quality. The flesh of both grades should be cherry red and marbled with little veins of fat. The covering fat should be pure white and firm to the touch. For stews, boiled beef, braised beef, and meat loaves, Good grade beef should be sufficient because of the long cooking needed for these recipes.

3. *Be sure the meat is well aged.*

4. *Understand the various cuts of beef and how they should be used.* The cooking method should determine the cut of beef to be used. Your butcher can help you choose from among the various cuts. When you order, be sure to tell your butcher what dish you want to prepare,

so that he can provide you with the proper piece of beef. Here is a general guide matching methods with cuts:

Grilling and Broiling: fillet, porterhouse, sirloin, top sirloin, Delmonico

Roasting: short loin (boned), standing rib roast, whole fillet, rump roast

Sautéing: all steaks, but not cut too thick

Stewing: rump, leg, shin

Braising: rump, chuck

Soups and Stock: neck, shin, and buttock

Pot-au-Feu de Boeuf aux Légumes
Boiled Beef with Vegetables

From this recipe you will have a good clear soup and boiled vegetables to serve with the beef. If you reduce the leftover soup, you will also have an excellent bouillon that can substitute for brown stock in many sauces. On French farms, the Pot-au-Feu is reheated day after day until all of it is eaten. Only the potatoes have to be eaten the first day, as they are not good when reheated.

The meat you use is of fairly inexpensive cut. It can be the brisket, plate, chuck, or round. Also ask your butcher for some shinbones and some chicken feet and giblets.

SERVES 6 TO 8.

5 *pounds or more shinbones*
2 *pounds chicken giblets and feet*
3 *to 4 pounds soup meat (beef brisket, plate, chuck, or round)*
Bouquet garni in a cheesecloth bag: 1 sprig of fresh parsley,
       6 *celery leaves,* 2 *bay leaves,* ½ *teaspoon peppercorns,*
       4 *cloves,* ¼ *teaspoon thyme*
1 *tablespoon salt*
5 *quarts water*
6 *medium-sized carrots, cut in half lengthwise*
4 *medium-sized yellow onions*
3 *stalks celery*
4 *white turnips*
4 *parsnips*

4 *leeks, outside leaves discarded*
½ *medium-sized cabbage (new cabbage if in season)*
8 *new potatoes*
Garnishes: 2 *tablespoons chopped fresh chervil for consommé
and* 2 *tablespoons chopped fresh parsley for meat*

1. In a large soup kettle, place the shinbones, chicken giblets, chicken feet, soup meat, bouquet garni, salt, and water. Bring to a boil and skim the top of the liquid often.

2. Reduce the heat and let the liquid simmer for at least 3 hours, or until you can pierce the meat with a fork and feel it is almost tender.

3. Add all the vegetables and resume the simmering for 1 more hour, or until the vegetables are tender. Skim the fat on top of the broth which can result if the meat contained excessive fat. Strain.

4. Serve the broth hot with some chopped fresh chervil, if you can get some. Chervil gives the soup a distinctive flavor. Otherwise, use some chopped fresh parsley.

5. Put the soup meat in the center of a large platter and place the vegetables all around it. Sprinkle with fresh parsley, chopped fine. Serve after soup course.

Boeuf à la Mode
Beef à la Mode

This dish is a very popular one in France and can be made a couple of hours before serving. You just put it in a 200° oven while you are drinking a cocktail with your guests, or you can even prepare the entire recipe in advance and reheat it. It is a long procedure but makes a delicious meal.

SERVES 6 TO 8.

1 *4½-pound rump of beef, larded*

Marinade:
3 *carrots, thinly sliced*
3 *small white onions, sliced*
3 *celery stalks, sliced*

½ *cup minced fresh parsley*
1 *teaspoon thyme*
3 *bay leaves*
2 *whole cloves*
2 *cloves of garlic*
2 *teaspoons salt*
1 *teaspoon freshly ground black pepper*
1 *bottle Beaujolais wine or other light red wine*
½ *cup brandy*
1 *cup vegetable oil*

1. Ask your butcher to cut a nice piece of beef from the rump and to lard it with strips of pork fat inserted into the meat.

2. Put the carrots, onions, celery, parsley, thyme, bay leaves, cloves, and garlic in the bottom of a dish. Rub the beef with some salt and pepper and place the beef on top of the vegetables. Add enough red wine to cover the meat. Pour the brandy and ½ cup oil over the beef. Cover and marinate for 24 hours. Turn the meat and baste every hour during the day.

3. Drain the meat 1 hour before cooking and dry it thoroughly. Set aside the marinade for further use. Place the beef in a flat roasting pan; pour another ½ cup cooking oil over the meat and place it in a preheated 400° oven. Baste often with the oil and turn the meat every 2 or 3 minutes. The browning should take about ½ hour. Discard the oil and fat.

Sauce:
1 *veal knuckle*
1 *calf's foot, split*
4 *cups Brown Stock (p. 4) or canned beef consommé*
½ *cup tawny port*

4. Cook the reserved marinade until reduced by half. Strain out all the vegetables. Add the veal knuckle, calf's foot, Brown Stock, and tawny port to the marinade liquid and simmer for 1 hour.

5. Put the meat in a quart baking dish. Add enough sauce, together with the veal knuckle and calf's foot, to come to more than ½ way up the meat. Cover the dish; place it in a moderate 250° oven and simmer gently, turning the meat every 10 minutes. About 3 hours should be enough for slow braising. If a fork pierces the meat easily, it is done. Strain the juices and reduce by simmering to 3 cups. Set aside.

Vegetables:
24 *small white onions*

½ *cup sweet butter*
1 *bunch carrots, sliced*

6. While your meat is braising, you can prepare your vegetables. Sauté the onions in 4 tablespoons of the butter until lightly browned. Parboil the carrots in 1 quart of boiling water for 5 minutes, and then drain. Sauté in 4 more tablespoons of the butter until done. I always reheat my vegetables a few minutes before serving. Always keep the vegetables separate until serving time, as they change their flavor when heated in the sauce.

7. The three cups of sauce should be slightly thickened. If necessary add a little cornstarch mixed with an equal part of water or stock, a little at a time. If the sauce becomes too thick, add some more port wine and stock and simmer gently. Place the heated vegetables around the sliced meat on a platter and pour the sauce over the meat and vegetables.

Boeuf à la Bourguignonne
Beef Bourguignonne

Beef Bourguignonne is a beef stew that should be prepared a day or two in advance of when you plan to serve it, since it will gain taste when it is slowly reheated

SERVES 8 TO 10.

4 *pounds lean rump of beef cut in 2½-inch square pieces*
3 *cups Brown Stock (p. 4) or canned beef consommé*
3 *cups Beaujolais or light red Burgundy wine*
1 *cup tawny port*
24 *small white onions*
9 *tablespoons sweet butter*
1½ *pounds fresh mushrooms*
8 *ounces good-quality bacon (lean, with rind removed)*
1 *tablespoon vegetable oil*
2 *sliced young carrots*
6 *shallots, minced*
3 *celery stalks, sliced*
½ *teaspoon salt*
½ *teaspoon freshly ground black pepper*

3 *tablespoons flour*
2 *tablespoons tomato puree*
3 *cloves mashed garlic*
1 *large bay leaf*
¼ *tablespoon thyme*
5 *sprigs fresh parsley*
Garnish: *boiled potatoes, noodles, or rice*

1. Take the meat out of the refrigerator and let it stand at room temperature for 2 hours.

2. Meanwhile, simmer the Brown Stock or consommé and the wines together slowly until the volume is reduced to ⅔ of its original quantity (4 cups in total).

3. Sauté the onions in a pan with 3 tablespoons of the butter, until entirely cooked and browned. Set aside.

4. Wash and quarter the mushrooms and sauté them in 3 more tablespoons of the butter until all their liquid has evaporated. Add to the onions and set aside.

5. Cut the bacon in little strips, ¼ inch thick and 1½ inches long, and simmer in water for 15 minutes to remove the strong smoky taste. Drain and set aside. When dry, sauté the bacon in the oil until slightly browned. Remove; drain and set aside.

6. Sauté the pieces of beef in the oil and bacon fat in a large skillet until entirely browned on all sides. Do not burn or scorch. Set the beef aside with the bacon.

7. In the same pan, sauté the carrots, shallots, and celery until browned. Remove them and add them to the reduced wine and stock mixture to simmer for another ½ hour. Then, strain the liquid and set aside. Discard the vegetables.

8. In a large skillet on top of the stove melt the remaining 3 tablespoons of butter. Add the pieces of beef and the bacon and sprinkle with a little of the salt and pepper. Sprinkle with the flour and toss the meat around so that it is covered with flour. Turn the meat every 2 minutes until the flour is nicely browned and the beef is covered with a crust.

9. Add some of the wine-stock liquid, just enough to barely cover the meat. Add the tomato puree, garlic, bay leaf, thyme, and parsley and transfer to a covered casserole. Put in a preheated 300° oven and simmer *very slowly* for about 3 hours. Regulate the oven heat throughout so that the liquid never boils but merely simmers. If the liquid gets too thick, add more stock.

10. When your meat is done, taste for seasoning, and add more of

the salt or pepper if necessary. If the liquid is too thin, remove the liquid and boil it down separately in a saucepan until it is of the right consistency. Then add the cooked onions and mushrooms to the meat and pour the sauce over them.

11. Cover and keep in the oven at 200° until ready to serve. Garnish the stew platter with boiled potatoes, noodles, or plain rice.

Daube de Boeuf
Daube of Beef

You can prepare the Daube of Beef a day or two before serving, just as you can the Beef à la Mode and the Beef Bourguignonne. All are better when reheated.

This dish is prepared in various ways in the different provinces of France. It can be varied by the addition of tomatoes, mushrooms, or olives, depending on your taste. I never cook the vegetables along with the Daube, but add them just before serving. You can serve the beef on a platter, with the vegetables around it. Add some boiled or mashed potatoes or noodles, if you wish.

The meat is marinated before braising. A cut from the rump or shoulder of beef will be fine for Daube of Beef. The proper way to prepare the meat is first to lard it with strips of salt pork. Ask your butcher to lard the beef for you, but if he cannot for some reason, skip the larding.

I know that you probably do not have a *daubière*. It is a large covered casserole. I usually use a Pyrex dish, 9 by 4½ inches, which is big enough to hold five quarts. You can use any large covered casserole you happen to have.

SERVES 8 OR MORE.

4 *pounds beef rump or shoulder, cut in 2-inch squares*
¼ *teaspoon thyme*
2 *bay leaves, broken into small pieces*
8 *sprigs fresh parsley, chopped fine*
½ *cup brandy*
3 *tablespoons olive oil*
3 *cups dry red wine*
6 *carrots, sliced*

6 *white onions, sliced*
8 *peppercorns*
2 *cups Brown Stock* (*p. 4*) *or canned beef consommé*
1 *cup flour*
8 *strips thick bacon, cooked in boiling water for a few minutes, and cut in pieces*
2 *cloves garlic, minced*
Salt and freshly ground black pepper (*optional*)

1. Put the larded pieces of beef on the bottom of a large covered casserole. Sprinkle with the thyme, bay leaves, and parsley. Pour the brandy and olive oil over the beef. Stir and mix well. Add the wine, carrots, onions, and peppercorns, and marinate overnight in the refrigerator.

2. Take the meat and the marinade out of the refrigerator. Remove the meat and strain the liquid. Discard the vegetables and spices. Add the Brown Stock or consommé to the liquid and simmer for 1 hour, or until the liquid is reduced to about ⅔ of its original quantity.

3. When your marinade is finished cooking, strain it through a fine sieve.

4. Dry the pieces of beef on paper towels while the marinade is cooking and roll them in the flour until they are well coated. Shake off the excess flour.

5. In the bottom of your casserole, place a layer of the blanched bacon, cut in small pieces, then a layer of meat. Repeat until all the bacon and meat are in the dish. Pour the hot marinade over the meat— you should have enough liquid to cover the beef and bacon.

6. Cover the dish tightly and put it in a preheated 300° oven and simmer until done, from 2½ hours to 4 hours, depending on the meat. The meat should be easily pierced with a fork when done. Regulate the oven heat throughout so that the liquid never boils, but merely simmers.

7. About 10 minutes before taking the dish out of the oven, add the crushed cloves of garlic and stir.

8. Before serving the meat, skim the fat off the top and taste for addition of some salt and pepper if needed.

Filet de Boeuf Stroganoff
Beef Stroganoff

When my grandmother had leftover beef from the Pot-au-Feu, she would serve it a day later with a sour-cream sauce similar to Stroganoff. It tasted delicious to me, perhaps because I was young and always hungry. I prefer to use the tips of fillet of beef for Beef Stroganoff. You can keep the center cut of the fillet for Chateaubriand with Béarnaise Sauce (p. 130); however, should you feel that the fillet is too expensive, try using a sirloin or *contre-filet*.

SERVES 6.

2 *pounds front end of 7- or 8-pound fillet of beef*
Salt and freshly ground black pepper
5 *tablespoons sweet butter*
2 *tablespoons flour*
1½ *cups Brown Stock (p. 4) or canned beef consommé*
1½ *teaspoons Dijon mustard*
4 *to 5 tablespoons sour cream*
2 *small white onions, chopped*

1. Cut the meat across the grain, not more than ½ inch thick, and make the strips approximately 2 inches long by ¾ inch wide. Sprinkle them lightly with some salt and pepper and refrigerate for 3 hours.

2. In a saucepan, melt 2½ tablespoons of the butter with the flour. Cook over medium heat, stirring constantly. Do not scorch the flour. Slowly add the Brown Stock, stirring with a wire whisk until the sauce is thickened and smooth.

3. Add the mustard and blend well.

4. Add the sour cream and stir well. Set aside.

5. In a heavy skillet, melt the remaining 2½ tablespoons of the butter. Cover the bottom of the skillet with the meat and onions. Brown quickly on all sides. Do not put more than 1 layer of meat and onions in at a time. If you have more meat and onions, repeat the operation. The meat should be well browned, but do not overcook.

6. Discard the onions and add the meat to the sour-cream sauce. Taste to see if more seasoning is needed before serving. Serve with rice, noodles, or mashed potatoes.

NOTE: You can also add a little Brown Stock to the skillet after the meat has been browned; reduce it by simmering and strain the liquid. Taste it. If it is not bitter, add it to the sour-cream sauce. It will add a lovely taste. However, if the onions have been burned during the browning operation, this will make the sauce bitter and the stock should not be used.

Chateaubriand à la Béarnaise
Chateaubriand with Béarnaise Sauce

SERVES 5 OR 6.

6 *pounds center fillet of beef, cut into 5 or 6 steaks, 1½ to*
    1¾ inches thick
Salt and freshly ground black pepper
1 *cup vegetable oil*
1½ *cups Béarnaise Sauce (p. 17)*

1. Sprinkle the steaks lightly with some salt and pepper. Place them in a baking dish and marinate them in oil for 2 hours at room temperature before broiling.

2. Before broiling the meat, it is absolutely necessary that your broiler be preheated to a temperature of 500° or higher on your thermometer.

3. Broil the beef for about 5 minutes on each side, keeping the broiler door ajar.

4. If your broiler does not get hot enough, you can pan-broil the steak as follows: Put a little vegetable oil in a thick-bottomed skillet (preferably an iron skillet). When the oil starts to smoke, add the chateaubriand. Cook for 5 minutes on each side, less or more, depending on how you like your beef—rare, medium rare, done, or well done. My timing of 5 minutes on each side is for medium rare.

5. Serve immediately on a platter with the Béarnaise Sauce in a sauceboat as an accompaniment.

Tournedos Rossini
Fillet Steaks with Foie Gras and Madeira Sauce

Tournedos are slices of fillet of beef, about 1 to 1¼ inches thick. You will sometimes see them on restaurant menus under the name "Medallions of Fillet of Beef." Since the fillet is a tender but rather tasteless cut of meat, in my opinion, the foie gras, Madeira, and truffles give it just the finishing touch it needs. Tournedos Rossini is expensive to make but exceedingly delicious to eat.

SERVES 6.

2 *cups Brown Stock (p. 4) or canned beef consommé*
⅓ *cup plus 2 tablespoons Madeira wine*
½ *pound fresh mushrooms, sliced thin*
6 *tablespoons sweet butter*
6 *slices canned block foie gras*
1 *tablespoon arrowroot or cornstarch*
6 *canned artichoke bottoms or 6 round slices French bread,*
        fried in butter (cut the same size as the fillet steaks)
Salt and freshly ground black pepper
6 *1- to 1¼-inch-thick fillet steaks (practically a whole fillet*
        of beef)
2 *tablespoons vegetable or olive oil*
3 *truffles, sliced into 24 pieces*
Garnishes: buttered potato balls, asparagus tips

1. In a saucepan, simmer the Brown Stock or consommé with the ⅓ cup of Madeira until the mixture is reduced to 1½ cups. Set aside.

2. Sauté the mushrooms in a skillet with 2 tablespoons of the butter, until their liquid has evaporated. Add the mushrooms to the reduced stock-wine liquid.

3. Place the slices of foie gras in a pan. Cover them with some of the reduced stock-wine mixture. Set aside.

4. In a saucepan, blend the arrowroot or cornstarch with the extra 2 tablespoons of Madeira. Add the hot stock with the mushrooms gradually, stirring to make a smooth sauce. Simmer gently for a few minutes. Set aside.

5. If you are using the canned artichoke bottoms, wash them in hot water; drain; sprinkle salt and pepper lightly on them and set them

in a covered pan with 2 tablespoons of the butter. Keep them hot over moderate heat.

6. If you are using croutons, fry the rounds of French bread on both sides in butter until golden brown.

7. Dry the steaks with paper towels. In a skillet large enough to hold the 6 portions, put 2 tablespoons oil and 2 tablespoons of the butter. Set over moderately high heat. When the butter begins to foam, set the steaks in the skillet and raise the heat high enough to sear the meat quickly, 5 minutes on each side, for medium-rare meat.

8. While the meat is cooking, warm the foie gras and truffles in the stock mixture, just enough to heat gently.

9. Set the artichoke bottoms or the croutons on a hot platter. Place a cooked steak on each, and sprinkle lightly with some salt and pepper. On top of each steak, place a slice of the foie gras and 4 slices of truffle.

10. Removing the oil and butter from the skillet, pour in the stock mixture from the foie gras and truffles and simmer it for a few minutes. Then add it to the mushroom sauce. Taste for seasoning. Pour the sauce over the 6 tournedos and serve immediately. Potato balls cooked in butter and asparagus tips placed around the meat are nice accompaniments.

Bifteck à la Bordelaise
Broiled Steaks with Bordelaise Sauce

Another way of serving grilled steaks is with Bordelaise sauce. You just pour the sauce over the steaks as they come out of the broiler, and serve them immediately to your hungry guests.

SERVES 6.

4 *shallots, minced*
3 *tablespoons sweet butter*
¾ *cup red wine*
Pinch of thyme
Pinch of marjoram
¾ *cup Brown Stock (p. 4) or canned beef consommé*
Few drops lemon juice
1 *tablespoon chopped fresh parsley*

Salt and freshly ground black pepper
Grilled steaks

1. Sauté the shallots in 2 tablespoons of the butter until they are transparent, but not browned.
2. Add the wine, thyme, and marjoram and simmer rapidly until reduced to ½ of its quantity.
3. Add the Brown Stock or consommé and reduce again by ½.
4. Add the lemon juice and parsley and simmer for 5 minutes. Strain the sauce and add the remaining 1 tablespoon of the butter. Taste for seasoning. Pour the sauce over the grilled steaks; sprinkle with some extra parsley and serve.

Steak Sauté au Beurre Maître d'Hôtel
Pan-Sautéed Steak with Maître d'Hôtel Butter

Before the modern broiler was invented, the French housewife cooked on top of a wood, coal, or gas stove. So, of course, she pan-broiled all of her steaks.

I can assure you that it is a quick and wonderful method for cooking small steaks. Even today, though I have a modern broiler, I like to pan-broil my steaks unless they are more than 1¼ inches thick.

SERVES 4.

4 *Delmonico steaks, cut ¾-inch thick*
Seasoned salt
Freshly ground black pepper
½ cup vegetable or olive oil
2 tablespoons rendered fresh beef suet, or fat
½ cup Maître d'Hôtel Butter (p. 22)
Garnishes: French-fried potatoes, buttered string beans,
    watercress

1. Trim any excess fat off the steaks. If there is a layer of gristle around the steak, cut incisions into it to prevent the steak from curling. If the steak is moist, dry it thoroughly with paper towels.
2. Season the steaks with the salt and pepper. Pour 2 tablespoons of the oil over each steak. Cover them with wax paper and marinate at room temperature for 1 hour. *Note:* It is most important to have the

steaks at room temperature before you start cooking. If you attempt to prepare a steak medium rare when it has just come out of the refrigerator, the center will invariably be ice-cold when you serve it.

3. Place the suet or fat in a heavy skillet over moderately high heat. When the fat starts smoking, it will be hot enough to sear the meat.

4. Sauté the steaks on one side 2½ to 4 minutes, turn over, and sauté the other side the same amount of time. If you are fast enough in cooking and serving pan-broiled steaks, none of the juice essences will be lost.

5. When your steaks are ready, put them on a hot platter and divide the Maître d'Hôtel Butter among the four steaks. Serve with French-fried potatoes and buttered string beans, and 2 or 3 sprigs of watercress on each of the steaks.

Contre-filet Rôti au Porto
Roast Sirloin with Port

Too many women have been scared away from preparing elaborate meals after reading fancy cookbooks. A case in point is the following recipe, which calls for brown stock. Earlier, in Chapter 1, I described how to make homemade country-style brown stock. Although some of you may want to try the homemade stock, your leisure time may be limited. Instead of trying to accomplish the ultimate in French cooking, you should avail yourself of the many good substitutes on the market, such as the canned consommés and bouillons. When they are simmered together with port wine, as described in this recipe, the resulting sauce is excellent.

At Monblason we used short loin of beef for this roast; we kept the fillet for tournedos and used the *contre* part of the fillet for chateaubriand and roasts. *Contre-filet* is an expensive cut of meat, particularly if you ask your butcher for prime beef. The butcher should bone the meat and leave just a little layer of fat on the outside.

SERVES 8.

1 8-*pound* contre-filet *or sirloin roast*
Seasoned salt and freshly ground black pepper
½ *cup vegetable oil*

3 *cups Brown Stock* (*p.* 4) *or canned beef consommé*
2 *cups tawny port*
1½ *pounds fresh mushrooms, sliced*
4 *tablespoons sweet butter*
Garlic salt
Garnishes: pan-roasted potatoes and minced parsley

1. Let the meat stand in a roasting pan at room temperature for 2 hours before roasting. Sprinkle some salt and pepper all over the meat. Pour the vegetable oil over the roast and set aside.

2. Simmer the Brown Stock or consommé and port wine together, long enough to reduce it to ½ its original quantity. Sauté the mushrooms in 3 tablespoons of the butter until all the liquid has evaporated. Do not burn, or the mushrooms will become bitter. Add a little garlic salt, and pour the port wine sauce over the mushrooms. Set aside.

3. About 2 hours before the guests arrive, start to roast the meat in a preheated 500° oven, leaving the door of the oven ajar. Every 5 minutes or so, turn the roast and baste it frequently with the oil. As this is a preliminary cooking operation, do not overcook the roast. The fast searing will help keep the juices inside the meat. It takes approximately 20 to 30 minutes, not more, to sear it. The roast must be crisp on the outside. When seared, take the meat out of the oven and place it in another roasting pan. Put the remaining 1 tablespoon of butter on top and set aside.

4. It will take another 30 to 45 minutes, depending on how you like your meat, to finish roasting the beef.

5. Have the oven temperature at 350°. As soon as the beef starts to roast, remove the mushrooms from the port-wine sauce and set aside. Baste the roast frequently with the port-wine sauce. Turn the meat many times. When ready, let the roast stand outside the oven for 10 minutes before serving. In cooling off, the juices will remain inside.

6. Pour the remaining port wine over the mushrooms and keep it hot on the stove without boiling. Slice your meat and arrange on a hot platter. Place the mushrooms on the sides of the platter and pour the sauce over the meat. Serve with pan-roasted potatoes. Sprinkle with minced parsley.

Filet de Boeuf Wellington
Fillet of Beef Wellington

To make Fillet of Beef Wellington successfully, you cannot rush through the various stages. You can, however, do the initial cooking of the fillet and cover it with the pastry dough early in the day. Let it stand at room temperature until you are almost ready to serve your meal, then do the final roasting. You can also make the sauce in advance and then slowly reheat it just as the fillet is about cooked.

SERVES 6 TO 8.

1 *4- to 5-pound fillet of beef (with 2 end pieces removed and*
    reserved for sauce)
¼ *cup cognac*
Salt
Seasoned salt
Freshly ground coarse black pepper
¼ *to ½ cup vegetable oil*
Purée de Foie Gras Truffé (Louis Henry brand Strasbourg
    en Timbale)
2 *black truffles, minced*
¼ *teaspoon rosemary*
1 *recipe Pastry Dough (p. 137)*
1 *egg yolk*
¼ *cup heavy cream*
1 *recipe Madeira Sauce (p. 138)*

1. Rub the fillet all over with the cognac. Season with some salt, seasoned salt, and coarse black pepper. Let the fillet stand at room temperature for at least 1 hour.

2. Pour some vegetable oil over the fillet and roast in a preheated 450° oven for approximately 20 minutes. Do not overcook. After removing the roasted fillet from the oven, let it cool to room temperature.

3. When the fillet is cool, spread over it the foie gras *truffé* mixed with the minced truffles and season with the rosemary.

4. Cover the fillet with the Pastry Dough by placing the meat in the center of the pastry and sealing the center seam and the end flaps with a little water and/or beaten egg. Place the meat on a baking sheet, seam-side down. Make 5 or 6 small openings on top of the crust to give steam

FILLET OF BEEF
WELLINGTON •

a chance to escape during baking and use the leftover scraps of dough to attach to the top with water or beaten egg as decorations.

5. Roast in a preheated 450° oven for 10 minutes. Brush the pastry several times with a mixture of egg yolk and cream to make the crust golden brown. After the 10 minutes reduce the heat to 350° and roast for another 20 minutes or more, until the pastry is well cooked and the fillet medium rare and hot. Remove from oven; let stand a few minutes and then slice. Pass the Madeira Sauce separately.

Pastry Dough

2 *cups flour*
½ *teaspoon salt*
½ *cup sweet butter*
3 *tablespoons shortening*
Approximately 5 tablespoons ice-cold water

1. Sift together the flour and the salt.
2. With a pastry blender or 2 forks, cut in the cold butter and the shortening, until the mixture is mealy.
3. Add the cold water a little at a time, gathering the dough together into a ball. Chill dough for several hours in the refrigerator.
4. Roll the dough out thinly, approximately ⅛ inch thick. Place the fillet on the dough and carefully roll it up, wrapping the dough completely around the fillet.

Madeira Sauce

End pieces cut from the fillet of beef
8 *tablespoons sweet butter*
5 *shallots, minced*
2 *cups Brown Stock (p. 4) or canned beef consommé*
½ *cup Madeira wine*
6 *fresh parsley sprigs*
1 *bay leaf*
¼ *teaspoon thyme*
2 *tablespoons flour*
1 *pound fresh mushrooms, sliced and sautéed in butter*
1 *truffle, sliced*

1. Cut the 2 ends of the fillet in small pieces and sauté them in 6 tablespoons of the butter until the meat is cooked and nicely browned.
2. Add the minced shallots and sauté them until slightly browned.
3. Add the Brown Stock or consommé and the Madeira wine, parsley sprigs, bay leaf, and thyme. Bring to a boil. Reduce heat and simmer for 1 hour. Strain the liquid.
4. Melt the remaining 2 tablespoons of butter; add the flour, stir, and cook slowly together until golden. Add the strained Madeira-stock mixture slowly to make a smooth sauce. Simmer for ½ hour and then add the sliced, sautéed mushrooms and the sliced truffle.

Hamburgers à la Orson Welles
Hamburgers à la Orson Welles

I discovered this recipe for hamburgers in Hollywood when I was working for Orson Welles. The boss told me one day that he had eaten some hamburgers in Dave Chasen's Restaurant, and that they were simply *formidable!* He suggested that I ask Dave for the recipe. Knowing how many deliberately distorted recipes had been handed to the public by restaurant chefs, I decided that I would use some other method to find out of what these sensational Chasen hamburgers were made.

One day shortly after Mr. Welles mentioned it to me, I walked into Chasen's dining room and ordered that special hamburger. I have never eaten a meal so slowly, practically dissecting the hamburger piece by piece. I found the taste of ham, a hint of onions, and of course, the beef.

Back in my own kitchen, it took me several sessions before I came up with my own recipe. I sincerely hope Mr. Welles won't object to the dedication of this recipe. Humorous gourmets and Orson Welles fans may say, "No wonder there is ham in it!"

SERVES 8.

4 *small white onions, minced*
7 *tablespoons sweet butter*
2 *pounds ground lean chuck*
½ *pound boiled ham, ground fine*
2 *eggs, slightly beaten*
1½ *teaspoons salt*
½ *teaspoon freshly ground black pepper*
¼ *teaspoon thyme*
Flour
1 *tablespoon vegetable oil*
¼ *cup Brown Stock (p. 4) or canned beef consommé*
¼ *cup dry white vermouth*
3 *tablespoons sweet butter*
Garnish: chopped fresh parsley

1. Sauté the minced onions slowly in 2 tablespoons of the butter until tender but not browned.

2. In a mixing bowl, put the cooked onions, 3 tablespoons of melted butter, the beef, ham, eggs, salt, pepper, and thyme. Mix well to blend thoroughly. Taste for seasoning and correct if necessary. Form the mixture into patties 1 inch thick and keep in the refrigerator until ready to cook.

3. When ready, dip the patties lightly in flour and shake off the excess flour.

4. In a large frying pan or iron skillet melt the remaining 2 tablespoons of butter with the vegetable oil. When the fat is hot enough to sauté the meat, the butter foam will start to disappear. Just be careful not to burn the butter.

5. Put the patties in the skillet immediately and sauté them approximately 5 minutes on each side, depending on how rare or well done you like them. Arrange on a platter and keep warm in a 200° oven while you make the sauce.

6. Remove the fat remaining in the skillet after the hamburgers have been removed.

7. Add Brown Stock or consommé and vermouth and reduce by simmering until you have a syrupy sauce.

8. Take the skillet off the stove immediately and swirl into the sauce the 3 tablespoons of butter.

9. Pour the sauce over the hamburgers; sprinkle on some finely chopped parsley and serve.

Meat Loaf Monblason
Meat Loaf Monblason

I never could understand why so many people turn up their noses at the mention of meat loaf. If made properly and served with the right sauce, meat loaf can be a marvelous culinary accomplishment.

SERVES 8 OR MORE.

8 *small white onions, chopped finely*
1 *green pepper, chopped finely*
4 *tablespoons sweet butter*
1½ *pounds ground lean chuck*
¾ *pound ground lean pork*
¾ *pound ground lean veal*
3 *eggs, beaten*
1 *cup Brown Stock (p. 4) or canned beef consommé*
1½ *cups bread crumbs or toasted wheat germ*
1½ *cups finely chopped fresh parsley*
¼ *teaspoon thyme or basil*
2 *teaspoons salt*
1 *teaspoon freshly ground black pepper*
2 *or 3 strips of bacon*
3 *to 4 cups Tomato Sauce Provençale (p. 12) or Brown*
    Mushroom Sauce (p. 14)
2 *tablespoons chopped fresh parsley*

1. Sauté chopped onions and green pepper together in the butter until soft and transparent.

2. Combine the ground beef, pork, veal, the eggs, Brown Stock or

consommé, and bread crumbs. Add the onion-pepper mixture; season with the parsley, thyme or basil, salt, and pepper, and blend well.

3. To shape the loaf, you can place the mixture in a buttered rectangular Pyrex baking dish and unmold the uncooked loaf into a larger roasting pan.

4. Place the strips of bacon on top.

5. Place the meat loaf in a preheated 325° oven and bake for 1½ hours. Remove bacon and degrease the pan.

6. Pour either the Tomato Sauce Provençale or the Brown Mushroom Sauce over the meat loaf. Bake for another ½ hour, basting often with the sauce. Sprinkle with chopped parsley and serve hot.

Hachis à la Parmentier
Hash à la Parmentier

This dish takes its name from Antoine Augustin Parmentier, French agronomist-economist, who promoted the culture of potatoes in France at the end of the eighteenth century. Anytime you see a recipe with Parmentier in its title, you can be sure that potatoes are a major ingredient.

Although I have included this recipe in the chapter on beef, it can also be made with other cooked meat leftovers such as pork, veal, or turkey. Hash à la Parmentier is for the more adventurous cooks—those of you who enjoy a little experimentation with food. You will not be confined to strict measurements when you prepare this dish. Instead, you can use your leftover pieces of beef, pork, or poultry and those all-important potatoes with your own bit of individual seasoning and ingenuity to make a wholesome and mouth-watering main dish.

SERVES 4.

2 to 3 cups leftover meat, finely ground
Few minced onions, sautéed in butter until golden
1 to 2 eggs
Handful of finely chopped fresh parsley
Some Brown Stock (p. 4) or canned beef consommé
Bread crumbs and seasonings to your taste
4 medium-sized potatoes
4 tablespoons sweet butter
1 cup grated Swiss Gruyère cheese

Light cream
Salt and freshly ground black pepper

1. Mix together the ground meat leftovers with the sautéed onions.

2. Add 1 egg or 2, if you wish, the parsley, some Brown Stock or consommé, and some bread crumbs and seasonings.

3. Line the bottom of a long, shallow Pyrex dish with the meat mixture. Set aside.

4. Cook the potatoes in boiling water. When they are tender, mash them well, add the butter, almost all of the cheese, and a little cream to make the mashed potatoes smooth, but still firm. Add some salt and pepper to your taste.

5. Cover the meat mixture with the mashed potatoes, spreading the potatoes evenly to cover the meat completely. Sprinkle more cheese on top.

6. Bake in a preheated 325° oven for 45 minutes, then brown under the broiler until the cheese is melted and browned.

CHAPTER 7

Veal

Veau

Noix de Veau Rôtie
Poitrine de Veau Rôtie et Farcie
Roulade de Veau Braisée aux Tomates

Blanquette de Veau
Sauté de Veau Marengo
Ragoût de Veau à la Tourangelle

Côtes de Veau du Midi
Côtes de Veau à la Chasseur

Escalopes de Veau à l'Anglaise
Escalopes de Veau au Marsala
Escalopes de Veau à la Crème
Escalopes de Veau à l'Estragon
Escalopes de Veau Cordon Bleu

Veal is the flesh of the calf. The best-quality veal comes from a milk-fed calf between six and twelve weeks old. The flesh of milk-fed veal should be firm, smooth, fine grained, and a very pale pink color. Much of the veal found in American markets has been fed on grass or grain. Hence, its color ranges from dark pink to light red. It tastes reasonably good, but it never has the flavor and tenderness of entirely milk-fed veal. In France, the calves are allowed to drink only from the mother cow, and between meals a muzzle is put on the animals to prevent them from eating hay, straw, or any other food which will change the texture and color of its flesh.

There are a few American butchers who carry only milk-fed veal. Prime, milk-fed veal is the only kind to ask for, and your butcher will cut it in any style you wish.

Veal is always light and lean, and for that reason a veal roast, rack of veal, or breast of veal should always have a rich sauce to accompany it. Chops or scallops of veal can be prepared *au naturel,* but because the meat of the milk-fed calf is very tender, it must never be overcooked.

Noix de Veau Rôtie
Roast Rump of Veal

For this recipe, have the meat rolled and tied nicely by the butcher. Let it stand at least three hours at room temperature before roasting.

SERVES 6 TO 8.

1 *4-pound rump of veal*
Salt and freshly ground black pepper to taste
Oregano (*optional*)
9 *tablespoons sweet butter, melted*
1½ *cups Brown Stock* (*p.* 4) *or canned beef consommé*
¾ *cup cream sherry*
12 *to* 16 *small white onions*
Garnishes: green peas, carrots, and noodles, rice, or mashed potatoes

1. Season the veal with salt, pepper, and oregano and place it in a roasting pan in a preheated 350° oven. Every 5 minutes or so, turn the meat and baste it with 6 tablespoons of the melted butter. The meat should be well browned in about 45 minutes.

2. While the meat is roasting, simmer the Brown Stock or consommé with the cream sherry until it is reduced by about half.

3. Sauté the white onions in the remaining 3 tablespoons of butter very slowly until they are browned.

4. Continue to roast the veal for another 45 minutes, this time basting frequently with the reduced stock-sherry mixture.

5. Place the roasted veal in a covered baking dish; add the cooked onions and remaining stock-sherry mixture and cook slowly at 250° for another ½ hour, basting frequently with the liquid.

6. About 5 minutes before serving, pour all the gravy into a saucepan and boil it down to ½ its quantity. Taste for and add extra seasoning if necessary.

7. Slice the meat and place it on a heated platter with the onions. Pour the gravy over the slices. Serve with green peas, carrots, and noodles, rice, or mashed potatoes.

Cold Roast Veal

Mix leftover cold roast veal with French Dressing (p. 21) and serve with a salad of Romaine lettuce or Belgian endive.

Poitrine de Veau Rôtie et Farcie
Roast Stuffed Breast of Veal

Breast of veal is an inexpensive cut. Try to get one which comes from a milk-fed calf. With just a little care, you can make your friends a splendid meal. This is really a family-style dish, popular in French rural districts.

SERVES 6 TO 8.

1 *4-pound breast of veal*
1½ *cups Brown Stock (p. 4) or canned beef consommé*
¾ *cup cream sherry or white wine*
1 *recipe Stuffing (see below)*
Garnishes: green peas, carrots, and mashed potatoes or noodles

Ask your butcher to bone the breast and remove the excess fat. Have him make a pocket in the thickest part of the breast. Stuff the pocket with the following:

Stuffing:
2 *small white onions, chopped and lightly sautéed in butter*
10 *fresh mushrooms, sliced finely and sautéed in butter*
1 *pound hot Italian sausage, cooked to render the fat*
½ *cup bread crumbs, seasoned with salt and pepper*
1 *egg, beaten*
1 *tablespoon chopped fresh parsley*
2 *teaspoons chopped fresh tarragon*
2 *teaspoons chopped fresh chives*
Extra salt and freshly ground black pepper to taste

1. Mix the onions, mushrooms, sausage, bread crumbs, and egg together. Season with the parsley, tarragon, chives, salt, and pepper and fill the pocket in the breast of veal. Close securely with thread.

ROAST STUFFED
BREAST OF VEAL •

2. Simmer together the Brown Stock or consommé and the cream sherry until it is reduced to about ½ its quantity.

3. Place the stuffed breast of veal in an open roasting pan; bake in a 275° oven, basting often with the reduced stock-sherry mixture. It will take approximately 3 hours to roast a 4-pound stuffed breast of veal.

4. When the meat is ready, reduce the gravy in a saucepan, by simmering, to a light syrup.

5. Pour the gravy over the veal and glaze the meat under the broiler for 2 minutes. Serve with peas, carrots, and mashed potatoes or noodles.

NOTE: This recipe can also be made with shoulder of veal.

Roulade de Veau Braisée aux Tomates
Braised Veal Roll with Tomato Puree

SERVES 6.

2 *pounds leg of veal, cut into 4 slices and pounded* ¹⁄₁₆ *inch thick*
Several slices imported boiled ham, preferably Polish type
½ *cup seasoned, fresh bread crumbs*
3 *cloves garlic, minced finely or crushed*
3 *medium-sized white onions, minced and sautéed in
    2 tablespoons sweet butter*

¾ *teaspoon dried basil*
½ *cup minced fresh parsley*
8 *tablespoons melted sweet butter*
Salt and freshly ground black pepper to taste
1 *recipe Tomato Puree (see below)*

1. Ask your butcher to cut 4 large, thin slices from the leg of veal, weighing approximately 2 pounds altogether. After pounding them, they should not be over 1/16 inch thick. Put them side by side with the lengths overlapping.

2. On top of them, put some very thin slices of imported ham.

3. Make a stuffing of the bread crumbs, garlic, onions, basil, pars-

BRAISED VEAL ROLL
WITH TOMATO PUREE·

ley, and 4 tablespoons of the melted butter. Mix well and add some salt and pepper.

4. Cover the meat evenly with the stuffing and roll up the veal. Tie the roll securely in a few places.

5. Roast the veal in a preheated 325° oven until slightly browned, about 20 minutes, basting with the remaining 4 tablespoons of melted butter. Add the Tomato Puree and bake slowly, basting often, for 1 more hour. Skim off the excess fat and serve.

Tomato Puree

10 *ripe tomatoes*
5 *tablespoons sweet butter*

½ cup dry white wine
¼ teaspoon dried basil
Salt and pepper to taste

1. Chop the ripe tomatoes and combine with the butter. Cook slowly in a covered saucepan until the mixture is the consistency of a smooth puree, approximately 1½ hours.
2. Add the dry white wine, basil, salt, and pepper.
3. Simmer for 10 minutes and use the sauce to baste the veal.

Blanquette de Veau
Veal Blanquette

At home when I was a kid, we had this tasty dish once every week. Even today, I am still enjoying it. When I prepare this blanquette in my own kitchen, it is a change from roasts and broiled meats and it can be reheated and served the next day.

SERVES 6.

3 pounds veal shoulder or breast, cut in 1-inch cubes
3 carrots, sliced thin
2 yellow onions, sliced
1 leek, sliced
2 stalks celery
4 sprigs fresh parsley
¼ tablespoon thyme
2 bay leaves
4 cloves
5 cups White Stock (p. 6) or canned chicken consommé
    (or enough to cover veal)
24 small white fresh mushrooms
12 small white onions
3 tablespoons sweet butter
3 tablespoons flour
Salt and freshly ground black pepper
3 egg yolks
½ cup heavy cream

Garnishes: steamed white rice, 2 tablespoons chopped fresh
parsley, green peas

1. Place the veal in a large saucepan with the carrots, onions, leek, celery, parsley, thyme, bay leaves, and cloves. Add the White Stock or consommé to cover. Bring to a boil and let it simmer for 45 minutes or until the meat is cooked. While the meat is cooking, remove the scum from time to time with a large spoon. When cooked, remove the meat from the broth and set aside.

2. Strain the liquid and cook the mushrooms in it for about 3 minutes. Remove the mushrooms and add them to the veal.

3. Cook the small white onions until tender in the same liquid and add them to the veal and mushrooms.

4. Reduce the stock to ½ its volume by simmering.

5. Melt the butter and add the flour, cooking and stirring for about 3 minutes, being careful not to let the mixture get brown.

6. Add the stock little by little, stirring constantly, to make a smooth sauce. Taste and add salt and pepper if necessary.

7. Put the meat, mushrooms, and onions back in the sauce and heat through.

8. Just before serving, beat together the egg yolks and cream and add to the stew. Heat gently. Do not let it boil!

9. Decorate a heated platter with a ring of steamed white rice. Place the meat and sauce in the center with parsley on top and serve. Peas are nice with it, too.

Sauté de Veau Marengo
Veal Stew Marengo

Here is another stew that can be prepared the day before, but reheat it gently.

SERVES 8.

¼ *cup vegetable oil*
4 *pounds veal from the shoulder, neck, or lower leg, cut in*
   2-inch pieces
Salt and freshly ground black pepper to taste
4 *tablespoons sweet butter*
3 *tablespoons flour*

8 *small white onions, sliced*
3 *cups dry white wine*
1 *cup Tomato Puree (p.* 149) *or canned tomato puree*
1 *teaspoon tarragon*
½ *teaspoon thyme*
3 *cloves garlic, crushed*
2 *tablespoons orange liqueur*
1 *pound fresh mushrooms, quartered and sautéed in butter*
    until their liquid has evaporated
Cornstarch mixed with a little water (optional)
Garnishes: chopped fresh parsley, buttered noodles

1. In a skillet heat the oil until quite hot. Brown the veal pieces in the oil on all sides.

2. Season the veal with some salt and pepper. Add the butter and when it melts, sprinkle the flour over the veal. Stir over moderate heat for about 6 minutes to brown the flour lightly. Remove from heat. Arrange the veal in a baking casserole and set aside.

3. Sauté the onions with the remaining oil in the same skillet as the veal over moderate heat until slightly browned.

4. When the onions are lightly browned, remove the oil and add the wine to the skillet with the onions. Boil for 2 or 3 minutes, stirring to dissolve the coagulated juices from the sautéed veal.

5. Pour the wine and onions over the veal in the casserole and bring to the simmering point, stirring to mix the flour with the liquid.

6. Add the Tomato Puree, tarragon, thyme, garlic, and orange liqueur.

7. Cover the casserole and bake it in a preheated 250° oven for 1½ hours. The liquid should just simmer during that time.

8. Add the mushrooms and return the casserole to the oven for 10 minutes longer.

9. Remove the casserole from the oven. Drain the liquid and reduce it to approximately 2 cups by simmering it in a saucepan. Skim off the fat.

10. The sauce should be slightly thickened. If it is too thin, add some cornstarch which has been dissolved in a little water and stir until thickened. Combine the sauce with the veal, onions, and mushrooms. Arrange on a hot platter. Sprinkle with chopped parsley and serve with buttered noodles.

Ragoût de Veau à la Tourangelle
Veal Stew Tourangeau

This is a popular dish among the rural people of Touraine and shows that not only beef but also veal can be prepared with a red wine sauce.

SERVES 4 TO 6.

1 *4-pound breast of milk-fed veal*
2 *cups Brown Stock (p. 4) or canned beef consommé*
5 *tablespoons sweet butter*
4 *tablespoons flour*
2 *cups dry red wine*
14 *small white onions, cooked lightly in butter*
4 *sprigs fresh parsley*
1 *bay leaf*
Pinch thyme
2 *garlic cloves*
1 *bunch small carrots, diced*

1. Cut the breast of veal in 1½-inch pieces. Simmer it in the Brown Stock or consommé for approximately 1 hour.
2. Meanwhile, melt the butter over low heat and stir in the flour, cooking slowly for 1 or 2 minutes, until the roux is golden, but not browned.
3. Add the wine a little at a time and stir well until the sauce is thickened and smooth.
4. When the veal is cooked, remove from the stock. Skim the fat from the stock and add the stock to the wine sauce.
5. Put in the veal, onions, parsley sprigs, bay leaf, thyme, garlic cloves, and carrots and simmer for 1 more hour until the meat is tender and the carrots and onions cooked. Remove the garlic, parsley, and bay leaf before serving.

Côtes de Veau du Midi
Veal Chops Southern France Style

The south of France has a distinctive cuisine. Green peppers, onions, garlic, and tomatoes are used in 75 percent of the preparations. I love that style of cooking. I have traveled quite extensively through Provence and along the Pyrenees up to the Basque country and have enjoyed many dishes cooked with the flavor of the South. Here is a recipe you can prepare the day before and reheat in a 350° oven 40 minutes before serving. It is a blessing, as the preparation takes quite a while.

SERVES 8.

2 cups Brown Stock (p. 4) or canned beef consommé
1 cup cream sherry
1 16-ounce can stewed tomatoes
10 to 14 tablespoons sweet butter
8 small white onions, sliced
1 pound fresh mushrooms, quartered
3 green peppers, minced
Salt and freshly ground black pepper
Flour
8 loin or rib veal chops, cut 1¼ inches thick
½ cup brandy or cognac
1 cup minced fresh parsley
24 black olives, pitted and halved
3 cloves garlic, minced
1 bay leaf
¼ teaspoon thyme

1. Simmer the Brown Stock or consommé and sherry slowly until reduced to ½ its quantity. Set aside.
2. Simmer the tomatoes until nearly all the liquid has evaporated. Set aside.
3. Sauté the onions in 3 tablespoons of the butter until slightly browned. Set aside.
4. In the same skillet sauté the mushrooms in 3 more tablespoons of the butter if necessary or as needed until their liquid has evaporated. Do not burn them. Set aside.

5. Cook the green peppers in more butter if necessary until soft and their liquid has also evaporated. If the liquid from the tomatoes, onions, green peppers, and mushrooms has not completely evaporated, drain. Otherwise, you will have a stew.

6. Sprinkle some salt, pepper, and flour lightly on the chops. Sauté the chops in 5 tablespoons of butter very fast until all the chops are nicely browned, but not entirely done. Place them in a casserole.

7. In a skillet, heat and flame the brandy or cognac. Stir in the stock-sherry mixture. Keep stirring for 2 minutes.

8. Add the drained tomatoes, onions, mushrooms, green peppers, parsley, olives, garlic, bay leaf, thyme, and salt and pepper to taste. Stir and pour this mixture over the chops. Taste for seasoning.*

9. Bake the covered casserole in a preheated 250° oven for 45 minutes. Skim off the excess fat and serve.

Côtes de Veau à la Chasseur
Veal Chops Chasseur

The white wine gives a distinctive and different flavor to the sauce. I have always been prejudiced against wine made with Concord grapes. I suggest a good California Chablis if you cannot obtain a French Chablis.

SERVES 6.

8 *veal chops, cut 1 inch thick*
4 *tablespoons sweet butter*
4 *shallots, chopped*
8 *large fresh mushrooms, sliced*
1 *clove garlic, minced*
1 *cup dry white wine*
1 *cup White Stock (p. 6) or canned chicken consommé*
2 *tablespoons Tomato Puree (p. 149) or canned tomato puree*

---

* If you intend to serve the dish later or the next day, after pouring the mixture over the chops and seasoning it, cover the casserole and let it cool. Then place in the refrigerator. When ready to serve, bake in a 350° oven for 40 minutes.

1 *teaspoon chervil*
1 *teaspoon tarragon*

1. Sauté the chops in 3 tablespoons of the butter until lightly browned on both sides. Do not overcook. Put the chops aside.

2. Sauté the shallots, mushrooms, and garlic in the same frying pan, lightly browning them over a moderate fire.

3. Pour in the wine and simmer to ½ its quantity.

4. Then add the stock and the Tomato Puree.

5. Boil it for 2 to 3 minutes, then add the chervil, tarragon, and the remaining tablespoon of butter.

6. Put the chops in a covered baking dish and pour the sauce over them. Bake in a preheated 300° oven for 15 minutes and serve.

Escalopes de Veau
Veal Scallops

When you prepare veal scallops, the cooking is always done the same way. Sauté the veal in butter first and then set it aside while you prepare the sauces. The sauces can be quite different, depending on what appeals to you—wine sauce, cream sauce, tarragon-flavored sauce, or just lemon and butter. Here are several for you to try.

Escalopes de Veau à l'Anglaise
Breaded Veal Scallops

If you want to keep away from heavy sauces, try this simple recipe. It can be made a few minutes before sitting down at the table.

SERVES 6.

2 *pounds veal, cut from the leg into* 12 *scallops and*
    pounded ¹⁄₁₆ *inch thick*
Salt and freshly ground black pepper
Flour for dredging
2 *eggs*

1 *tablespoon water*
2 *cups fresh bread crumbs*
¾ *cup sweet butter*
1 *tablespoon lemon juice*
Garnishes: chopped fresh parsley, lemon wedges, mashed
    potatoes, and buttered green peas

1. Ask your butcher to cut you some veal scallops from the leg and to pound them ⅟₁₆ inch thick. Sprinkle them with some salt and pepper and dredge thoroughly with flour.

2. Dip the scallops in the eggs, which have been beaten together with the water.

3. Coat the meat on both sides with the bread crumbs. Tap lightly with a spatula to make the crumbs stick. Put the meat on a wire rack and cool in the refrigerator for 2 to 3 hours.

4. Place ½ cup of the butter in a large skillet and heat. Do not let it get brown.

5. Sauté the scallops in it on both sides until crisp and brown. Do not overcook; otherwise the veal will get dry. Arrange the veal on a heated platter.

6. Add 4 tablespoons of the butter to the skillet plus the lemon juice. Strain the juice over the meat and garnish with parsley and lemon wedges. Serve with mashed potatoes and buttered green peas.

The three veal scallop recipes which follow are cooked approximately the same way. Only the seasonings and types of wine and stock change. Various herbs may be used with veal but I suggest you experiment with them one at a time. All recipes for veal scallops go nicely with mushrooms, rice, noodles, mashed potatoes, or potatoes lyonnaise as accompaniments.

Escalopes de Veau au Marsala
Veal Scallops Marsala

SERVES 4 TO 6.

2 *pounds veal, cut from the leg into* 12 *scallops and pounded*
    ⅟₁₆ *inch thick*
Salt and freshly ground black pepper
Flour for coating veal

4 *tablespoons sweet butter*
2 *shallots, minced*
1 *clove garlic, minced*
4 *sprigs fresh parsley, minced*
1½ *tablespoons flour*
½ *cup Marsala wine*
1 *cup White Stock* (*p. 6*) *or canned chicken consommé*

1. Buy milk-fed leg of veal and ask your butcher to cut the veal into pieces 4 to 5 inches square and to flatten them. (You can do this yourself by placing the veal scallops between two pieces of wax paper and pounding them.) Sprinkle with some salt and pepper and coat on both sides with flour.

2. Melt the butter in a large frying pan over a high heat, taking care not to let it brown. Put in the veal scallops and brown on both sides. Do not overcook. It should take about 5 or 6 minutes altogether.

3. Take the frying pan off the heat. Place the meat in a flat roasting pan and keep warm in a preheated 250° oven.

4. Return the frying pan to the heat. Add the shallots, garlic, and parsley and sauté for 5 minutes. Do not scorch.

5. Add the flour and cook for 5 minutes longer, stirring constantly.

6. Slowly add the Marsala and the White Stock or consommé. Lower the heat and stir a little longer to eliminate the lumps in the sauce. If it is too thick, add more stock.

7. Strain the sauce over the veal. Keep warm in a 250° oven until ready to serve.

Escalopes de Veau à la Crème
Veal Scallops with Cream

SERVES 4 TO 6.

2 *pounds veal, cut from the leg into* 12 *scallops and pounded*
     ⅟₁₆ *inch thick*
Salt and freshly ground black pepper
Flour for coating veal
4 *tablespoons sweet butter*
2 *shallots, minced*
1 *clove garlic, minced*
4 *sprigs fresh parsley, minced*

1½ *tablespoons flour*
1 *cup White Stock (p. 6) or canned chicken consommé*
¼ *cup cream sherry*
¼ *cup dry vermouth*
½ *pound fresh mushrooms, sliced and sautéed in butter*
¾ *cup heavy cream*

1. Have the scallops cut and prepared as in the recipe for Veal Scallops Marsala (p. 157).

2. Melt the butter in a large frying pan over high heat, taking care not to let it brown. Put in the veal scallops and brown on both sides. Do not overcook. It should take about 5 or 6 minutes altogether.

3. Take the frying pan off the heat. Place the meat in a flat roasting pan and keep warm in a preheated 250° oven.

4. Return the frying pan to the heat. Toss in the shallots, garlic, and parsley and sauté for 5 minutes. Do not scorch.

5. Add the flour and cook 5 minutes longer, stirring constantly.

6. Slowly add the White Stock or consommé, cream sherry, and vermouth. Lower the heat and stir a little longer to eliminate the lumps in the sauce. Then strain the sauce to remove lumps of flour and the garlic, shallots, and parsley. If it is too thick, add a bit more stock.

7. Add the mushrooms to the sauce and just before serving, add the heavy cream. Stir and heat gently. Pour over the veal and serve.

Escalopes de Veau à l'Estragon
Veal Scallops with Tarragon

SERVES 4 TO 6.

2 *pounds veal, cut from the leg into 12 scallops and pounded*
    ¹⁄₁₆ inch thick
Salt and freshly ground black pepper
Flour for coating veal
4 *tablespoons sweet butter*
3 *tablespoons minced shallots*
4 *sprigs fresh parsley, minced*
1 *tablespoon chopped fresh or ½ tablespoon dried tarragon*
1 *cup plus 2 tablespoons Brown Stock (p. 4) or canned*
    beef consommé
¾ *cup dry white wine*

¼ cup dry vermouth
1 tablespoon cornstarch, dissolved in the 3 tablespoons
    Brown Stock

1. Have the scallops cut and pounded as in the recipe for Veal Scallops Marsala (p. 157).
2. Melt the butter in a large frying pan over a high heat, taking care not to let it brown. Put in the veal scallops and brown on both sides. Do not overcook. It should take about 5 or 6 minutes altogether.
3. Take the frying pan off the heat. Place the meat in a flat roasting pan and keep warm in a preheated 250° oven.
4. Return the frying pan to the heat. Add the shallots, parsley, and tarragon and sauté for 5 minutes. Do not scorch.
5. Slowly add the Brown Stock or consommé, wine, and vermouth and cook together for a few minutes.
6. Add the dissolved cornstarch and continue cooking and stirring over low heat until the sauce becomes thickened and smooth. Strain the sauce, pour over the veal, and serve.

Escalopes de Veau Cordon Bleu
Veal Scallops Cordon Bleu

SERVES 6.

2 pounds veal, cut from the leg into 12 scallops and pounded
    ⅟₁₆ inch thick
6 thin slices boiled Polish ham or prosciutto
6 thin slices Swiss Gruyère cheese
9 tablespoons sweet butter
Salt and freshly ground black pepper
¾ cup bread crumbs, seasoned with salt and pepper
½ cup flour
3 eggs beaten with 5 tablespoons heavy cream
¼ cup vegetable oil
1 recipe for Cordon Bleu Sauce (p. 161)

1. Brush 1 side of each veal scallop and each slice of ham and cheese with 4 tablespoons of the butter, melted. Place a slice each of ham and cheese between 2 of the veal scallops, buttered sides on the

inside. Do this with all the scallops and trim them to make 6 neat sandwiches.

2. Sprinkle veal sandwiches on both sides with a little salt and pepper. Dredge the veal sandwiches in a mixture of the seasoned bread crumbs and flour and refrigerate for 2 to 3 hours. The butter on the insides will congeal and hold the sandwiches together.

3. When you are ready to cook them, dredge the scallops in the bread-crumb mixture again, then in the egg-cream mixture and again in the bread crumbs.

4. Melt 3 tablespoons of the butter with 2 tablespoons of the oil in a frying pan over high heat. Brown the scallops on both sides for about 2 to 3 minutes on each side.

5. Put the scallops in a baking dish. Add the remaining 2 tablespoons butter and 2 tablespoons oil and bake the veal for about 15 minutes in a preheated 375° oven. Pour the sauce over and serve.

You can prepare the same sauce while the veal is in the oven.

Cordon Bleu Sauce

4 shallots, minced
1 clove garlic, minced
4 sprigs fresh parsley, minced
2 tablespoons sweet butter
2 tablespoons flour
2 tablespoons brandy
1 tablespoon Tomato Puree (p. 149) or canned tomato puree
¾ cup cream sherry or ½ cup Marsala
1½ cups Brown Stock (p. 4) or canned beef consommé
Salt and freshly ground black pepper

1. In the frying pan where the veal was sautéed, sauté the shallots, garlic, and parsley, adding 2 more tablespoons of butter if necessary. Brown slightly.

2. Add the flour and make a roux, keeping the color golden but not allowing it to brown.

3. Stir and add the brandy and the Tomato Puree. Cook for 1 minute and add the cream sherry or Marsala.

4. Cook and stir, adding the Brown Stock or consommé little by little. Simmer for 5 minutes. If it is too thick, add a little more stock.

5. Season to taste with salt and pepper. Strain the sauce into a saucepan and keep warm until ready to pour over the veal.

CHAPTER 8

Lamb

Agneau

Carré d'Agneau Rôti au Vin de Xérès

❋

Gigot d'Agneau à l'Ail
Gigot d'Agneau en Marinade au Chevreuil
Gigot d'Agneau aux Câpres

❋

Épaule d'Agneau aux Flageolets

❋

Noisettes d'Agneau aux Champignons

❋

Côtelettes d'Agneau Grillées à l'Anglaise

❋

Navarin d'Agneau à la Printanière

❋

Sauté d'Agneau à l'Indienne

The meat of the lamb is young, pink, and tender. Mutton is the flesh of older sheep and is reddish in color. It is classified as lamb up to one year, and mutton if the sheep is older than one year.

In the United States more of the young lamb is consumed, but in Europe it is exactly the opposite, with mutton being eaten more often. I have never tasted anything better than the French *pré-salé,* or salt meadow mutton, which comes from the pasture close to the sea coast of France. These aromatic plants are prolific and the spray of the sea on those plants gives the flesh of the mutton a distinctive salty taste which is highly prized.

In some parts of the world, particularly hot climates, mutton tends to retain the taste of wool fat. I have tasted mutton in Africa and Asia, and imported lamb from New Zealand and Australia, and if I may say so, stick to the U.S. lamb. You will pay more for it, but you will like it a lot better.

Always buy Prime or Choice lamb. First-quality lamb has a great deal of white fat spread evenly over the flesh and muscles. In second-quality lamb there is less fat; in third-quality lamb a very thin layer of fat covers the meat. Poor-quality mutton, usually the imported variety, is a pitiful sight—skinny carcass, yellowish fat, and it is tough to cook and eat, unless it is stewed for hours. Like beef, mutton or lamb should be hung and aged. Your butcher should be able to tell you if the lamb has been aged enough for eating.

Carré d'Agneau Rôti au Vin de Xérès
Roast Rack of Lamb with Sherry

SERVES 4 TO 6.

2 *cups Brown Stock (p. 4) or canned beef consommé*
½ *cup cream sherry*
15 *small white onions*
9 *tablespoons sweet butter*
½ *pound fresh mushrooms, cut in half*
1 *clove garlic, minced*
2 *3-pound racks of lamb, with bone between each rib*
Seasoned salt
Freshly ground coarse black pepper
4 *tablespoons vegetable oil*
Garnishes: small new potatoes and buttered carrots

1. Simmer the Brown Stock or consommé and sherry together until the liquid is reduced by half. Set aside.
2. Sauté the onions in 4 tablespoons butter slowly until golden brown and thoroughly tender. Set aside.
3. Lightly sauté the mushrooms in 3 tablespoons butter.
4. Mix together the stock-sherry mixture, onions, mushrooms, and garlic. Set aside.
5. Rub the lamb with some seasoned salt, coarse pepper, and the vegetable oil.
6. Roast the lamb in a preheated 400° oven for about 15 minutes or until it is browned. Reduce the heat to 300°.
7. Remove all the fat from the pan. Pour the wine sauce with the onions and mushrooms over the lamb, and add 2 tablespoons of butter. Roast for another 20 to 25 minutes at 300°, basting the meat frequently. The meat should be crisp and brown on the outside and pink on the inside.
8. Slice the lamb and arrange on a hot platter with the onions and mushrooms, small new potatoes, and buttered carrots around it. Pour the pan juices over it.

Gigot d'Agneau à l'Ail
Leg of Lamb with Garlic

SERVES 6 TO 8.

1 5- to 7-pound leg of lamb, with outside skin removed
8 cloves garlic, cut lengthwise into slivers
Seasoned salt
Freshly ground coarse black pepper
Vegetable oil
3 cups Brown Stock (p. 4) or canned beef consommé
2 cups cream sherry
8 small new potatoes
4 tablespoons sweet butter
Garnishes: lima beans and chopped fresh parsley

1. Take the leg of lamb out of the refrigerator 3 to 5 hours before cooking time. Meat must always be at room temperature before roasting or broiling.

2. Insert the pieces of garlic all around the leg by making tiny incisions and pushing the garlic underneath. Season the meat with seasoned salt and coarse black pepper. Pour on a little vegetable oil and let the meat marinate until ready to roast.

3. Meanwhile, simmer together the Brown Stock or consommé and the cream sherry until the liquid is reduced by half. This will be your basting sauce and gravy base.

4. Place the leg of lamb in a roasting pan, and roast in a preheated 450° oven with the oven door ajar. Turn frequently and baste with the vegetable oil and the fats accumulated during roasting. When the outside is brown and crisp, approximately 45 minutes later, take the meat out of the oven and place it in another roasting pan. Use the pan with the accumulated lamb fat to roast potatoes (separately from the lamb) for 1 to 1½ hours.

5. Put the butter on the meat and let it stand until 1 hour before you are ready to eat.

6. Reduce the oven temperature to 300°. The lamb should roast slowly now so that it will remain rare and juicy.

7. Place the lamb in the oven and turn it every 10 minutes, basting with the stock-sherry sauce. Compute the approximate roasting time by

figuring 20 minutes per pound, subtracting the 45 minutes for the first roasting.

8. When cooked, take the meat out of the oven and let stand for 10 minutes. This helps to keep the meat juices inside. Then slice the meat and arrange on a hot platter.

9. You should have approximately 2 cups of gravy left. Pour some of it, piping hot, on top of the meat. The rest should be served in a sauceboat. Surround the meat with lima beans and small potatoes which have been roasted in the lamb fat from the first roasting. Sprinkle the top with chopped parsley. Serve immediately.

Gigot d'Agneau en Marinade au Chevreuil
Marinated Leg of Lamb Stew

Only the experts will recognize this as lamb. It looks and tastes like venison.

SERVES 6 TO 8.

4 *medium-sized white onions, sliced*
3 *carrots, sliced thin*
1 *rib celery, sliced*
3 *cloves garlic, sliced*
½ *cup olive oil*
1 *bottle Beaujolais, more if necessary to cover the meat*
¾ *tablespoon salt*
1 *tablespoon peppercorns*
8 *sprigs fresh parsley*
5 *bay leaves*
½ *teaspoon thyme*
1 *teaspoon rosemary*
1 *6- to 7-pound aged leg of lamb, with skin and fat removed*
½ *cup vegetable oil*
2½ *cups Brown Stock (p. 4) or canned beef consommé*
4 *to 5 tablespoons sweet butter*
Freshly ground coarse black pepper
Garnish: Chestnut Puree (p. 292)

1. Simmer the vegetables and garlic in the olive oil in a covered saucepan for about 5 minutes. Do not let them brown. Then add the

wine, salt, peppercorns, and herbs. Simmer for another 15 minutes. Let cool.

2. Place the meat in an enamel or Pyrex dish which is large enough to hold the meat and the marinade and vegetables. Pour in the marinade and cover. Refrigerate it for 3 or 4 days and turn the meat 5 or 6 times a day.

3. Take the lamb out of the marinade. Drain and pour the vegetable oil over it.

4. Simmer the marinade 15 minutes and then discard the vegetables and herbs. Simmer liquid slowly for about 2 hours more.

5. Add 2½ cups Brown Stock or consommé to 2½ cups of the marinade. Simmer and reduce to ⅔ of the quantity.

6. Start roasting the lamb in a preheated 375° oven, basting often with the vegetable oil. Turn the meat every 10 minutes. It should take 45 minutes to 1 hour for the meat to brown well and be crisp on the outside.

7. Take the meat out of the pan; discard the fat or oil and place meat in another pan. Put the butter on top and let cool.

8. About 1½ hours before serving, put the meat in a preheated 325° oven with ½ of the marinade sauce and baste often. Turn the meat every 10 minutes, adding more sauce if necessary.

9. When the meat is ready, the marinade will be reduced to about ½ the quantity. Add some good freshly ground black pepper to the sauce. The meat should be sliced and arranged on a platter with some of the hot sauce over it. It will look dark, just like venison. This can be served with Chestnut Puree.

Gigot d'Agneau aux Câpres
Leg of Lamb with Capers

SERVES 6 TO 8.

6 *cups White Stock (p. 6) or enough to cover the lamb*
1 *5- to 6-pound leg of spring lamb, boned and rolled*
6 *medium-sized carrots, sliced*
6 *small white onions, sliced*
Bouquet garni: 1 stalk celery, 4 sprigs fresh parsley, 1 bay leaf, 2 cloves, all tied together in a cheesecloth bag
½ *teaspoon thyme*
2 *cloves garlic*

1. Bring White Stock to a boil.

2. Put the leg of lamb into the boiling stock with the carrots, onions, bouquet garni, thyme, and garlic.

3. Bring the stock to a second boil. Cover and let the meat cook gently. Allow approximately 2 hours for cooking, or 20 minutes per pound. Test with a fork to determine if the lamb is tender. Remove the lamb from the stock.

4. Skim the fat off the top of the stock and simmer until there are 3 cups left. Use the clear stock as the base for the following sauce. Meanwhile, keep the leg of lamb warm.

White Sauce with Capers

6 *tablespoons sweet butter*
6 *tablespoons flour*
3 *cups stock*
4 *tablespoons capers*
¾ *cup heavy cream*
Salt and freshly ground black pepper

1. In a heavy saucepan, melt the butter and stir in the flour. Cook for about 3 minutes over moderate heat until the mixture is golden, but not brown.

2. Gradually add the stock, a little at a time, stirring constantly, until you have a smooth, thick sauce.

3. Stir in the capers and cream and add salt and pepper to taste.

4. Slice the lamb. Arrange it on a platter and spoon on some of the sauce. Pass the rest of the sauce separately in a sauceboat.

Épaule d'Agneau aux Flageolets
Braised Shoulder of Lamb with White Beans

Late in the year, after the lamb or mutton has reached maturity, braising is the best cooking method to use. With a little care, you can make a succulent dish. For easy carving, have the butcher bone and truss the lamb. Remember to reserve the lamb bones. When cooked with meat, they add great flavor to the sauce.

SERVES 8.

5 *tablespoons vegetable oil*
4½ *to 5½ pounds shoulder of lamb, boned*

Reserved bones from lamb shoulder
4 medium-sized carrots, sliced
4 small white onions, sliced
2 stalks celery, sliced
2 cups dry sherry or dry white wine
½ teaspoon salt
½ teaspoon freshly ground black pepper
6 to 8 sprigs fresh parsley
2 medium-sized bay leaves
¼ teaspoon rosemary
¼ teaspoon thyme
4 cloves garlic, sliced
3 cups Brown Stock (p. 4) or canned beef consommé
3 cups White Beans (see below)

1. Heat the oil in a roasting pan and brown the meat and the bones on all sides in a preheated 400° oven. Be certain your lamb has a nice crusty cover when finished. This will take approximately 20 minutes.

2. Remove the bones and meat from the roaster and prepare the sliced vegetables the same way you prepared the meat, but roast only for 3 or 4 minutes. Remove them from the roaster and add to the meat. Discard the oil. Reduce oven temperature to 325°.

3. Pour the wine or sherry into the roaster. Melt the coagulated juices by bringing the wine to a boil and stirring. Simmer the wine in the roaster until it is reduced by about half.

4. Place the meat in the roaster. Add the bones, vegetables, salt, pepper, parsley, bay leaves, rosemary, thyme, garlic, and enough Brown Stock or consommé to cover ¾ of the lamb. Bring to a boil on top of the stove.

5. Immediately put your roaster into the 325° oven and simmer slowly; do not boil. Turn the shoulder every 20 minutes and baste often with the sauce. When the meat can be pierced easily with a fork, it is done. Remove the roast lamb. Strain the sauce and discard the vegetables. Skim the fat from the sauce.

6. Slice and arrange the meat on a platter with the sauce poured on. Pass extra sauce in a gravy boat.

White Beans

2 cups dried white beans
Bouquet garni: 3 sprigs parsley and 2 bay leaves, tied together in a cheesecloth bag

¼ teaspoon thyme
2 carrots, sliced
2 onions
2 cloves garlic, minced
Lump of sweet butter
½ to 1 cup sauce from the lamb

1. Soak the dried white beans in cold water for 1 to 2 hours.
2. Drain the beans. Wash them again and add enough water to more than cover them.
3. Add the bouquet garni and thyme.
4. Add the sliced carrots, onions, and garlic.
5. Bring the water to a boil. Cover and simmer slowly until done. Drain the surplus water.
6. Add some butter to the beans; stir and set aside until ready to be served with the braised lamb. When reheating the beans, add some sauce from the lamb to moisten them. Surround the sliced meat with the beans.

Noisettes d'Agneau aux Champignons
Loin Lamb Chops with Mushrooms

Noisettes d'agneau are loin lamb chops that have been boned. They can also be cut from the rib chops. The thickness should be between ¾ inch and 1 inch. Your butcher should prepare them properly for you. The usual serving is 2 noisettes per person. The arrangement of the food for this dish is beautiful, and the combined tastes will delight your guests.

SERVES 6.

12 noisettes of lamb, cut ¾ to 1 inch thick
Salt
Freshly ground black pepper
4 tablespoons vegetable oil
2 cups Brown Stock (p. 4) or canned beef consommé
½ cup dry white wine
12 large fresh mushrooms (caps and stems separated)

2 *tablespoons sweet butter*
Garlic salt
Garnishes: Garlic Tomatoes (p. 309) and Country-Style
Potato Cake (p. 305)

1. Season the noisettes with salt and freshly ground black pepper. Pour the vegetable oil over them and marinate at room temperature for 1 to 2 hours.

2. Simmer the Brown Stock or consommé with the wine until it is reduced to ½ its quantity. Add the mushroom stems and set aside to use as the sauce for the lamb.

3. Sauté the mushroom caps in the butter, adding a little garlic salt to taste. When the juices have evaporated, set aside and keep warm.

4. Prepare the Garlic Tomatoes. When they are half done, begin preparing the Country-Style Potato Cake.

5. When the potatoes, tomatoes, and mushrooms are all ready, keep them warm and prepare the noisettes. Broil or sauté the noisettes over high heat. Since it is a tender cut, do not overcook them. About 3½ to 4 minutes on each side should be enough, as the meat should remain pink.

NOISETTES D'AGNEAU
WITH MUSHROOMS•

6. Slice your Country-Style Potato Cake into 6 wedges like a pie. On a large, heated platter, place 1 slice for each guest. In between, place the noisettes, each one covered by a mushroom cap, with 1 tablespoon of sauce spooned over. Place the Garlic Tomatoes on the platter equally spaced between the potato wedges and the noisettes. Serve the balance of the sauce in a gravy boat.

Côtelettes d'Agneau Grillées à l'Anglaise
Broiled Lamb Chops with Butter and Lemon

SERVES 6.

6 *1-inch-thick double-rib lamb chops (French cut)*
Salt
Seasoned salt
Garlic salt
Freshly ground black pepper
6 *tablespoons vegetable oil*
6 *small chunks sweet butter*
Juice from ½ lemon
2 *tablespoons chopped fresh parsley*
Garnishes: fresh watercress and French-fried potatoes

1. Trim the chops, leaving as little fat as possible.
2. Season each chop with salt, seasoned salt, garlic salt, and pepper. You only need to sprinkle a little of each on each chop.
3. Place 1 tablespoon of vegetable oil on each chop and marinate for 2 hours.
4. Preheat the broiler to at least 500°. Broil the lamb about 5 minutes on each side for rare chops, 7 or 8 minutes on each side if you like them medium rare, and 10 minutes on each side for well-done lamb.
5. Place the chops on a heated platter. Put a small chunk of butter, a few drops of lemon juice, and a sprinkling of parsley on each chop. Garnish with fresh watercress and French-fried potatoes.

Navarin d'Agneau à la Printanière
Spring Lamb Stew

Navarin à la Printanière is a springtime dish in France. In the spring, the lamb is young and fresh vegetables become available. Today, it is not as seasonal a dish as it used to be. Now, with frozen vegetables and imported baby carrots on the market, you can prepare it any time.

Did you ever walk through Les Halles, the Central Market in Paris, in the springtime when young, tasty vegetables were on display? Those were the days. Now the market is gone, but the French still cultivate the marvelous ingredients for this type of stew.

The American cook can certainly duplicate the French version. Just be sure to use young spring lamb and fresh vegetables in season. This dish can be prepared in the morning and the green vegetables added a few minutes before serving.

SERVES 6.

3 *pounds lamb shoulder, breast, or neck, cut in 1½-inch cubes*
6 *tablespoons vegetable oil*
1½ *tablespoons superfine sugar*
1 *teaspoon salt*
¼ *teaspoon freshly ground black pepper*
3 *tablespoons flour*
3 *cups White Stock (p. 6) or canned chicken consommé*
2 *large fresh tomatoes, peeled and chopped, or ¼ cup*
    Tomato Puree (p. 149)
2 *cloves garlic, minced*
2 *small bay leaves*
¼ *teaspoon rosemary*
8 *small baby carrots*
12 *small white onions*
8 *turnips, cut in 1½-inch pieces*
6 *small new potatoes, peeled*
1 *cup fresh peas, shelled*
16 *fresh string beans*
Chopped fresh parsley

1. Dry the meat on paper towels so that it will brown well.
2. Heat the vegetable oil in a skillet; put a few meat pieces at a time into the hot oil. Repeat until all the pieces are browned and place the meat in a casserole.
3. When all the meat is in the casserole, sprinkle the pieces of meat with the sugar, salt, and pepper and cook slowly until the sugar starts to caramelize. This will give a nice color and add sweetness to your sauce.
4. Sprinkle the flour over every piece of meat and brown the meat by cooking over moderately high heat, stirring often. The meat should be coated evenly with a crust.

5. Remove the excess oil from the skillet the lamb was cooked in and add the White Stock to the juices. Pour the liquid into the casserole over the lamb.

6. Add the tomatoes, garlic, bay leaves, and rosemary.

7. Cover the casserole and bake in a preheated 325° oven for 1 hour. Adjust the oven temperature, if necessary, to prevent the liquid from coming to a boil.

8. Add the carrots, onions, turnips, and potatoes. Stir and cook in the oven for 1 more hour. Taste for seasonings and tenderness. Your meat is ready when pierced easily with a fork.

9. Cook the peas and string beans in boiling salted water for 5 minutes, uncovered, or until they are almost tender. Drain and add to the casserole. Keep warm until ready to serve.

10. Arrange the meat on a platter surrounded by the vegetables and sprinkle with fresh parsley.

Sauté d'Agneau à l'Indienne
Curried Lamb

When making a curried dish, I always use an imported Indian curry powder and I never have any trouble. I have had some nasty experiences in restaurants, however. The curry should be hot, but not so hot as to kill your taste buds. A vague direction like "season to taste" where curry is concerned makes more sense to me than "add ¼ teaspoon curry," as the strengths of the various curry powders differ widely. Remember, a recipe is just a guide to cooking, not a strict regulation.

SERVES 6.

4 *small white onions, finely chopped*
1 *clove garlic, minced*
6 *tablespoons sweet butter*
2 *large cooking apples, peeled, cored, and finely chopped*
3 *tablespoons flour*
2½ *cups Brown Stock (p. 4) or canned beef consommé,*
     heated

3 *pounds lean lamb shoulder, boned and trimmed,*
   cut in 1-inch cubes
Vegetable oil
Imported curry powder to taste
Garnishes: boiled white rice and green peas

1. In a large skillet, sauté the onions and garlic in the sweet butter until tender.

2. Add the apples and cook until you have a soft, mushy mixture.

3. Sprinkle the flour on top and blend. Cook slowly for 10 more minutes, or until the mixture is golden. Do not scorch.

4. Slowly add the Brown Stock or consommé and stir continuously until all the liquid is absorbed. Strain through a fine sieve, pressing the onion and apple pulp through into the sauce. Your sauce should be smooth. If it seems too thick, add a little bit more stock.

5. Brown the meat in a skillet in some vegetable oil. When all the pieces are well browned, drain the oil and place the lamb and the sauce in a Pyrex baking dish, with a little curry powder added.

6. Mix well; cover and simmer in a preheated 325° oven for 1 hour. Taste and add more curry powder if necessary. Use extreme caution in adding the curry.

7. Return the dish to the oven and cook until the lamb is tender. Add more salt, pepper, curry, or even a little sugar to taste. Serve with rice and tender green peas.

CHAPTER 9

Pork

Porc

Jambon de Porc Frais Rôti
Jambon Braisé au Madère

Porcelet Rôti et Farci

Carré de Porc Rôti à la Piquant
Carré de Porc en Marinade

Côtes de Porc Braisées Charcutière
Côtes de Porc Braisées à la Moutarde
Côtes de Porc Braisées aux Pommes
Côtes de Porc Sautées à la Normande

Plat de Côtes de Porc à la Piquant

Cassoulet de Porc aux Haricots Blancs à la Virion

Ragoût de Porc aux Légumes

Choucroute Garnie

Mousse au Jambon

For centuries in Europe the consumption of pork was greater than that of any other meat. This was particularly true in farm districts like Lorraine, where for five days out of seven, you would be certain that for dinner you would have La Potée au Lard. Here we call it New England Boiled Dinner. Pigs, when they are fed the proper food and slaughtered by complete bleeding, can produce meat with flavor as delicious as the other meats we eat. Today there are so many breeds of pigs that it is difficult to know every one of them. In England and France alone, there are at least twenty varieties.

The pork you find in the markets generally comes from hogs six to twelve months old. The meat should be quite white, and the fat even whiter. Do not buy rosy or pink pork, as it is not good enough for roasting. The best cuts are the loin, fillet chops, and ham. All can be eaten fresh or cured.

Pork is no problem to cook but it takes more time than chicken, veal, or beef. The latter meats, when overcooked, will get dry. However, a roast loin of pork which has been basted with the proper sauce, then covered and left in the oven at low heat, will keep well while you are drinking cocktails with your guests. Whether roasted or boiled, pork must be cooked thoroughly so that its delicious flavor will be fully developed. Thanks to the strict meat inspection in the United States today, fewer cases of trichinosis are being reported. Always roast a loin slowly for 2½ to 3 hours at 325° so that the internal temperature in the center of the roast is more than 140°. This temperature will always kill the trichina if it is present in the pork.

Jambon de Porc Frais Rôti
Roast Fresh Leg of Pork

SERVES 8.

1 8- or 9-pound fresh leg of pork, trimmed (can be boned)
Salt and freshly ground black pepper to taste
3 tablespoons vegetable oil
2 cups dry white wine
2 cups Brown Stock (p. 4) or canned beef consommé
4 tablespoons sweet butter
1 clove garlic, minced (optional)
Garnish: pan-roasted potatoes

1. Three hours before roasting, sprinkle meat with salt and pepper. Pour the vegetable oil over it, and let it stand at room temperature in the roasting pan, covered.

2. When ready to roast, place the fresh pork in a preheated 350° oven for 1 hour. Baste and turn the meat every 15 minutes until nicely browned on all sides.

3. Drain and reserve the fat. It can be used to roast potatoes in another pan.

4. Add ½ the wine and Brown Stock or consommé and the butter and reduce the heat to 300°. Baste often, and when the sauce is reduced to half, add the rest of the wine and stock. The total cooking time should be close to 4 hours, and the meat thermometer should read at least 180° when the meat is ready.

5. The meat can be kept covered in the oven another hour or so until you are ready to serve, but reduce the heat to 250° so that the sauce barely simmers and keep on basting every 15 minutes. Add more stock if necessary and the garlic if you wish. Discard excess fat. Taste sauce for seasoning and serve hot.

Jambon Braisé au Madère
Ham Braised with Madeira Wine

Some brands of ham are quite salty. Tell your butcher to give you a good-quality ham. Trim the excess fat.

SERVES 10 TO 12.

6 *medium-sized carrots, sliced*
4 *medium-sized onions, sliced*
6 *tablespoons sweet butter*
1 *7½- to 10-pound cooked ham*
2½ *cups Madeira wine*
2½ *cups Brown Stock (p. 4) or canned beef consommé*
2 *small bay leaves*
¼ *teaspoon thyme*
2 *basil leaves*
8 *sprigs fresh parsley*
½ *cup superfine sugar*
2 *to 3 medium-sized potatoes, peeled and sliced (optional)*
2 *tablespoons arrowroot*
2 *tablespoons cold Brown Stock (p. 4) or canned beef consommé*

1. Braise the carrots and onions in 3 tablespoons of the butter until tender and slightly browned.

2. Place the ham in a large roasting pan. Add the braised vegetables.

3. Boil the wine and the 2½ cups Brown Stock or consommé in the pan in which the vegetables were browned for 1 or 2 minutes. Pour the liquid over the ham. Add the bay leaves, thyme, basil leaves, and parsley sprigs.

4. Cover the pan and bake in a preheated 300° oven for 2½ to 3 hours. While the meat is roasting, turn every 15 minutes and baste with the juices.

5. When the meat is ready, sprinkle the sugar over it and place under a hot broiler to glaze. Be careful not to burn the sugar.

6. Strain the liquid from the roasting pan, discarding the herbs and vegetables, and reduce the liquid to ½ its quantity by simmering. If the ham has made the sauce too salty, add the potatoes and cook

them in the sauce while reducing it. The potatoes will absorb some of the saltiness. Strain the sauce and discard the potatoes.

7. Blend the arrowroot and the cold Brown Stock or consommé. Stir it into the braising sauce.

8. Simmer the sauce slowly for 10 minutes. Then stir in the remaining 3 tablespoons of butter. Serve hot with the braised ham.

Porcelet Rôti et Farci
Roast Stuffed Suckling Pig

A suckling pig or piglet is approximately two months old when it reaches the market. It usually has to be specially ordered and weighs ten to fifteen pounds. To roast it whole in an oven may be a problem, as your roasting pan and your stove may be too small. The best way to cook it would be on a spit outdoors. In that way, the skin will be golden brown and crusty when ready to be carved. I have eaten roast suckling pig on many occasions and every time it was a delicious success. A savory stuffing, a nicely seasoned gravy, and a crusty, roasted skin highlighted the feast.

I had no intention of including this recipe in the book, but recently something unusually funny happened to me in Kona, Hawaii, the site of one of the largest chain hotels. I had heard for years about the magnificent way the Hawaiians prepared and cooked the famous luau. I had seen some color films of the festivities. No sooner had I set foot on Hawaiian soil than I saw the great publicity employed to advertise these mammoth culinary festivals. I said to myself, "How can I stay away?"

I immediately made reservations for my wife and myself to be guests at the next luau held on the grounds of the hotel at which we were staying. The day came. Approximately fifty other tourists were drinking and eating appetizers around the fire pit and I could see the smoke escaping between the hot stones. I was perplexed. Something did not click. Why the stones on top of the piglet? Then somebody threw some dirty rags full of mud over the stones and some large leaves over the rags. I took another drink to brace myself against the inevitable. Were we going to eat some suckling pig meat which had come in contact with that dirty water and mud? That I had to see.

We were told to go to a dining room inside our hotel where we

would be served, as the festivities were about to begin. Everyone obeyed
the orders but me. I couldn't leave the vicinity of the fire pit. The personnel told me that I would miss great happenings in the dining room,
but I was obsessed by one thought: Why don't they take the piglet
out of the fire pit and carve it in the dining room? I again refused to
move. My professional instinct told me that I had been taken (never
mind the fifty other tourists), and for the money it had cost me for my
reservation, I was going to wait until the final curtain came down on
the last act of the show—the unveiling of the roast suckling pig.

Finally, they gave up trying to persuade me to leave. Two busboys
uncovered the muddy rags and the leaves and finally removed the top
stones. Looking me straight in the eye was the piglet, minus his apple,
minus everything but his head and four feet. After looking at the strange
sight for a few seconds, I exploded into laughter. *There* was the famous
Hawaiian barbecue promoted so cleverly by travel agents and public
relations personnel.

I have seen great deterioration in the food industry during the last
thirty years but this was the best example of fooling the customers I
have ever seen in any eating place. I rejoined my fellow tourists in the
dining room where the food was served buffet style. On two large platters hundreds of little pieces of pork were waiting for our culinary pleasure. The piglet, minus his legs and head, had been roasted without
stuffing or gravy in the main kitchen long before I had settled myself in
front of the fire pit.

SERVES 10 TO 14.

Salt
Freshly ground black pepper
1 *piglet, as small as you can buy it (approximately 12 pounds)*
1 *recipe Stuffing (p. 186)*
3 *tablespoons sweet butter, softened*
2 *cups Brown Stock (p. 4) or canned beef consommé*
2 *cups dry white wine*

1. Sprinkle salt and pepper inside and outside the piglet. Fill the
cavity loosely with the Stuffing. Close the opening with skewers and tie
tightly with string. With a brush, spread the butter all over the skin.

2. Place the piglet in a kneeling position in a large shallow pan.
Pour 1 cup of Brown Stock or consommé and 1 cup of wine into the
pan and roast in a preheated 350° oven for approximately 5 hours,

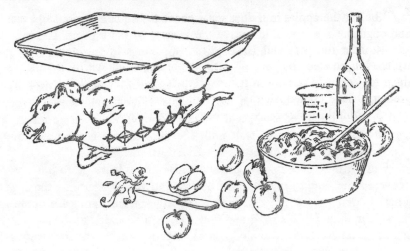

ROAST STUFFED
· SUCKLING PIG ·

or until done. Baste every 15 minutes with the sauce and add the balance of the stock and wine as often as necessary.

3. When the meat is done, degrease the pan and discard any fat.

4. Simmer the sauce until it is reduced and slightly thickened to a creamy consistency. Season to taste. Carve the piglet and serve with the Stuffing and the sauce.

Stuffing

1 *pound hot Italian sausage*
10 *Rome, Northern Spy, or tart green apples, peeled, cored,*
    and quartered
¼ *cup granulated sugar*
½ *teaspoon cinnamon*
½ *teaspoon sage*
½ *teaspoon salt*
⅓ *cup cognac*
½ *cup port wine*
½ *cup Brown Stock (p. 4) or canned beef consommé*
2 *cups croutons, sautéed in butter*

1. Cook the sausage in a skillet until it renders its fat and is slightly browned. Break the meat into small pieces in a large mixing bowl.

2. Cook the apples in the sausage fat until slightly browned and tender. They should retain their shape. Discard the excess fat.

3. Put the apples in a dish and add the sugar, cinnamon, sage, salt, and cognac.

4. Mix the port and Brown Stock or consommé in the skillet in which you cooked the sausage and the apples. Boil the liquid and reduce to ½ cup. Pour the liquid over the sausage meat. When your ingredients have cooled, lightly mix croutons, sausage meat, and apples.

5. Stuff the inside of the piglet loosely and skewer the opening.

Carré de Porc Rôti à la Piquant
Roast Loin of Pork with Piquant Sauce

SERVES 6 TO 8.

Piquant Sauce

¾ cup ketchup
½ cup water
½ cup dark corn syrup
1 8-ounce can tomato sauce
½ cup wine vinegar
½ cup light brown sugar
1 teaspoon chili powder
1½ tablespoons cornstarch
6 tablespoons Cointreau

1 5-pound center-cut loin of pork, with bone cut between
    each rib
3 to 4 large cooking apples, peeled, cored, and sliced
    crosswise to make rings
½ cup sweet butter
⅓ cup granulated sugar
½ teaspoon freshly grated or ground nutmeg
Garnishes: pan-roasted potatoes, apple rings

1. Combine the ketchup, water, dark corn syrup, tomato sauce, wine vinegar, brown sugar, and chili powder. Simmer over low heat for 10 minutes.

2. Blend the cornstarch with 4 tablespoons of the mixture and

then add it to the rest of the sauce. Cook the sauce slowly and stir until it is slightly thickened.

3. Add the Cointreau and continue stirring. Simmer gently for 20 minutes and set aside.

4. Roast the pork in a shallow pan in a preheated 325° oven for 2 hours. The roast will be nearly done and golden brown. Remove the pan drippings and use them to roast the potatoes.

5. Reduce the oven temperature to 250°.

6. Put the roast pork in a covered roasting pan and pour ½ of the sauce over it. Put the pan in the oven again. Continue to roast at 250° for ½ to 1 hour.

7. About 10 minutes before serving, pour the remaining sauce over the roast.

8. Sauté the apple rings in the butter in a heavy skillet until lightly browned on both sides. Sprinkle with the granulated sugar and nutmeg.

9. When ready to serve, slice the pork and place on a hot platter. Spoon the hot Piquant Sauce over the meat. Garnish with pan-roasted potatoes and apple rings.

Carré de Porc en Marinade
Marinated Loin of Pork

SERVES 8.

1 5-pound center-cut loin of pork, with bone cut between
   each rib
4 medium-sized yellow onions, sliced
6 medium-sized carrots, sliced
3 medium-sized bay leaves
½ teaspoon thyme
2 basil leaves
8 sprigs fresh parsley
8 cloves
10 peppercorns
1 bottle Chablis or dry white wine
4 tablespoons vegetable oil
2 cups White Stock (p. 6) or canned chicken consommé
Salt and freshly ground black pepper (optional)
Sugar to taste

Garnishes: pan-roasted potatoes, braised carrots, peas, and applesauce

1. For this recipe, ask your butcher to cut the bone between each rib.

2. Put the pork into a large casserole. Add the onions, carrots, bay leaves, thyme, basil, parsley, cloves, and peppercorns and pour the wine over all.

3. Cover the casserole and refrigerate at least 1 or 2 days. Turn the meat every 6 hours and baste with the wine.

4. About 3 or 4 hours before you are ready to roast the pork, take the casserole out of the refrigerator, and allow it to reach room temperature.

5. Take the meat out of the marinade. Put it into a roasting pan and pour the vegetable oil over it. Cover the pan with wax paper or foil and let it stand at room temperature until ready for roasting.

6. Meanwhile, strain the wine marinade, reserving the vegetables and herbs for later use. Add the White Stock or consommé and simmer the liquid until reduced to ½ its quantity. If you use canned chicken consommé, do not add salt and pepper until the roast is nearly done, as the chicken consommé is already highly seasoned.

7. Put the vegetables and the seasonings in the roasting pan with the meat and bake in a preheated 400° oven for 1 hour. Turn the roast and baste with the juices every 10 minutes. After 1 hour your vegetables should be braised and brown.

8. Remove the vegetables and the fat and return the roast to the oven. Reduce the oven temperature to 300°. Roast for 1 to 1½ hours more.

9. Meanwhile, put the vegetables into the reduced marinade. Cover the pot and simmer slowly for about 40 minutes.

10. Strain the marinade through a very fine sieve, as your sauce should be clear of all the little pieces of seasonings and vegetables.

11. Remove all the fat from the roasting pan and pour ½ of the marinade over the roast. Continue to roast at 300°, basting often.

12. About ½ hour before the meat is ready, pour the rest of the sauce over the roast and taste for seasoning. If the sauce is slightly acid from the wine, add 2 lumps of sugar. Add salt and pepper if necessary.

13. Your meat is ready when easily pierced with a fork. You can keep the meat warm for 1 more hour by reducing the heat to 225° and continuing to baste every 10 minutes. With the sliced roast pork you

can serve potatoes roasted in the fat that was discarded from the roast, along with braised carrots, peas, and applesauce.

Côtes de Porc Braisées Charcutière
Braised Pork Chops with Fresh Tomato Sauce

Pork chops are more tender and juicy if they are browned first in hot fat or oil and then roasted at a low temperature in a covered casserole. This slow steaming helps to tenderize the meat and get rid of the fat.

SERVES 6.

6 1¼-inch-thick pork chops
2 medium-sized yellow onions, sliced
3 medium-sized carrots, sliced
1 bay leaf
5 peppercorns
¼ teaspoon thyme
1 basil leaf
4 cloves
4 sprigs fresh parsley
½ teaspoon salt
½ teaspoon freshly ground black pepper
½ bottle dry Chablis
3 tablespoons vegetable oil
3 tablespoons sweet butter
4 small white onions, minced
1½ tablespoons flour
2 cups fresh ripe tomatoes, peeled, seeded, and sliced
2 cloves garlic, minced
2 tablespoons tomato paste
4 sour pickles, sliced
⅓ cup capers
2 tablespoons chopped fresh basil, or 2 tablespoons chopped
   fresh parsley

1. Place the pork chops in a shallow dish with the yellow onions,

carrots, bay leaf, peppercorns, thyme, basil leaf, cloves, parsley sprigs, salt, and pepper and add wine over all. Marinate overnight, turning and basting every 6 hours.

2. Remove the chops from the marinade, and cook the liquid with the vegetables slowly in a covered saucepan for 45 minutes. Strain through a fine sieve and set the sauce aside. Discard the vegetables.

3. Dry the chops well. Heat the oil in a large skillet and brown the chops on both sides.

4. Pour out the fat; add the butter and the white onions and sauté them slowly for 10 to 15 minutes without burning the onions.

5. Sprinkle the flour over the chops and simmer for 5 minutes.

6. Shake the skillet; turn the chops over and add the tomatoes and garlic. Cover the skillet and simmer for 10 minutes.

7. Add the cooked marinade and the tomato paste. Cook for 5 more minutes.

8. Arrange the chops in a baking dish or casserole; pour the sauce over them, then cover and bake in a preheated 300° oven. Adjust the heat if necessary so the meat and the sauce will simmer slowly for 30 to 40 minutes.

9. When ready to serve, add the pickles and capers. Taste for additional salt and pepper.

10. Arrange the chops on a hot serving platter. Skim the excess fat from the sauce and simmer it for a few minutes to thicken it if it is watery. Pour the sauce over the chops and sprinkle with some basil or parsley.

Côtes de Porc Braisées à la Moutarde
Braised Pork Chops with Mustard Cream Sauce

SERVES 6.

6 1¼-*inch-thick pork chops, trimmed of excess fat*
1 *cup dry white wine*
Salt
1½ *cups heavy cream*
1 *tablespoon Dijon mustard*
2 *tablespoons Tomato Puree (p. 149) or canned tomato puree*
Freshly ground black pepper
3 *tablespoons vegetable oil*

1 *clove garlic, minced*
¼ *cup fresh chopped chervil, basil, or parsley*

1. Marinate the chops overnight in the wine with a pinch of salt.
2. Strain the wine and simmer until it is reduced to ½ cup.
3. Simmer the cream separately until it is reduced to 1 cup.
4. Mix the wine, mustard, and Tomato Puree. Add the cream and beat well. Season with salt and pepper and set aside.
5. Dry the pork chops thoroughly with paper towels.
6. Heat the oil in a skillet and when it is very hot, sauté the chops for 5 minutes on each side until brown. Transfer them to a casserole.
7. Discard the fat from the skillet. Pour in the cream mixture and simmer for 4 to 5 minutes to absorb the meat juices sticking to the skillet.
8. Add the garlic and chervil, basil, or parsley. Cook for another 2 minutes, then strain the sauce over the chops. Season to taste.
9. Cover the casserole and bake in a preheated 275° oven for another 10 minutes, or until ready to serve. Regulate the oven temperature so that the sauce barely simmers, in case you have to delay your meal.

Côtes de Porc Braisées aux Pommes
Braised Pork Chops with Apples

SERVES 8.

8 *rib pork chops, 1 inch thick*
Salt and freshly ground black pepper
4 *tablespoons sweet butter*
3 *medium-sized tart green apples*
1 *cup White Stock (p. 6) or canned chicken consommé*
2 *sprigs fresh parsley, chopped*

1. Trim the excess fat from the chops and sprinkle lightly with salt and pepper.
2. Melt 2 tablespoons butter in a large, heavy skillet over moderately low heat and brown the chops on both sides. Transfer the meat to a long, shallow baking dish that will hold the 8 chops side by side. Do not wash the skillet; it will be used to prepare the sauce.
3. Wash and core the apples and cut 8 slices crosswise, ⅝ inch thick. Set 1 slice on each chop.

4. Melt 2 more tablespoons of the butter and brush on the apples.

5. Bake the chops, covered, for 40 minutes in a preheated 350° oven, or until the chops are tender, basting a few times. Set the chops and apples on a hot platter and keep them warm in a moderately hot oven while you prepare the sauce.

6. Heat the White Stock or consommé and pour it into the baking dish used earlier. Stir and scrape loose any congealed juices clinging to the pan and pour the liquid into the skillet. Bring the liquid to a boil.

7. Simmer and reduce liquid to ⅔ of its quantity and pour the gravy over the pork chops and apples on the hot platter. Sprinkle with parsley and serve hot.

Côtes de Porc Sautées à la Normande
Pork Chops with Apples in Cream Sauce

SERVES 8.

9 *tablespoons sweet butter*
2 *to 3 medium-sized tart green apples, cut crosswise into*
    16 *slices*
½ *cup granulated sugar*
8 *1-inch-thick loin pork chops*
Salt and freshly ground black pepper
¼ *cup dry white wine*
¼ *cup White Stock (p. 6) or canned chicken consommé*
1½ *cups heavy cream*
½ *tablespoon lemon juice*
2 *sprigs fresh parsley, chopped*

1. Set a baking dish or roasting pan in a preheated 350° oven. Add 5 tablespoons of the butter.

2. When the butter is melted, place the slices of apple side by side and sprinkle the sugar evenly on the slices. Bake for 5 minutes. Turn the slices over repeatedly until the apples are tender and slightly browned.

3. Reduce the heat to 250° and keep the apples warm.

4. Trim the excess fat from the pork chops and sprinkle some salt and pepper on both sides of the chops.

5. Melt 4 tablespoons of the butter in a skillet and cook and brown the chops over moderately high heat until they are well done.

6. Set the meat on a platter and keep warm in the oven with the apples.

7. Discard fat from the skillet. Add the wine and stock to the skillet. Bring to a boil and simmer until liquid is reduced to ¼ cup.

8. Add the cream and simmer until liquid is reduced to ¾ cup. Season to taste with more salt and pepper and add the lemon juice.

9. Take the pork chops and apples out of the oven. Arrange the apple slices around the pork chops on the platter. Pour the sauce evenly over each pork chop, sprinkle parsley on top, and serve.

Plat de Côtes de Porc à la Piquant
Spareribs with Piquant Sauce

Since there is not too much meat on the bones of spareribs, you should allow a full pound per serving.

SERVES 6.

6 *pounds spareribs, cut into single-rib pieces*
Piquant Sauce (*p.* 187)
3 *or* 4 *large Rome, Northern Spy, or tart green apples, peeled,*
    cored, and sliced crosswise
½ *cup sweet butter*
⅓ *cup sugar*
½ *teaspoon freshly grated or ground nutmeg*

1. Roast the spareribs in a shallow baking pan in a preheated 350° oven. Baste with the Piquant Sauce and turn every 10 minutes. Total baking time will be about 1½ to 1¾ hours.

2. Sauté the apple rings in the butter in a heavy skillet until lightly browned on both sides. Sprinkle with sugar and nutmeg. Serve with the spareribs.

Cassoulet de Porc aux Haricots Blancs à la Virion
Pork and Bean Casserole à la Virion

What is a cassoulet? There are so many ways to prepare this dish that I would not attempt to give you the original recipe. Many different cooks have come up with different versions of cassoulet. I have traveled throughout the southwestern part of France where the cassoulet originated, and I know that if you don't have cassoulet in the right restaurant, you may be disappointed.

In and around Toulouse in the Languedoc region of France, they make their cassoulet with "confit d'oie," or preserved goose, an ingredient found in the original version of the dish. It is an elaborate preparation which naturally tastes delicious; however, be aware of your own tastes and use whichever available ingredients you like the best: pork, goose, mutton, duck, or sausage. I do not believe that a good cassoulet is a difficult dish to make. My advice is not to make it when you are pressed for time. You should follow a slow cooking procedure all the way through except during the initial browning of the meat.

SERVES 8.

Beans:
4 *cups dried white beans*
Bouquet garni: 2 *sprigs fresh parsley,* 2 *bay leaves,* 1 *stalk celery,* 3 *cloves garlic, and* 4 *cloves, all tied together in a cheesecloth bag*
¼ *teaspoon thyme*
2 *medium-sized carrots, whole*
3 *small white onions, whole*
½ *pound salted breast of pork*
½ *pound fresh bacon*

1. Soak the beans in cold water for 3 to 4 hours, or until they start to swell. If they are soaked in the water too long, they will start to ferment. Drain the water from the beans.

2. Put the beans, bouquet garni, thyme, carrots, onions, pork, and bacon in a large pot. Cover with boiling water and barely simmer over low heat until your beans are nearly done and unbroken.

3. Remove the pork and bacon (to be used with the other meats);

discard the vegetables and the bouquet garni and keep the beans in the liquid until ready to use.

Meats:
½ *cup vegetable oil*
1½ *pounds loin of pork, boned and cut into 1½-inch pieces*
1½ *pounds loin of mutton, boned and cut into 1½-inch pieces*
1 *Polish sausage or any other garlic sausage, parboiled and*
        sliced 1 inch thick
4 *tablespoons sweet butter*
6 *medium shallots, minced*
2 *medium-sized tomatoes*
4 *tablespoons Tomato Puree (p. 149) or canned tomato puree*
1½ *cups dry white wine*
2 *cups Brown Stock (p. 4) or canned beef consommé*
3 *cloves garlic, minced*
¼ *teaspoon thyme*
2 *bay leaves*
1 *teaspoon salt*
½ *teaspoon freshly ground black pepper*
Leftover roast goose or duck, sliced (optional)

1. Pour some vegetable oil into a large skillet. When it is hot, brown the pork, mutton, and sausage. Brown them quickly only 1 layer at a time. If the skillet is not large enough to do it all at once, do it in several stages. When the pieces of meat are nicely browned, put them aside. Discard the oil and fat but let the juices from the meat remain in the pan.

2. In the same skillet, over moderate heat, add the butter and the shallots to the meat juices. Stir and sauté them until slightly browned.

3. Add the tomatoes and Tomato Puree. Cook and stir for 2 minutes.

4. Add the white wine. Reduce the sauce by simmering to about ⅔ of its quantity, stirring constantly.

5. Add the Brown Stock or consommé, garlic, thyme, bay leaves, salt, pepper, and the liquid from the beans and simmer for 15 minutes longer, uncovered.

6. Strain the liquid through a sieve and pour it over the meat in a saucepan. Simmer slowly until the meats are half-done—approximately 30 minutes. Add the parboiled sausage and set aside.

Assembling and Baking the Cassoulet

1. Place a layer of beans in the bottom of a Pyrex baking dish or a casserole. Then cover with some of the meats and sausages, another layer of beans, the rest of the meats and sausages, and top with the rest of the beans.

2. Cover the casserole and simmer in a preheated 300° oven for 1 hour. Season to taste and check for tenderness. Add more stock if necessary. The pork and mutton should be tender. The beans should have the consistency of Boston baked beans—firm but tender. There should be enough thick sauce to serve with the cassoulet. If you have any leftover goose or duck, you can put some small pieces in the casserole ½ hour before serving.

Ragoût de Porc aux Légumes
Pork Stew with Vegetables

SERVES 8.

1 3-*pound shoulder of pork, boneless and lean*
5 *tablespoons sweet butter*
Flour
1½ *cups dry white wine*
1½ *cups White Stock (p. 6) or canned chicken consommé*
Bouquet garni: 4 sprigs parsley, 1 small bay leaf, 2 cloves
        garlic, and 6 peppercorns, all tied together in a
        cheesecloth bag
Pinch of thyme
6 *small carrots, quartered*
16 *small white onions*
4 *medium-sized turnips, quartered*
8 *small new potatoes (optional)*
1 *teaspoon salt*
½ *teaspoon freshly ground black pepper*
Cornstarch (optional)

1. Remove the excess fat from the meat and cut the meat into 1½-inch cubes.

2. Melt 3 tablespoons of the butter in a Dutch oven and sauté the meat until nicely browned on all sides. Be careful not to burn the butter or scorch the meat.

3. Sprinkle some flour over the meat and stir until the flour adheres to the meat and is slightly browned.

4. Add the wine, mixed with the White Stock or consommé, the bouquet garni, and the thyme. Bring to a boil, cover, and simmer for 1¾ hours.

5. Meanwhile, clean and peel the carrots, onions, and turnips.

6. Sauté the onions in 2 tablespoons of the butter in a covered pan for 15 minutes over moderately high heat. Uncover and simmer gently until the onion juice has evaporated.

7. Add the onions, turnips, and carrots to the stew. Add the peeled potatoes if you are using them. Cover and simmer until all the vegetables are tender, approximately 45 minutes. Season with the salt and pepper and test the meat for tenderness.

8. If the sauce is too thick, add a little more stock. If it is too thin, dissolve a little cornstarch in a small amount of cold water and blend in with the stew until slightly thickened.

Choucroute Garnie
Sauerkraut with Smoked Pork

Sauerkraut is a finely shredded cabbage which has been fermented in brine. In certain provinces of France like Lorraine and Alsace, practically every farm family makes its own sauerkraut, or *choucroute,* to be eaten during the off-season in place of fresh vegetables.

Choucroute Garnie is generally made with a variety of pork cuts like sausages, spareribs, and smoked ham. In Alsace they have an outstanding regional recipe for pheasant and sauerkraut. The main seasonings used in such dishes are juniper berries and salt.

SERVES 6 TO 8.

2½ *pounds prepared sauerkraut, well drained*
½ *pound smoked pork rind, cut into pieces*
2 *carrots*
3 *small white onions*

Bouquet garni: 4 *sprigs parsley,* 8 *peppercorns,* 1 *bay leaf,*
    3 *cloves, and* 8 *juniper berries*
6 *slices bacon*
1 *cup dry white wine*
1 *cup White Stock* (*p.* 6) *or canned chicken consommé*
Salt to taste
2 *pounds spareribs,* 2 *pounds precooked smoked ham,* 1 *pound*
    parboiled Polish sausage, 12 *frankfurters*
Small new potatoes (*optional*)

1. Soak the sauerkraut in cold water for 2 hours. Drain and extract all the water.

2. In the bottom of a casserole, place the smoked pork rind. Add the sauerkraut. Tie the carrots, onions, and the bouquet garni in some cheesecloth and place on top of the sauerkraut. Add the thyme, bacon, wine, White Stock, and salt.

3. Bring to a boil; cover and simmer the casserole in a preheated 300° oven for 3 hours.

4. If you wish to add 1 or all of the meats to the sauerkraut, you can do so 1 to 1½ hours before the sauerkraut is ready. New potatoes can also be added an hour before the cooking is completed. If none of these are desired, the sauerkraut can be cooked alone and used as a garnish for a roast ham or roast loin of pork.

5. Before serving the sauerkraut, remove the pork rind, vegetables, and seasonings. If there is too much liquid, discard it.

Mousse au Jambon
Ham Mousse

SERVES 6 TO 8.

2 *cups White Stock* (*p.* 6) *or canned chicken consommé*
1 *bay leaf*
½ *teaspoon thyme*
6 *sprigs fresh parsley*
5 *shallots, minced*
2 *tablespoons sweet butter*
⅓ *cup dry vermouth*

2 *envelopes unflavored gelatin*
1 *tablespoon Tomato Puree (p.* 149) *or canned tomato puree*
2 *tablespoons cognac*
2½ *cups boiled Polish or American ham, finely diced*
½ *teaspoon salt*
½ *teaspoon freshly ground black pepper*
1 *cup heavy cream*
Garnishes: lettuce leaves or watercress and sliced tomatoes

1. Put the White Stock or consommé, bay leaf, thyme, and parsley into a saucepan. Cover and simmer for 15 minutes. Strain and set aside.

2. Sauté the minced shallots in the butter. When lightly wilted, add them to the strained stock.

3. Pour the vermouth into a large bowl. Sprinkle the gelatin into the vermouth and wait a few minutes until the gelatin absorbs the liquid and softens.

4. Now add the stock, Tomato Puree, and cognac and mix well. Add the ham.

5. Pour the mixture into a blender and blend until you get a puree. Season with salt and pepper if necessary. Pour the puree into the same bowl and refrigerate.

6. Whip the cream until stiff and refrigerate.

7. When the ham puree starts to set, stir it and put it back in the refrigerator. When it becomes slightly stiff again, fold in the whipped cream and pour into a mold or a rectangular 9 by 5 by 3-inch Pyrex dish. Return it to the refrigerator.

8. When the puree is firmly set, unmold it on a bed of lettuce leaves or watercress and surround it with sliced tomatoes.

AN ADDITIONAL SUGGESTION: Jellied stock can be used to make this mousse even more attractive. You make jellied stock by dissolving 1 envelope unflavored gelatin in a little cold water and then adding 2 cups heated white stock and stirring until it is completely blended and dissolved. Pour a thin layer of jellied stock on the bottom of the mold and refrigerate until set. Then pour in the mousse. Refrigerate again until the mousse is firm and pour in the other half of the jellied stock. Refrigerate until firm and then unmold. You can use either the large mold or Pyrex dish, as indicated above, or individual ramekins or custard cups. The individual molds with the jellied stock on the top and bottom look especially appetizing when unmolded on little beds of lettuce leaves or watercress and tomatoes.

CHAPTER 10

Chicken and Poultry

Volaille

Poulet Grillé
Poulet Sauté
Poulet Sauté au Chablis
Poulet Sauté aux Fines Herbes
Poulet Rôti à la Vallée d'Auge

Poularde Braisée à l'Alsacienne
Poularde Rôtie à la Grand-mère
Poularde Rôtie à la Provençale

Coq au Vin
Cari de Poularde à l'Indienne
Fricassée de Poularde à la Suprême
Ragoût de Poularde à la Créole
Poularde avec Riz à la Mornay

Soufflé de Volaille
Mousse de Volaille à la Velouté

Croquettes de Volaille ou Dindonneau

Capon à la Suprême

Dinde Rôtie à l'Américaine

Caneton aux Navets
Caneton à l'Orange

Caneton Montmorency
Caneton aux Pêches

❀

Oie Rôtie Farcie

❀

Pigeonneaux Rôtis en Casserole

❀

Coqs de Bruyère Rôtis sur Croûtons

❀

Farce de Pain à l'Américaine
Farce de Marrons

Poultry generally refers to domesticated birds, such as chicken, turkey, duck, squab, and goose. Chicken, which is inexpensive and easy to cook, is the most popular. Chickens can be pan-fried, broiled, roasted, and stewed. The versatility of the appropriate accompanying gravies and sauces and the ingredients from which they can be made is almost unlimited.

As for determining the weight, size, and age of chickens, you will have to rely largely on your butcher for more information. He can also tell you the differences between one chicken and another. Here is a general guideline to the various types of chickens you will find in the market:

Broiler-Fryers	1½ to 3 pounds. Usually very young, 8 to 10 weeks old.
Roasting Chickens	3½ to 6 pounds. A little fatty but still young.
Capons	4½ to 8 pounds. Castration makes the meat more tender, but you will have to discard a large amount of fat in cooking.
Fricassee Chickens	3 to 6 pounds. Retired poultry, too old to lay eggs.

From the very young chicken to the roasting chicken, look for birds with flesh that is tender, but not flabby. One way to recognize age and tenderness is to press the breastbone from side to side. If it gives easily, it is a young chicken. Capons are in a category by themselves, since they are raised mainly for eating. You cannot be too finicky in choosing a capon. Fricassee chickens are usually too old for laying eggs and for roasting, but they make excellent chicken broth. In addition, fricassee chickens can be used for blanquettes, or stews, with a rich creamy sauce, accompanied by onions, mushrooms, young carrots, and green peas.

Unfortunately, the feeding of poultry in the United States leaves a lot to be desired. The best-flavored chickens and poultry come from special farms which feed their birds a generous diet of grains and substantial bird food. This type of poultry usually costs twice as much as the ordinary broiler or fryer sold in the supermarkets, but you pay for the flavor. The flavor of poultry raised in a synthetic environment is tasteless in comparison.

Here are a couple of tips which may help you when you are preparing chicken or other poultry for your family:

When roasting poultry, it is important to protect the breast. It is the most delicate part of the bird and will dry out if it is overcooked or if it is not properly basted. A good way to keep the breast moist when roasting a large bird is to cover the entire breast with thick, fatty bacon.

The best way to roast a large chicken or a capon is to start at a high oven temperature to brown the bird all around and then continue at a lower temperature to complete the cooking. You can begin roasting at 450° for 30 to 40 minutes and continue at 325° until done. A chicken or capon usually needs about 18 minutes per pound to be well cooked.

Poulet Grillé
Broiled Chicken

The broiler-fryer can be cooked very quickly under a broiler, pan-fried in a skillet, or deep-fried in oil. A wide variety of sauces can be served with the broiler-fryer, just by varying the stocks and wines and adding tomatoes, heavy cream, sour cream, mushrooms, or cognac.

Here is the method I use for broiling chickens:

SERVES 8.

1 *cup cream sherry*
1 *cup White Stock (p. 6) or canned chicken consommé*

2 2½-pound broilers, quartered
Salt and freshly ground black pepper
3 tablespoons sweet butter, melted
½ cup heavy cream or ½ cup sour cream or 2 tablespoons
    Tomato Puree (p. 149) or ½ pound fresh mushrooms,
    sliced and sautéed in butter
Garnishes: 4 sprigs fresh watercress and French-fried or
    mashed potatoes

1. Simmer the sherry and White Stock or consommé together until they are reduced to 1 cup.

2. Sprinkle the chicken lightly with some salt and pepper and pour the butter over each piece.

3. Broil under a hot preheated 450° broiler until nearly cooked and nicely browned on all sides.

4. Reduce the heat and baste the chickens on both sides several times with some of the sherry-stock mixture until they are done. Remove the chickens.

5. Add the juices in the pan to the rest of the sherry-stock mixture and simmer it until reduced to a syrupy consistency. If you wish, you may add the cream or sour cream to the sauce and simmer for a few minutes, or add the Tomato Puree or the mushrooms.

6. When the sauce is ready, arrange the chickens on a platter and pour the sauce over it. Garnish with 2 sprigs of fresh watercress on each end of the platter and surround the chickens with French-fried or mashed potatoes.

Poulet Sauté
Fried Chicken

The French do not prepare fried chicken as a rule, but occasionally they bread the young chicken and sauté the parts in butter and serve it with a sauce. Here in the United States the young chickens are often breaded and deep-fried in shortening or oil.

You do not have to be a colonel from Kentucky to fry a chicken. Knowing how to bread the chicken properly is the only trick. Here is a simple way to prepare the fryer for either sautéeing in the French way or frying Kentucky-style. I served this recipe many times to John Ringling North.

SERVES 6.

2 *young fryers, cut in pieces*
Salt and freshly ground black pepper
2 *eggs, slightly beaten*
2 *tablespoons water*
1 *cup flour*
1 *cup soft bread crumbs*
*Oil or shortening for deep-frying or ½ cup sweet butter
    for sautéeing*
Garnish: Velouté Sauce (p. 10)

1. Sprinkle the chicken parts with some salt and pepper.
2. Beat the eggs and the water lightly together.
3. Dip the chicken pieces in the flour and then in the eggs and water.
4. Then cover all the parts with the bread crumbs.
5. Heat the oil or shortening to 400°, using a deep-fry thermometer or an electric deep-fry pan, and fry the chicken parts, a few at a time, for about 20 minutes, or until brown and crisp and cooked throughout.
6. If you wish to sauté the breaded chicken, melt some butter in a large, heavy skillet and place the chicken pieces in side by side over moderate heat. When the chicken is well browned on both sides, cover the skillet, then lower the heat and continue cooking for about 15 minutes, or until the chicken is cooked throughout.
7. Serve the deep-fried or sautéed chicken with Velouté Sauce.

Poulet Sauté au Chablis
Sautéed Chicken with Chablis Wine

SERVES 6 TO 8.

16 *small white onions*
4 *tablespoons sweet butter*
¾ *pound fresh mushroom caps*
1 *cup Chablis*
Salt and freshly ground black pepper

8 *chicken legs (fryers)*
8 *chicken thighs (fryers)*
4 *tablespoons sweet butter, melted, mixed with 2 tablespoons oil*
1 *clove garlic, minced*
4 *shallots, minced*
1 *cup heavy cream*
¼ *cup chopped fresh parsley*

1. Sauté the white onions slowly in 2 tablespoons of the butter until they are tender, but not brown. Set aside.
2. Sauté the mushroom caps in 2 tablespoons of the butter until their juices have evaporated. Set aside.
3. Simmer the wine, uncovered, in a saucepan until reduced to ½ cup.
4. Sprinkle some salt and pepper on the chicken. Place the chicken parts in a shallow roasting pan and into a preheated 400° oven. Turn on the broiler. Pour the melted butter mixed with the oil over each piece and broil until browned on both sides.
5. Place the browned chicken parts in a casserole with the onions, mushrooms, and garlic and keep warm.
6. Sauté the shallots in the roasting pan with the juices from the chicken. When transparent and tender, add the reduced wine. Stir and cook for 2 minutes and strain the sauce over the chicken. Cover the casserole and bake in a 325° oven for 45 minutes.
7. Take out the chicken, onions, and mushrooms and place on a heated platter. Place the platter in a 225° oven to keep warm. Immediately pour the cream into the sauce in the casserole and cook together quickly until your gravy has the consistency of heavy cream. Taste for seasoning.
8. Pour the sauce over the chicken. Sprinkle on some parsley and serve.

Poulet Sauté aux Fines Herbes
Sautéed Chicken with Herbs

SERVES 6.

2 *2½-pound fryers, cut in pieces*
Salt and freshly ground black pepper

8 *tablespoons sweet butter*

1 *cup dry white wine*

4 *shallots, minced*

1 *cup White Stock (p. 6) or canned chicken consommé*

2 *tablespoons flour*

1 *tablespoon lemon juice*

1 *tablespoon finely chopped fresh or ½ tablespoon dried parsley*

1 *tablespoon finely chopped fresh or ½ tablespoon dried chervil*

1 *tablespoon finely chopped fresh or ½ tablespoon dried tarragon*

1. Sprinkle the chicken pieces lightly with some salt and pepper and sauté them in 6 tablespoons of the butter until cooked and browned. Remove pieces to a warm platter and keep warm in a preheated 250° oven.

2. Add the wine and the shallots to the juices in the pan and simmer until reduced to ½ the original quantity.

3. Add the White Stock or consommé and boil down until you have only 1¼ cups. Strain the liquid.

4. Melt 2 tablespoons of the butter in a saucepan and blend in the flour. Cook slowly for about 3 minutes until golden and bubbly and gradually stir in the strained liquid. Cook and stir until you have a smooth sauce. If it is too thick, add a little more stock.

5. Stir in the lemon juice, parsley, chervil, and tarragon and simmer for 1 more minute. Pour the sauce over the chicken and serve.

Poulet Rôti à la Vallée d'Auge
Roast Chicken with Calvados and Cream

The province of Normandy in western France is noted for its pastures and cattle. Out of that combination came the famous Camembert and Pont l'Evêque cheeses, Isigny's butter and cream, *pré-salé* lamb, and Calvados.

The Vallée d'Auge, situated in the heart of Normandy, is well remembered by gourmets from all over the world for an outstanding dish.

Poulet Rôti à la Vallée d'Auge contains the butter, rich heavy cream, and applejack brandy for which the Normandy countryside is famous.

SERVES 6 TO 8.

3 2- to 3-pound fryers, split, or 2 3- to 4-pound roasting
    chickens, cut in pieces
6 shallots, minced
6 tablespoons sweet butter
¼ teaspoon thyme
½ cup dry white wine
½ cup White Stock (p. 6) or canned chicken consommé
Salt and freshly ground black pepper
5 tablespoons Calvados or applejack brandy
1 tablespoon Cointreau or orange liqueur
1½ cups heavy cream
¼ cup chopped fresh parsley

1. If you use fryers, have the butcher split them in half. Discard the tips of the wings and the knees. If you use roasters, have the butcher cut them in pieces for you. Allow 2 pieces for each serving.

2. Sauté the shallots in a saucepan with 2 tablespoons of the butter until slightly brown. Add the thyme, wine, and White Stock or consommé and simmer until reduced to ½ cup. Set aside.

3. Melt the remaining 4 tablespoons of the butter.

4. Sprinkle the chicken lightly with some salt and pepper and pour the melted butter on both sides. Bake the chicken in a shallow roasting pan in a preheated broiler until nicely browned and about ¾ done, approximately 15 minutes.

5. Pour the Calvados or applejack over the chicken and ignite. Baste the chicken with the liquid until the flames die out. Then place the chicken in a casserole; cover and keep warm.

6. To the juices and butter in the roasting pan, add the hot stock-wine mixture and cook for 5 minutes, stirring constantly to detach the coagulated juices from the sides of the baking pan.

7. Add the orange liqueur and cream.

8. Simmer until reduced to 1 cup of liquid, or until the sauce has the consistency of heavy cream. Taste for seasoning and skim off the excess butter if any.

9. Strain the sauce through a fine sieve over the chicken in the casserole. Lower the oven temperature to 300° and simmer the covered casserole in the oven for 20 more minutes. When ready, put the chicken

on a heated platter. Spoon the sauce over; sprinkle on the parsley and serve.

Poularde Braisée à l'Alsacienne
Braised Chicken with Cream and Wine

SERVES 6.

Salt and freshly ground black pepper
1 4- to 5-pound roasting chicken, cut in 12 small pieces
4 tablespoons sweet butter
3 tablespoons vegetable oil
18 small white onions
1 pound small fresh mushrooms, cut in halves
¼ cup White Stock (p. 6) or canned chicken consommé
4 shallots, minced
¾ cup Riesling or a light, dry white wine
¾ cup heavy cream
Chopped fresh parsley

1. Sprinkle some salt and pepper on all the chicken pieces.
2. Heat the butter and oil in a large frying pan and brown the chicken thoroughly. Cook until about ½ done. Add more butter if needed.
3. Place the chicken, onions, and mushrooms in a covered casserole.
4. Add the White Stock or consommé to the pan the chicken was browned in and boil up to remove the coagulated juices. Add to the chicken in the casserole.
5. Bake in a preheated 350° oven for 30 minutes, or until the chicken and vegetables are completely cooked. Transfer the chicken and vegetables to a warm platter, leaving the juices in the casserole.
6. Add the shallots to the casserole and cook on top of the stove until they are tender. Remove the excess fat from the top of the sauce.
7. Add the wine and cook until the liquid is reduced to half.
8. Stir in the cream and cook 5 minutes longer or until sauce is creamy.
9. Pour the sauce over the chicken and vegetables. Sprinkle with some parsley.

Poularde Rôtie à la Grand-mère
Roast Chicken à la Grand-mère

SERVES 6.

6 *strips lean bacon*
1 *4- to 5-pound roasting chicken*
Salt and freshly ground black pepper
6 *tablespoons sweet butter*
¼ *cup dry vermouth*
½ *cup White Stock (p. 6) or canned chicken consommé*
18 *very small white onions*
24 *small new potatoes, cut and rounded to the size of a walnut*
2 *tablespoons chopped fresh parsley*

1. Dice the bacon. Drop into boiling water and cook for 10 minutes to remove the strong smoky taste. Drain and set aside.
2. Sprinkle the chicken lightly with some salt and pepper.
3. Melt the butter in a casserole and place the chicken in it. Cover and roast in a preheated 350° oven for about 1 hour.
4. Mix together the vermouth and the White Stock or consommé and baste the chicken often during the roasting.
5. Add the diced bacon and the white onions and roast for another 20 minutes.
6. Then add the potatoes and roast until the potatoes are done, about ½ hour longer. Be sure to keep the casserole tightly covered during the cooking and continue to baste from time to time.
7. Set the chicken on a platter surrounded by the onions and potatoes, leaving the liquid in the casserole. Simmer the liquid to a nice consistency. Pour the liquid over the chicken and serve with the parsley on top.

Poularde Rôtie à la Provençale
Roast Chicken à la Provençale

This is a good dish to make for a buffet dinner, since you can keep the chicken warm in a chafing dish. This dish can be prepared the day before, and the baking can be done 1¼ hours before serving.

SERVES 8.

2 cups White Stock (p. 6) or canned chicken consommé
1 cup cream sherry
Bouquet garni: 2 bay leaves, 2 basil leaves, and 8 sprigs fresh
     parsley, all tied together in a cheesecloth bag
1/4 teaspoon thyme
6 small white onions, sliced
2 green peppers, chopped
9 tablespoons sweet butter
1 pound fresh mushrooms, sliced
4 cups Tomato Puree (p. 149)
2 tablespoons tomato paste
2 cloves garlic, minced
20 black olives, quartered
1 5- to 6-pound roasting chicken, cut into pieces (reserve neck,
     liver, gizzard, and wing tips for stock)
Salt and freshly ground black pepper
1/2 cup cognac
4 tablespoons chopped fresh parsley
Garnishes: Saffron Rice (p. 277) and green peas

1. Put the White Stock or consommé, sherry, bouquet garni, and thyme into a saucepan and simmer until reduced by half. Set aside.

2. Sauté the onions and green peppers together in 3 tablespoons of the butter, just until tender. Set aside.

3. Sauté the mushrooms in 2 more tablespoons of the butter until their water is completely evaporated. Do not burn the mushrooms, as they become bitter when scorched.

4. Combine the reduced stock, onions, peppers, mushrooms, Tomato Puree, tomato paste, garlic, and olives in a saucepan and set it aside.

5. In a flat roasting pan, large enough to place the chicken pieces side by side, set the chicken, which has been salted and peppered and brushed all over with the remaining 4 tablespoons of butter, melted. Place in a preheated broiler and broil until the chicken is well browned on both sides. Do not overcook, as the chicken will complete cooking with the sauce. Remove chicken from broiler.

6. Pour the cognac over the chicken and ignite it. Baste the meat with the burning cognac until the flames die out. Strain the juices and add to the ingredients in the saucepan.

7. Heat the sauce and taste it for seasoning. Add some salt and

pepper if necessary and distribute the sauce evenly over the pieces of chicken so that it is well covered by it.

8. Cover the roasting pan with heavy-duty aluminum foil to prevent the chicken from getting dry. Place the roasting pan in a 300° oven for 1¼ hours.

9. Skim the excess fat from the top of the sauce and place the chicken pieces on a warm platter. Spoon the sauce over the chicken and sprinkle the parsley on top. As a garnish, Saffron Rice can be placed in a ring around the chicken. Green peas or another green vegetable can also serve as an accompaniment.

Coq au Vin
Chicken with Red Wine

This recipe calls for a fine bottle of red wine from Burgundy, a full-bodied one such as Chambertin. Other good, less expensive Burgundies, such as a Beaujolais or Côtes du Rhône can be used as well. Keep the more costly Chambertin to drink at the table.

SERVES 6.

¾ bottle Chambertin, Beaujolais, Côtes du Rhône, or other good Burgundy wine
2 cups White Stock (p. 6) or canned chicken consommé
Bouquet garni: 2 bay leaves and 6 sprigs parsley, tied in a cheesecloth bag
¼ teaspoon thyme
½ pound bacon, in one piece
6 cups boiling water
12 tablespoons sweet butter
12 small white onions, peeled
¾ pound fresh mushrooms, sliced
1 3- to 3½-pound roasting chicken, cut in pieces (reserving neck, liver, and gizzard)
Salt and freshly ground black pepper
⅓ cup cognac
4 tablespoons flour
1 tablespoon tomato paste

3 *cloves garlic, minced*
1 *recipe Pastry Dough* (*p.* 137) *and* 1 *egg yolk beaten with*
　　¼ cup heavy cream, or 4 *slices white bread, cubed and*
　　sautéed in 4 *to* 5 *tablespoons sweet butter until crisp*
Garnishes: parslied potatoes, green peas, and carrots

1. In a saucepan, simmer the wine and the White Stock or consommé together with the bouquet garni and the thyme until reduced to 3½ cups. Set aside.

2. Remove the rind from the bacon and cut it into ¼-inch-thick pieces. Put the bacon into a saucepan with 6 cups of boiling water and boil for a few minutes. This blanching process will remove the strong smoky taste. Drain well. Slowly sauté the bacon in 1 tablespoon of the butter until it is lightly browned. Set aside.

3. Sauté the onions in 2 tablespoons of the butter until golden brown and tender but do not burn. Very slow simmering is the best way to cook onions. Set aside.

4. Sauté the mushrooms in 2 tablespoons of the butter until their liquid has evaporated. Do not brown. Set aside.

5. Add some of the wine-stock mixture to all the saucepans and skillets used to cook the preceding ingredients. Boil it up and return the stock-wine mixture to the saucepan. They will pick up the aroma, butter, and juices sticking to the cooking utensils and add them to the final sauce.

6. Place the chicken pieces, including the gizzard, neck, and liver, in a baking pan. Sprinkle lightly with some salt and pepper and brush each piece with 3 tablespoons of the butter, melted. Preheat the broiler and brown on both sides under the broiler. It is very important not to overcook the chicken. The browning is just to give the meat more flavor to blend into the sauce.

7. Pour the cognac over the chicken and ignite it, keeping the oven door open while the cognac is flaming. Shake the pan and baste with the cognac until the flames die down. Put the chicken on a platter and set aside.

8. Pour some wine-stock mixture into the pan the chicken was cooked in, boil it up to pick up the coagulated juices and the cognac, and return the mixture to the saucepan with the rest of the stock. By now the stock has a very full aromatic flavor. Remove the bouquet garni.

9. Melt the remaining 4 tablespoons of the butter in a saucepan and blend in the flour until you have a smooth paste. Cook over moderate heat, being careful not to scorch the flour. Cook until very slightly brown

as this will take away some of the flour taste. To do this properly, you must stir constantly, never leaving the saucepan alone even for 1 second. Add the hot aromatic wine-stock mixture, a little at a time, stirring constantly to get a smooth sauce, the consistency of heavy cream. Add the tomato paste and garlic. Simmer for 5 minutes longer and taste for seasoning.

10. In a 4- to 5-quart casserole or round Pyrex baking dish, put half the mushrooms and onions, and some of the bacon. Set the chicken pieces over them and then the rest of the bacon, mushrooms, and onions. Pour all the sauce into the casserole. Taste for seasoning.

11. Cover the casserole and bake at 350° for 20 minutes. Stir gently and degrease the sauce from time to time during the baking.

12. Let the chicken and vegetables cool, skim any accumulated fat off the top, and transfer the mixture to another casserole. At this point you can either cover the casserole or place pastry dough on top of the Coq au Vin as a lid. Pierce some holes in the pastry to let the steam escape. Brush it with the egg yolk, mixed with the heavy cream. The golden crust lends beauty to the Coq au Vin. However, if you do not wish to use the dough topping, cover the casserole tightly.

13. If you are using the pastry-dough lid, bake the casserole in a 400° oven for 10 minutes. Then reduce to 300° and simmer slowly for 1 hour. If you are not using a pastry-dough lid, bake the covered casserole in a 325° oven for 1 hour. Adjust the heat if necessary so the sauce does not boil.

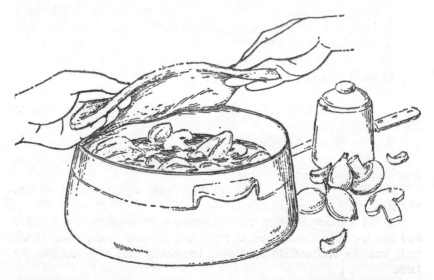

COQ AU VIN.

14. If you have not used the pastry-dough cover, sprinkle the sautéed bread cubes on top. Serve on a platter with parslied potatoes, green peas, and carrots. If you have used the pastry-dough cover, serve the Coq au Vin in its own casserole and serve the vegetables separately.

Cari de Poularde à l'Indienne
Chicken Curry

This dish can be prepared the day before and reheated in a 250° oven for 45 minutes. I use curry powder "to taste" rather than a specific amount, as it should be added to suit your own taste buds and to add flavor to the chicken, not to overpower it. Be sure to use a good brand of imported curry powder.

SERVES 6.

5 *small white onions, sliced*
2 *stalks celery, finely chopped*
½ *cup sweet butter*
4 *Rome, Northern Spy, or tart green apples, sliced but not*
   peeled
4½ *cups White Stock (p. 6) or canned chicken consommé*
3 *tablespoons flour*
1 *5-pound roasting chicken, cut into serving pieces*
¼ *cup vegetable oil*
Imported curry powder, to taste
Garnish: boiled rice

1. Sauté the sliced onions and chopped celery in 4 tablespoons of the butter until tender.
2. Add the sliced apples and simmer until done.
3. Add 4 cups of the White Stock or consommé and cook for ½ hour longer. Set aside to cool.
4. When partly cooled put the stock and vegetables in a blender and blend for 1 minute and strain.
5. In a saucepan, melt the remaining 4 tablespoons of the butter and add the flour. Cook together for 1 to 2 minutes until golden. Gradually add the strained stock, stirring constantly until it is smooth. Set aside.
6. Put the pieces of chicken into a roasting pan; pour the vegetable

oil on top and put into a preheated broiler. Broil until well browned and roasted on all sides. Baste often. Discard the fat; pour the remaining ½ cup of White Stock over the chicken and cook for 5 minutes longer. Strain the juices into your sauce. Reduce the oven to 300°.

7. Add the curry powder, a little at a time, to the sauce, until the taste is to your liking.

8. Place the chicken in a 5-quart Pyrex baking dish. Add the curry sauce, cover, and bake at 300° for 1 hour or longer, stirring a few times. Serve on a platter surrounded by boiled rice.

Fricassée de Poularde à la Suprême
Chicken Fricassee with Suprême Sauce

The French word *fricassée* applies to a chicken dish made with a white sauce, very similar to a blanquette of veal. Usually a fowl, an older bird is used for this recipe, but that is no reason for trying to get the toughest bird on the market. If you can make a fricassee with a roasting chicken, so much the better, and the poaching will take less time. This, too, is a dish which lends itself to advance preparation and can be completed one hour before serving time.

SERVES 6 TO 8.

4 *tablespoons sweet butter*
1 *5-pound roasting or stewing chicken, cut into serving pieces*
4 *cups White Stock (p. 6) or canned chicken consommé*
Bouquet garni: 6 sprigs parsley, 2 small carrots, 2 small onions,
    2 stalks celery, 6 peppercorns, and 1 bay leaf, all tied in
    a cheesecloth bag
Pinch of thyme
12 *small white onions*
1 *pound fresh mushrooms, cut in halves*

Suprême Sauce:
4 *tablespoons sweet butter*
4 *tablespoons flour*
3 *cups reserved White Stock (see above)*
1 *cup heavy cream*
Salt and freshly ground black pepper

3 *egg yolks*
Juice of ½ *lemon*

1. Melt the butter in a frying pan and lightly brown the chicken pieces evenly on all sides.

2. Put the chicken pieces and the White Stock or consommé in a large saucepan along with the bouquet garni and thyme. Bring to a boil and simmer until the meat is tender, approximately 1½ hours. Remove the chicken and bouquet garni and skim the fat off the top of the liquid.

3. In the same stock simmer the onions until tender, approximately 45 minutes.

4. Add the mushrooms and let them simmer for 10 minutes. Strain. Reserve the onions, mushrooms, and chicken.

5. Simmer the stock until it is reduced to 3 cups of liquid and set aside.

6. To make the sauce, melt the butter in a saucepan. Add the flour. Stir and cook for 2 minutes until golden. Be careful not to burn the flour. Add the hot stock, a little at a time, stirring to form a smooth, thick white sauce. Add ½ cup of the cream and stir.

7. Put the chicken, onions, and mushrooms in a quart casserole or Pyrex baking dish and pour the sauce over it. Taste for seasoning. Now the dish can be set aside until 1 hour before you are ready to serve. Cover and refrigerate.

8. Be sure your fricassee is at room temperature before it is baked. Take it out of the refrigerator 1 hour or so earlier. Bake in a preheated 275° oven for about 1 hour. The sauce should barely simmer, so check it from time to time and adjust the oven temperature if necessary.

9. When ready to serve, beat together the egg yolks and the ½ cup of remaining cream. Stir the mixture into the sauce and heat gently until it is thickened. Then add the lemon juice to taste.

Ragoût de Poularde à la Créole
Chicken Stew à la Créole

SERVES 6.

1 4-*pound roasting chicken, cut in serving pieces*
Salt and freshly ground black pepper
4 *tablespoons bacon fat*
3 *shallots, minced*

6 *medium tomatoes, peeled and chopped, or 2 cups canned*
  tomatoes
1 *package frozen okra, defrosted and sliced, or ½ pound*
  fresh okra, sliced
2 *pimentos, chopped*
2 *sprigs fresh parsley*
2 *cups White Stock (p. 6) or canned chicken consommé*
1½ *cups cooked long-grain rice*

1. Sprinkle the chicken pieces lightly with some salt and pepper.
2. In a skillet, brown the chicken thoroughly with the bacon fat and set the chicken aside.
3. In the same pan, sauté the minced shallots until tender, but not browned.
4. Add the tomatoes and simmer for 10 minutes.
5. Add the okra, pimento, and parsley and cook for 10 minutes longer.
6. Put back the chicken pieces. Add the White Stock or consommé and cook, covered, for 45 minutes, or until the chicken is tender.
7. Remove the parsley and add the rice. Taste for seasoning, adding more salt and pepper if necessary.

Poularde avec Riz à la Mornay
Chicken and Rice with Mornay Sauce

SERVES 4 TO 6.

Mornay Sauce:
4 *tablespoons sweet butter*
4 *tablespoons flour*
1½ *cups White Stock (p. 6) or canned chicken consommé*
½ *cup grated Swiss Gruyère cheese*
½ *cup heavy cream*
½ *teaspoon salt*
½ *teaspoon freshly ground black pepper*

1 *pound sliced fresh mushrooms*
4 *shallots, finely chopped*
3 *tablespoons sweet butter*

4 *cups cubed, cooked chicken*
6 *cups cooked, long-grained rice*

1. Melt the butter in a saucepan over moderate heat and stir in the flour. Stir and cook until golden and bubbly.

2. Gradually add the White Stock or consommé, stirring and cooking until you have a smooth sauce.

3. Add the cheese and cream. Do not boil.

4. Season to taste with the salt and pepper.

5. Slowly sauté the mushrooms and shallots in the 3 tablespoons of butter until their liquid has evaporated, but be careful not to burn them.

6. Add the cooked chicken and the sauce and simmer until hot, but do not let it boil.

7. Set the mixture on a warm platter surrounded by a border of cooked rice.

Soufflé de Volaille
Chicken Soufflé

SERVES 4.

2 *shallots, minced*
3 *tablespoons sweet butter*
2 *tablespoons flour*
1 *cup White Stock (p. 6) or canned chicken consommé, heated*
¾ *cup light cream*
½ *cup soft bread crumbs*
1 *teaspoon Worcestershire sauce*
2 *cups finely shredded, cooked chicken*
4 *egg yolks, beaten*
1 *teaspoon salt*
½ *teaspoon freshly ground black pepper*
7 *egg whites*
Garnish: 1 *cup White Mushroom Sauce (p. 11) (optional)*

1. Sauté the shallots in the butter over moderate heat until tender.

2. Blend in the flour and cook for 1 to 2 minutes until golden.

3. Stir in the hot White Stock or consommé and then the cream and cook until the sauce is smooth.

4. Add the bread crumbs and the Worcestershire sauce and cook for 2 minutes more. Remove from the fire.

5. Add the chicken, egg yolks, salt, and pepper and stir well.

6. Beat the egg whites until stiff, but not dry. Fold them gently into the chicken mixture. Pour the blended mixture into a lightly buttered soufflé dish or 2½-quart Pyrex baking dish.

7. Bake in a preheated 325° oven for 30 to 40 minutes, or until done. Serve with White Mushroom Sauce if you wish.

Mousse de Volaille à la Velouté
Baked Chicken Mousse with Velouté Sauce

This fast and simple hot mousse should be baked in a ring mold, a regular mold, or ten individual molds or custard cups, 6 to 8 ounces each, and served with Velouté Sauce.

SERVES 8.

Velouté Sauce:
4 *tablespoons sweet butter*
4 *tablespoons flour*
2 *cups White Stock (p. 6) or canned chicken consommé,*
   heated
1 *cup heavy cream*
Few drops lemon juice
Salt and freshly ground black pepper (optional)

Chicken Mousse:
3½ *cups diced cooked chicken*
½ *cup Velouté Sauce (see above)*
3 *tablespoons cream sherry*
4 *egg yolks, lightly beaten*
Salt and freshly ground black pepper
4 *egg whites*
⅛ *teaspoon cream of tartar*

1 *cup heavy cream, whipped*
Garnish: asparagus or broccoli

1. In a saucepan over moderately high heat, melt the butter and stir in the flour. Cook together for 2 minutes without burning. Add the hot White Stock or consommé, a little at a time, stirring constantly until you have a smooth sauce. Add the cream and lemon juice and taste for seasonings. Add some salt and pepper if necessary but remember that your chicken stock is already seasoned, so add your own seasonings very cautiously.

2. Place the chicken in a blender. Add ¼ cup of the Velouté Sauce and the sherry and blend to make a smooth paste. Transfer to a mixing bowl.

3. Add the egg yolks and another ¼ cup of the Velouté Sauce and some salt and pepper to taste.

4. Beat the egg whites with the cream of tartar until they are stiff but not dry and stand in soft, stiff peaks.

5. Very gently alternately stir into the chicken mixture the beaten egg whites and the whipped cream. Pour the mixture into well-buttered molds or custard cups.

6. Place the molds in a flat roasting pan, with enough hot water to come ½ way up the molds. Bake in the center rack of a preheated 300° oven for about ½ to 1 hour, depending on the size of the molds. Test the mousse as you would a cake by inserting a pointed knife into the center. When the knife comes out clean, the mousse is ready to be served.

7. Have the remainder of the Velouté Sauce heated and pour it over the portions of chicken mousse. Asparagus or broccoli is especially nice served with it.

Croquettes de Volaille ou Dindonneau
Chicken or Turkey Croquettes

When you have some leftover chicken or turkey, try this recipe. It may be prepared in advance and chilled. A trick is to roll the croquettes in the flour, eggs, and bread crumbs *twice* so that they have a nice crust that seals all the flavor inside.

SERVES 4 TO 6.

3 *shallots, finely minced*
6 *tablespoons sweet butter*
6 *tablespoons cream sherry*
1½ *cups finely diced, cooked chicken or turkey*
½ *teaspoon dried oregano*
3 *tablespoons flour*
1 *cup light cream, scalded*
2 *tablespoons concentrated mushroom liquid* (*optional*)
2 *egg yolks*
¼ *cup light cream*
⅓ *cup grated Swiss Gruyère cheese*
Salt and freshly ground black pepper
2 *whole eggs*
2 *tablespoons vegetable oil*
Flour and bread crumbs for coating croquettes
2 *cups Tomato Sauce Provençale* (*p.* 12) *or White Mushroom Sauce* (*p.* 11) (*optional*)

1. Sauté the shallots in 3 tablespoons of the butter until tender, but not browned.
2. Add the sherry and reduce to 2 tablespoons liquid.
3. Stir in the chicken or turkey and the oregano and set aside.
4. Melt the remaining 3 tablespoons of the butter in a saucepan and blend in the flour. Simmer for 3 minutes without browning.
5. Stir in the scalded cream until you have a smooth, thick sauce. Add the mushroom liquid, if you are using it.
6. Beat the egg yolks together with the cream and stir into the white sauce. Remove immediately from the heat.
7. Add the chicken or turkey mixture, the cheese, and some salt and pepper to taste. Chill the mixture for 1 hour, or until it is firm enough to handle easily.
8. When ready to shape into balls, *at least* 1 *hour before frying,* beat together the eggs and the 2 tablespoons of vegetable oil.
9. Shape the chicken mixture into balls or little cylinders. This recipe should make between 25 and 30 croquettes.
10. Roll each croquette in some flour and then into the egg-oil mixture. Be certain that the mixture covers the croquette completely.

Then roll in the bread crumbs. Place the croquettes in the refrigerator for at least 1 hour.

11. Just before frying, repeat the above operation, dipping each croquette in flour, egg-oil mixture, and bread crumbs once again.

12. Add vegetable oil in a deep fryer or other pot until it reaches 1½ inches high. Heat to 375°. Fry the croquettes, a few at a time, until they are lightly browned. Set them in a preheated 350° oven to keep them hot while the others are frying. If you set them in an ovenproof platter or dish with paper towels under them, the excess oil will be absorbed and they can be served crisp and hot.

13. If you wish, you may serve them with Tomato Sauce Provençale or White Mushroom Sauce.

Capon à la Suprême
Capon with Suprême Sauce

SERVES 6 TO 8.

1 6- to 8-pound capon
4 medium-sized white onions, left whole and peeled
1 green pepper, sliced
4 stalks celery, chopped
4 carrots, sliced
2 bay leaves
¼ teaspoon thyme
8 sprigs fresh parsley
8 peppercorns
6 cups White Stock (p. 6) or canned chicken consommé,
      or enough to cover capon
1½ pounds small white fresh mushrooms
6 tablespoons sweet butter
6 tablespoons flour
1½ cups heavy cream
3 egg yolks
Lemon juice to taste
½ teaspoon salt

¼ teaspoon freshly ground pepper
Garnishes: green peas and boiled white rice

1. Place the capon in a large kettle. Add onions, green pepper, celery, carrots, bay leaves, thyme, parsley, and peppercorns and cover with the White Stock or consommé.

2. Bring to a boil; cover and simmer for 1½ to 2 hours. Skim the surface as often as necessary.

3. When the capon is cooked, remove from the stove and take the capon out of the liquid. Resume cooking the stock slowly until it is reduced to ½ its quantity. Strain the stock.

4. Cook the mushrooms in the stock. Strain and set aside.

5. Simmer the stock for another 10 minutes.

6. Melt the butter in a saucepan and stir in the flour. Blend well. Cook for about 3 minutes until golden. Add 3 cups of the hot stock, a little at a time, until you reach the right consistency. Simmer for 1 hour over a very low fire. Stir often. Do not scorch.

7. Put the cooked mushrooms in the sauce (which should be quite thick) and set it aside.

8. Beat the cream together with the egg yolks and set aside.

9. Heat the mushroom sauce slowly, stirring constantly. Add the lemon juice, salt, and pepper. Put the serving pieces of capon on a large heated platter. Place a ring of green peas around it and arrange another layer of rice around them. Add the egg-cream mixture to the sauce, stirring and heating very slowly. Pour the finished sauce over the capon and serve.

Dinde Rôtie à l'Américaine
Roast Stuffed Turkey à l'Américaine

The American traditional dish for Thanksgiving dinner is also served in France on special occasions and holidays like New Year's Day and Christmas. The French like to prepare a small young turkey (*dindonneau*) or a hen turkey of about eight to twelve pounds. In the United States large turkeys are more commonly served, and some weigh well over twenty pounds. Nowadays, you can find better and better turkeys in the market because of the new breeds being developed. If you order in advance, you may be able to get a fresh turkey.

For a small party of six to eight people, select a hen turkey weighing eight to ten pounds. The young hen turkeys are usually quite meaty. The method I use for roasting such a turkey can apply to both chicken and capon, too. It is a French method: fast roasting at 450° for about 40 minutes, and then slower roasting at 325° until done. If you are using a frozen turkey, it will have to be completely thawed overnight before you can begin the roasting.

SERVES 6 TO 8.

Turkey giblets, cut in small pieces
3 *tablespoons sweet butter*
3 *shallots, finely minced*
2 *cups White Stock* (*p. 6*) *or canned chicken consommé*
1 *8- to 10-pound hen turkey*
½ *teaspoon salt*
½ *teaspoon freshly ground black pepper*
1 *recipe Basic American Bread Stuffing* (*p. 237*)
½ *pound salt pork, sliced thin*
½ *cup melted butter*
1 *tablespoon cornstarch*

Basting Sauce

1. In a saucepan sauté the giblets (gizzard, liver, and heart) in the 3 tablespoons of butter to brown them.
2. Add the shallots and sauté them until they are transparent, but not browned.
3. Pour the White Stock or consommé into the pan. Cover and simmer for 1 hour.
4. Strain through a fine sieve and reserve the liquid for basting the turkey.

Stuffing and Roasting the Turkey

1. Sprinkle the cavity of the bird lightly with the salt and pepper and fill with the stuffing. Do not pack it too tightly as it will expand in cooking. Place skewers across the cavity to close it and tie the wings and drumsticks close to the body with string.
2. Lay the slices of salt pork over the breast.
3. Pour the ½ cup of melted butter all over the bird and roast in a preheated 450° oven for 20 minutes. Turn the turkey over and roast

the other side for 20 minutes. Baste often with the melted butter and the drippings from the pan.

4. Reduce the heat to 350° and roast until done. Do not forget to baste the turkey with the stock every 10 minutes. Total roasting time for a 10-pound turkey will be about 3 hours, or approximately 18 minutes per pound.

NOTE: In case of a delay in serving your meal, about ½ hour before the turkey is done, wrap it in heavy-duty aluminum foil and let it stand in a 250° oven until your guests are ready to eat. The foil will keep the turkey moist.

Gravy

1. Skim the fat from the roasting pan and discard. Strain the remaining juices into a saucepan along with any unused basting sauce. Taste for seasoning.

2. Simmer for a few minutes.

3. In another saucepan, place the cornstarch and just enough water to dissolve it. Very gently, pour the cornstarch into the hot turkey sauce. Stir and cook slowly until the gravy begins to thicken. If it is too thick, add a little extra stock. If too thin, add a bit more cornstarch dissolved in water.

Caneton aux Navets
Braised Duckling with Turnips

Because ducks usually contain so much fat, it is often a chore for housewives to prepare them properly. I sincerely believe my way of cooking duck is practical for both the amateur and the accomplished gourmet cook. Start with a nice plump duck. I prefer the New England ducks over the Long Island variety. If you buy a frozen duck, let it stand at room temperature overnight to thaw completely before you begin cooking.

SERVES 4.

1 *5-pound duck, with neck and giblets removed and reserved*
1 *cup dry white wine*

2 cups White Stock (p. 6) or canned chicken consommé
1 small bay leaf
¼ teaspoon thyme
2 sprigs fresh parsley
6 small white onions
6 peeled carrots, quartered
7 tablespoons sweet butter
4 tablespoons flour
4 white turnips, quartered
1 pound fresh sweet peas, cooked, or 1 10-ounce package
    frozen peas, cooked
Salt and freshly ground black pepper

1. Take out all of the loose fat from the inside of the duck and discard. Cut off the tail and discard. Chop off the ends of the wings and set aside with the neck and giblets.

2. Roast the unseasoned duck in a preheated 375° oven, approximately 1½ to 2 hours, until it is nicely browned all over and all the fat has been rendered. Keep discarding the fat from the pan while the duck is roasting. When the duck is finished, remove it from the oven and reduce the heat to 325°.

3. While the duck is roasting, simmer the wine and White Stock or consommé together with the neck and giblets from the duck, bay leaf, thyme, and parsley, until reduced to 2 cups. Discard the bay leaf and parsley.

4. In a covered saucepan sauté the onions and carrots in 3 tablespoons of the butter until nearly done and tender. Cover and keep warm.

5. Melt the remaining 4 tablespoons of butter in a saucepan and blend in the flour. Simmer the mixture for about 3 minutes over moderate heat, but do not burn the flour. Add the reduced wine-stock mixture a little at a time, stirring to make a smooth sauce.

6. Now that the duck is cool enough to handle, it can be carved. Cut the breast into 4 pieces, the legs into 4 pieces, and then cut off the 2 wings and the pieces from the carcass.

7. Put all the pieces into a covered casserole with the reduced stock, carrots, onions, and the uncooked turnips. Place in a preheated 325° oven and braise until the turnips are tender, about 45 minutes. Then add the peas. If the finished sauce is too thick, add a little more stock. Season with some salt and pepper and serve on a warm platter.

Caneton à l'Orange
Duckling with Orange Sauce

On the American market, you find fresh duck very rarely, but the frozen kind is satisfactory. It is always nicely plucked and cleaned and it can be thawed out overnight in the refrigerator. This recipe is especially nice for the housewife as it can be prepared for the most part the day before and completed an hour before dinner.

SERVES 2 TO 3.

1 *4½- to 5-pound duck, with giblets* (*at room temperature*)
2 *tablespoons vegetable oil*
3 *cups Brown Stock* (*p. 4*) *or canned beef consommé*
2½ *cups tawny port*
3 *to 4 tablespoons granulated sugar*
¼ *cup wine vinegar*
2½ *tablespoons arrowroot*
4 *oranges*
4 *tablespoons Cointreau or orange liqueur, more to taste*
Garnishes: Wild Rice à la Française (*p. 278*) *and buttered*
    asparagus

The Day before Serving

1. Take out all of the loose fat from the inside and neck of the duck and discard. Cut off the tail and discard. Chop off the end of the wings and set aside with the neck and giblets. You will use them to make the stock.

2. Be sure the duck is at room temperature. Place it in a roasting pan without any liquid and roast it in a 350° oven, approximately 1½ hours.

3. Every 10 minutes, turn the duck over so it will brown evenly. When ready it will be nicely browned and crisp and practically all the fat will be in the pan. Do not prick the skin. The meat will be nicely cooked without being dry.

4. Set the duck aside and let it cool off for ½ hour. Carve the wings first, then the legs and the breast. At Monblason we always used a whole duck for 2 people, but if you wish to serve 3, you can slice the breast and legs in smaller pieces.

5. Wrap the pieces of duck in aluminum foil and set aside in the refrigerator until 1 hour before serving.

Orange Sauce

1. Cut the giblets, neck, and wing tips in small pieces and brown them in the vegetable oil. Stir often so as not to burn the pieces.

2. When well done, remove the surplus oil and fat.

3. Add the Brown Stock or consommé and 2 cups of the tawny port and cook very slowly in a covered saucepan for about 2 hours.

4. Strain well through a fine sieve or clean linen towel and set aside.

5. In a saucepan put the sugar and wine vinegar and boil over moderately high heat until the mixture turns to a medium syrup. It should have the color and consistency of a caramel sauce. Do not let it get too dark, or it will taste bitter. It should have a sweet and sour flavor.

6. Immediately pour this caramel mixture into the strained stock and simmer for 10 minutes.

7. Mix the arrowroot with the remaining ½ cup of tawny port and cook slowly in a small saucepan, stirring constantly. As soon as it starts thickening, add the hot stock, a little at a time, until all of the stock has been added. Cook and stir until the sauce is of a nice consistency.

8. With a vegetable peeler, remove and reserve the rind from the oranges and slice the oranges. The orange slices will be used for decorating the platter.

9. Cut the orange rind into julienne strips ⅛ inch wide and put the strips into 1½ quarts of boiling water for a few minutes. Drain and put ½ of the strips into the sauce. Reserve the rest for decorating the platter along with the orange slices. Set your duck, sauce, orange slices, and rind into the refrigerator, tightly covered, until serving day.

Serving the Duck

1. About 2 or 3 hours before dinner, add the Cointreau or orange liqueur to the sauce and simmer for a short while. It should taste bitter-sweet. Depending on your taste, add more Cointreau or more strips of blanched orange rind.

2. Take the duck, orange slices, and rind out of the refrigerator and bring them to room temperature.

3. About 1 hour before serving your dinner, put some of the sauce in a baking dish. Place the duck pieces over the sauce and pour some

more of the sauce on top. Keep enough sauce hot on the stove for pouring over the finished duck on the platter.

4. When you are almost ready to serve dinner, put the baking dish into a 350° oven for 10 minutes. Then turn on the broiler. Leave the door open and watch the duck getting brown and crisp. Do not let it burn.

5. Place the duck in the center of a heated platter with the orange slices around it. Put some Wild Rice à la Française at the 2 ends of the platter and add the asparagus. Pour the rest of the hot Orange Sauce on the duck and scatter the remaining strips of orange rind on top.

Caneton Montmorency
Duckling with Cherry Sauce

SERVES 2 TO 3.

Ingredients and preparation are the same as for Duckling with Orange Sauce (p. 230), omitting the 4 oranges and the 4 tablespoons liqueur.

Substitute: 1 *can pitted black cherries, drained*
          1 *tablespoon lemon juice*
          ¼ *cup good cognac*
          3 *tablespoons granulated sugar*
          3 *tablespoons sweet butter*

1. Follow the recipe for Duckling with Orange Sauce, roasting the duckling as directed and preparing the sauce just until the stage where the orange rind is added.

2. Put the cherries in a saucepan with the lemon juice, cognac, and sugar and let them stand for 1 hour.

3. Add the cherry mixture to the finished sauce and let them simmer together for about 10 minutes. Use a very low heat; otherwise the cherries will shrivel.

4. About 1 hour before serving your dinner, put some of the sauce, *without the cherries,* in a baking dish. Place the duck pieces over the sauce and pour more of the sauce on top. Keep the rest of the sauce and the cherries for pouring over the finished duck on the platter.

5. When you are almost ready to serve, put the baking dish into a 350° oven for 10 minutes. Then turn on the broiler. Leave the door open and watch the duck brown and get crisp. Do not let it burn.

6. Slowly reheat the cherry sauce in the saucepan, adding the butter.

7. Place the duck in the center of a heated platter. Put some Wild Rice à la Française at the 2 ends of the platter, along with the other vegetables you are serving. Then pour the rest of the hot cherry sauce over the duck and serve.

Caneton aux Pêches
Duckling with Peaches

Follow the recipe for Duckling with Cherry Sauce (p. 232), substituting a good brand of canned freestone peaches or fresh poached peaches in season.

Oie Rôtie Farcie
Roast Stuffed Goose

Goose is the favorite bird served for Christmas in many European countries. In the United States goose must be ordered beforehand and may come frozen. If so, thaw the goose completely overnight before roasting it. Ask your butcher to get you a goose less than nine to ten months old, because as they get older they grow tougher. The weight should be from six to nine pounds. If it weighs more than nine pounds, it will have to be braised rather than roasted.

SERVES 6 TO 8.

1 6- to 9-pound goose
Salt and freshly ground black pepper
8 cups Chestnut Stuffing (p. 237)
Rendered chicken fat or goose fat
½ cup water
3 cups White Stock (p. 6) or canned chicken consommé
1 tablespoon cornstarch

1. Sprinkle the cavity of the goose with some salt and pepper and

fill loosely with the stuffing. Place skewers across the cavity to close it and tie the wings and drumsticks close to the body with string.

2. Rub the bird with chicken or goose fat.

3. Place the goose in a shallow roasting pan. Pour ½ cup water mixed with ½ cup White Stock or consommé over the goose and roast in a preheated 400° oven approximately 3 to 3½ hours. Baste the goose very often while it is roasting. If the liquid evaporates, add more water and stock. Do not let the juices get too brown and burn.

4. Every ½ hour turn the bird over, as it should brown very evenly.

5. If the goose is done and you cannot serve it immediately, cover it tightly with heavy-duty aluminum foil and lower the oven temperature to 250° until you are ready to eat.

6. Remove the goose to a serving platter. Skim the fat from the roasting pan and discard. Strain the gravy into a saucepan. Taste for seasoning. Add the rest of the stock.

7. Reduce by simmering to 1½ cups.

8. In another saucepan, place 1 tablespoon cornstarch and just enough cold water to dissolve it. Very gently, pour the cornstarch into the hot gravy. Stir and cook slowly until the sauce begins to thicken. If it is too thick, add a little extra stock. If too thin, add a bit more cornstarch dissolved in water. Serve the gravy with the goose.

Pigeonneaux Rôtis en Casserole
Casserole of Roast Squab

SERVES 6.

6 1-*pound squabs, cleaned and trussed*
Liver, gizzards, necks, and wing tips from 6 squabs
14 *tablespoons sweet butter*
4 *shallots, minced*
1 *cup cream sherry*
2 *cups White Stock (p. 6) or canned chicken consommé*
18 *small white onions*
1½ *pounds small white fresh mushrooms, whole*
4 *tablespoons vegetable oil mixed with 4 tablespoons melted*
    sweet butter
1 *teaspoon salt*
½ *teaspoon freshly ground black pepper*

2 *cloves garlic, finely minced*
Garnishes: green peas, baby carrots, and pan-roasted potatoes

1. Cut the neck, tips of the wings, livers, and gizzards in small pieces and sauté in 2 tablespoons of the butter.

2. When browned, add the shallots and simmer until the shallots are transparent.

3. Add the cream sherry and the White Stock or consommé. Simmer, covered, for 1 hour.

4. Take the lid off the saucepan and continue to simmer the stock until it is reduced by half. Strain.

5. Sauté the onions in 6 tablespoons of the butter in a covered pan until cooked through and slightly browned. Set aside.

6. Sauté the mushrooms in 6 tablespoons of the butter until their juices have evaporated. Do not brown them. Set aside.

7. Pour the 8 tablespoons of the oil-butter mixture over the squabs, which have been cleaned, trussed, and seasoned lightly with salt and pepper. Put them in a roasting pan and set them into a 350° oven.

8. When they start to brown, baste with the stock and turn the squabs every 10 minutes. Continue to baste and turn until completely browned, approximately 35 to 40 minutes. Reduce the oven heat to 300°.

9. Put the birds in a covered casserole with the sautéed onions and mushrooms, garlic, and stock. Simmer in a 300° oven for 1½ hours.

10. Degrease the accumulated fat from the surface of the sauce. Season to taste with more salt and pepper, if necessary. Pigeons are excellent when served with green peas, baby carrots, and small pan-roasted potatoes.

Coqs de Bruyère Rôtis sur Croûtons
Roast Rock Cornish Game Hens on Toast

Rock Cornish hens should be stuffed and basted frequently during the roasting, since this will add flavor and also prevent them from drying out.

SERVES 6.

Stuffing: 1 *recipe Mallard Duck Stuffing* (p. 242), *Basic American Bread Stuffing* (p. 237), *or simple apple*

*stuffing (cooking apples, peeled, cored, and cut in pieces,
sautéed in butter until tender but not mushy, and
seasoned to taste)*
1 *cup cream sherry*
½ *cup dry vermouth*
6 *1-pound Rock Cornish hens*
2 *cups White Stock (p. 6) or canned chicken consommé*
⅓ *cup lemon juice*
Salt and freshly ground black pepper
½ *cup sweet butter, melted*
6 *slices white bread, fried in butter*
Garnish: watercress or parsley sprigs

1. Make your stuffing and set aside.
2. Simmer the sherry, vermouth, and White Stock or consommé together until it is reduced to 2 cups of liquid.
3. Brush the hens with the lemon juice inside and out. The lemon juice tends to make the flesh more tender. Season lightly with salt and pepper; stuff the birds and truss.
4. Set them in a shallow roasting pan and pour the butter evenly over each bird. Roast in a preheated 400° oven for 30 minutes, basting often with the melted butter and the pan juices.
5. Reduce the heat to 325° and start basting the birds with the reduced stock-sherry mixture. Roast and baste for another 20 minutes, or until the birds are done.
6. Strain the sauce into a saucepan. Skim the excess fat and correct the seasoning.
7. Arrange the birds on the slices of bread, which have been fried in butter, and pour some of the sauce on top. Serve the rest of the sauce in a gravy boat. Decorate the platter with watercress or parsley.

Farces
Stuffings

Of all the stuffings I have ever tasted, I find the basic American bread stuffing the one that harmonizes best with turkey and chicken. Another delicious stuffing, and a great French favorite, is one made with a mixture of sausage, chestnuts, and some cognac (see below). With goose, this French version is excellent. Try it with turkey too.

Farce de Pain à l'Américaine
Basic American Bread Stuffing

MAKES 7 TO 8 CUPS.

2 *small white onions, minced*
2 *stalks celery, chopped*
½ *cup sweet butter, melted*
6 *cups stale bread cubes*
2 *teaspoons poultry seasoning*
¾ *cup White Stock* (p. 6) *or canned chicken consommé*
½ *cup chopped fresh parsley*
1 *clove garlic, finely minced* (*optional*)

1. Sauté the onions and celery in the butter until tender, but do not brown.
2. Combine with the bread cubes, poultry seasoning, White Stock or consommé, parsley, and garlic. Mix well.
NOTE: If you wish to use the packaged, prepared bread croutons that have already been seasoned, you can omit the poultry seasoning from the recipe.

Farce de Marrons
Chestnut Stuffing

It is not always easy to buy fresh chestnuts. Very often they are quite dry and wormy. I suggest you get the imported, canned whole chestnuts which are unsweetened. In large cities, any gourmet shop carries them.

MAKES 8 CUPS.

2 *small white onions, minced*
2 *tablespoons sweet butter*
1 *pound pork sausage*

3 *pounds chestnuts, drained (if canned, imported type)*
⅓ *cup cognac*
½ *teaspoon dried thyme*
½ *teaspoon dried marjoram*
1 *teaspoon salt*
½ *teaspoon freshly ground black pepper*
1 *cup bread crumbs*
¼ *cup White Stock (p. 6) or canned chicken consommé*

1. Sauté the minced onions in the butter until slightly browned.

2. Add the sausage and cook for 5 minutes, stirring constantly. Discard the fat rendered by the sausage.

3. In a large bowl, combine the sausage and onions with the chestnuts, cognac, thyme, marjoram, salt, pepper, bread crumbs, and White Stock or consommé. Mix well. Try not to mash the chestnuts. They should be coarsely broken.

4. Taste for seasoning and add more salt and pepper if necessary. Now stuff your bird.

CHAPTER 11

Game

Gibier

Canard Sauvage à la Lorraine

❄

Perdrix au Foie Gras sur Croûtons

❄

Faisan à l'Alsacienne
Jeune Faisan à la Périgourdine

❄

Côtelettes de Chevreuil Poivrade
Chevreuil Rôti
Chevreuil en Casserole

❄

Civet de Lièvre

❄

Choucroute Braisée

"Game" is a word generally applied to wild birds and animals which are usually hunted for their flesh and used as food. Their gamey taste is highly esteemed by many gourmets. Like poultry, game used as food should be young. Never try to roast an old cock pheasant or to prepare a piece of venison from a grandfather stag. A wild animal, always on the alert, running for his life, is usually a bundle of nerves. If he is killed young, the flesh will not be stringy and the flavor will probably be savory, depending on what types of wild berries, herbs, and leaves he has been feeding upon.

When I was a boy, my father and I would often go into the woods in search of mushrooms in season and follow the brooks. Sometimes, we would hunt game. There was one time in particular that I remember. My father had killed a fox and we decided to do something with the meat. Having eaten all sorts of game, including wild boar, I felt no hesitation when I began preparing the strongly scented meat of the fox. First, we hung the animal in a cold place where the meat could age and mellow. Then we marinated some cuts in good wine and spices and let them stand a few more days. We started cooking and discovered that we had not lost the gamey strength of the fox. It was tough. We tried some other ways of cooking, and the results were equally bad. My father and I never laughed as much as we did over our dismal failure. If the results had been successful, I could have claimed the credit for it all and called it "The Supreme of Fox à la Virion." No wonder I have never seen fox meat on a menu in any of the thousands of restaurants I have visited since that time.

Many people have asked me how you can tell the age of a game bird, how you prepare a venison roast, or how you cook a hare. There are no hard and fast rules, as meat from the same game varies in different parts of the world and in different sections of the United States, or even within a small country like France. The special regional climate and vegetation play a very important part in the taste and texture of the meat.

More and more wild bird farms are appearing throughout the country and their products are making their way to consumers in large cities. These birds do not taste as gamey as those which are killed in their natural habitats. They are also more tender and dependable for use by home cooks and good restaurants.

Canard Sauvage à la Lorraine
Mallard Duck à la Lorraine

This recipe also works well with a roast duckling, but I prefer using the stuffing for wild mallard ducks, as they are generally less fatty.

SERVES 4.

Mallard Duck Stuffing:
¾ *pound sausage meat*
Giblets from 2 mallard ducks or 1 *5-pound duckling*
6 *eating apples, peeled, cored, and quartered*
1½ *tablespoons sugar*
¼ *teaspoon salt*
¼ *teaspoon cinnamon*
¼ *teaspoon sage*
3 *tablespoons cognac*
⅓ *cup Brown Stock (p. 4) or canned beef consommé*
⅓ *cup port wine*

2 *mallard ducks or* 1 *5-pound duckling*
Salt and freshly ground black pepper
4 *tablespoons sweet butter, melted*

1. Fry the sausage meat in a skillet until it is slightly browned and it has rendered its fat. Put the meat in a mixing bowl. Sauté the duck giblets in the hot sausage fat and add to the reserved sausage meat.

2. Sauté the apples in the remaining hot sausage fat until slightly browned. They should hold their shape.

3. Set the apples in another mixing bowl and sprinkle the sugar, salt, cinnamon, sage, and cognac over them.

4. Discard the sausage fat from the skillet and pour in the Brown Stock or consommé and wine. Cook rapidly until the liquid has been reduced to ¼ cup.

5. Pour the wine-stock mixture over the sausage meat and mash the meat with a fork.

6. Mix gently with the apples and stuff loosely into the mallard ducks or duckling.

7. Sprinkle the ducks lightly with salt and pepper and brush the butter all over their skin. Roast the ducks in a preheated 375° oven until they are browned on all sides and then reduce the heat to 325° until they are done. Baste the ducks frequently with the pan juices. The mallard ducks should take approximately 1½ hours to cook, but if you are using a large roasting duck, it will take approximately 2½ hours. Pour some sauce over the ducks and serve hot. Serve the rest of the sauce in a sauceboat.

Port Wine Sauce

2 *cups Brown Stock* (*p.* 4) *or canned beef consommé*
1 *cup port wine*
3 *tablespoons sweet butter*

1. Simmer the Brown Stock or consommé and the port wine together until reduced to 1½ cups.

2. Just before serving, add the butter and stir. Serve hot but not boiling.

Perdrix au Foie Gras sur Croûtons
Roast Partridge on Toast with Foie Gras

SERVES 4.

½ *cup cream sherry*
½ *cup White Stock* (*p.* 6) *or canned chicken consommé*

4 *partridges*
Salt and freshly ground black pepper
½ *cup sweet butter, melted*
¼ *cup brandy*
4 *slices white bread*
4 *partridge livers, chopped*
1 *4-ounce can imported mousse of foie gras*
1½ *tablespoons finely chopped fresh parsley*

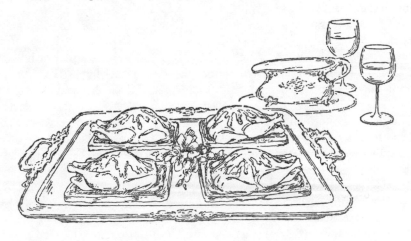

PARTRIDGE ON TOAST
WITH FOIE GRAS.

1. Simmer the sherry and White Stock or consommé together in a saucepan until reduced to ½ cup. Set aside.

2. Truss the partridges. Sprinkle them lightly with some salt and pepper and brush the butter all over the skin.

3. Set the partridges in a roasting pan and roast in a slow preheated 325° oven until tender, approximately 40 to 45 minutes. Baste often during the roasting.

4. Remove the partridges from the roasting pan and set aside. Drain the butter into a skillet. Reduce the oven temperature to 250°.

5. Pour the brandy over the partridges and ignite. When the brandy stops burning, put the partridges into the 250° oven to keep warm.

6. Sauté the bread in the butter remaining in the skillet, adding more butter if necessary. The toast should be well browned, like croutons. Keep the toast warm in the oven.

7. Sauté the chopped partridge livers in the same skillet, again adding more butter if necessary. Remove from the heat.

8. Add the foie gras and parsley to the partridge livers and mix well.

9. Spread the mixture on the toast and arrange the 4 slices on a platter. Set the birds on the platter, 1 bird on each slice.

10. Pour the reduced stock-sherry mixture into the skillet and roasting pan and boil up, scraping up any bits clinging to the pan. Strain into a saucepan. Bring to a boil. Pour over the partridges and serve.

Faisan
Pheasant

The word pheasant brings back to me many pleasant memories of the late Fred Bradna, ringmaster of the Ringling Bros. Barnum & Bailey Circus. "Freddie" was a remarkable character liked by everyone —a *bon vivant gastronome*—and his sincere friendship was certainly a great asset to me during my travels with the circus.

Alsatian by birth, and having traveled through Europe with Mrs. Bradna performing vaudeville circus acts, his knowledge of food was great, as was his insatiable taste for special dishes. Freddie was witty, and when the food and wine were exceptionally good, he did not have to tell you how grateful he was. *La joie de vivre* was written all over his face.

Quite often, he was the recipient of culinary gifts—game, meats, or exotic foods. Even in the remotest parts of the United States, he knew someone who would have some delicacy on hand when the circus arrived at that particular point. In August 1941, we were in Denver, Colorado, and after the last evening's performance he came to see me at the "Jomar," the private railroad car of Mr. North. He handed me four medium-sized pheasants, some fresh sauerkraut, and a bottle of Alsatian wine and told me they were for me. But, he said, if after preparing the Pheasants à l'Alsacienne I had too much to eat, I could send the leftovers to his room in another car halfway down the train. Very softly I cursed him and smiled. The worst punishment I could hand to the ringmaster was to cook his pheasants and keep them for myself.

During the night, the circus left for Salt Lake City, 600 miles away. Mr. and Mrs. John Ringling North and Mr. Henry North were on the

Jomar for the run. It was a Sunday with no performance, and a long train ride ahead. I started preparing the meals for my bosses first and then suddenly decided to braise that sauerkraut and have the pheasants ready for roasting for Freddie. Sometimes the train would run for hours without stopping and might make short, unscheduled stops at small railroad stations. But on long runs such as this, the stops were sometimes for an hour or so. Around noon we stopped at Green River, Utah, and I asked a railroad man how long we would be there. "One hour to an hour and a half" was his reply. Working fast on Bradna's pheasants, I made the finishing touches, and with a covered pan dashed to his quarters. Freddie was elated; his appreciation was overflowing. "You are the greatest," he said. "Have a drink with us."

I took a drink and was sipping it when the train started to move again—and move fast. We seemed to be on a steep decline. There was no communication between cars, and since Freddie's car was far back in the train, I could not take the chance of running forward to the Jomar, as the train was going at top speed.

I was expected to serve lunch at 1 P.M. in the Jomar. Now it was close to that and I could read anxiety on the ringmaster's face. If the boss was going to miss his chef, and more important, his lunch, Freddie would be in deep trouble when we reached Salt Lake City. He was so nervous that he could not even eat the sensational pheasant. I asked for another drink, hoping the train would stop again soon, wishing I would be only a few minutes late for lunch. But things did not work that way. The next stop came 1½ hours later. When I finally reached my post in front of the stove, René the butler told me, "Mr. North is happy to know you are not stranded in Green River. He and Mrs. North and his brother are starved and waiting impatiently for their meal."

Wherever you are, Freddie, I am still thinking of you and hope the food they are serving you now is as good as the pheasant I prepared for you in Utah. Here is the recipe for Faisan à l'Alsacienne that I prepared for Freddie Bradna aboard the circus train. This recipe can also be used for quail, doves, partridge, squab, and guinea hen.

Faisan à l'Alsacienne
Pheasant with Sauerkraut and White Wine

SERVES 8.

2 *cups White Stock (p. 6) or canned chicken consommé*
1 *cup Alsatian dry white wine*

4 1½-pound baby pheasants
Salt and freshly ground black pepper
4 tablespoons sweet butter, melted
1 recipe Braised Sauerkraut for Game (p. 254)

1. Simmer the White Stock or consommé and the white wine together until reduced to 1½ cups.

2. Split the pheasants along the back. Open and flatten them gently. Sprinkle them lightly with some salt and pepper. Brush the birds with the butter and set them in a roasting pan under a hot broiler.

3. Baste with the reduced stock-wine liquid. Broil for 5 minutes on each side, or until the split birds are nicely browned on each side.

4. Put some of the braised sauerkraut (about a 1-inch layer) in a large casserole. Place the pheasants on top and simmer, covered, for about ½ hour in a preheated 325° oven. The pheasants are ready when the flesh has lost its pink color. When overcooked, the pheasants become dry.

5. Place the halves of the pheasants on a large platter and surround with the braised sauerkraut. Pour the remaining wine sauce over the birds and serve.

Jeune Faisan à la Périgourdine
Baby Pheasant with Truffles

Usually these birds have to be ordered in advance, either fresh or frozen. They are raised on farms which specialize in game birds. The special feeding they get makes the flesh tender and not as gamey as the older, tougher pheasants killed during the hunting season.

SERVES 8.

4 1½-pound baby pheasants, with giblets
3 shallots, minced
8 tablespoons sweet butter, more if needed
1 cup cream sherry
2 cups White Stock (p. 6) or canned chicken consommé
4 tablespoons flour
1 cup heavy cream
2 black truffles, canned, with liquid
Salt and freshly ground black pepper to taste

4 *tablespoons sweet butter, melted*
Garnish: Wild Rice à la Française (*p.* 278) *or pan-roasted*
   new potatoes

1. Remove the neck and giblets from the pheasants. Cut off the
tips of the wings. Chop them all into small pieces and sauté with the
shallots in 2 tablespoons of the butter until cooked and slightly browned.
   2. Add the sherry and simmer until reduced to ½ its quantity.
   3. Add the White Stock or consommé and simmer until the liquid
has been reduced to 1½ cups. Strain the liquid and set aside.
   4. In a saucepan, melt 4 tablespoons of the butter and stir in the
flour. Cook and stir until slightly browned, being careful not to let it
burn. Combine the sherry and stock and add the liquid, a little at a time,
to make a smooth sauce.
   5. Simmer the sauce gently for ½ hour.
   6. Add the cream and simmer the sauce for another 10 minutes.
   7. Cut the ends off the truffles. Chop the ends into fine pieces and
add them to the sauce along with the juice from the can.
   8. Slice the remaining center parts of the truffles into 8 slices to be
used as decorations for the pheasants on the platter.
   9. Wash the pheasants and dry them thoroughly. Tie the wings
and the drumsticks to the body with string. Sprinkle some salt and
pepper on them and rub them with the remaining 2 tablespoons of
butter.
   10. Place the pheasants side by side in a roasting pan. Roast in a
preheated 400° oven, approximately 40 minutes. Turn the birds every
5 minutes and baste with the melted butter. Cook until nicely browned.
They should be slightly undercooked before the final operation.
   11. Remove the birds from the oven and let them cool. Add the
juices and butter from the pan to the reserved wine sauce. The sauce
should be fairly thick. If not, simmer it a little.
   12. With a large knife split each bird. Place the 8 halves side by
side in a roasting pan, with the breasts up. With a spoon spread ½ the
sauce over the pheasants. They should be completely covered with it.
   13. About 20 minutes before serving, put the roasting pan in a
400° oven. Bake for 15 minutes and then place under the broiler for
5 minutes more.
   14. When the sauce starts to brown, take the pan out and place
the pheasants on a large platter.
   15. Add whatever juices remain in the roasting pan to the remaining sauce. Reheat it and pour it, piping hot, over the birds. Place

a slice of truffle on each piece of pheasant and garnish with Wild Rice
à la Française or pan-roasted new potatoes.

Chevreuil
Venison

Venison should be aged for a period of two to three weeks before
being cooked. The meat of young deer is no problem to prepare. Roasts,
broiler steaks, and stews come to the table quite tender. However, you
may run into difficulty with an older animal, so those tougher cuts should
be marinated for a day or two. Here are a few ways you can prepare
different cuts of venison.

Côtelettes de Chevreuil Poivrade
Venison Steaks or Cutlets with Pepper Sauce

SERVES 6.

6 *1-inch thick loin steaks, fillets from the saddle, or
     venison cutlets*
Salt and freshly ground black pepper
4 *tablespoons sweet butter*
1½ *cups Pepper Sauce (see below)*

1. Sprinkle the steaks lightly with some salt and pepper on both
sides.

2. Melt the butter in a skillet and pan-fry the steaks, browning
them approximately 6 minutes on each side. Tender venison is excellent
medium-rare, but you will have to decide for yourself just how rare or
well done you like yours to be.

3. When the steaks are ¾ done, add the sauce. Reduce the heat and
cook for 5 minutes longer.

Pepper Sauce

⅔ *cup wine vinegar*
1½ *cups Brown Sauce (p. 12)*

12 *peppercorns*
3 *tablespoons red currant jelly*
½ *cup heavy cream* (*optional*)
Freshly ground black pepper (*optional*)

1. Simmer the wine vinegar until reduced to ⅓ cup.
2. Add the Brown Sauce and peppercorns to the wine vinegar and simmer gently for 20 minutes.
3. Add the jelly and stir until blended.
4. Strain the sauce and, if you wish, add the cream. Heat the sauce, but do not allow it to boil.
5. Taste the sauce; it should be fairly spicy. You can correct the seasoning by adding some freshly ground black pepper just before serving.

Chevreuil Rôti
Roast Venison

SERVES 8.

1 6-*pound leg of venison, boned*
2 *small white onions, sliced*
2 *carrots, sliced*
2 *small cloves garlic, crushed*
2 *small bay leaves*
Pinch of thyme
10 *peppercorns*
1 *teaspoon salt*
2 *cups red Burgundy wine*
1 *cup Brown Stock* (*p. 4*) *or canned beef consommé*
¼ *cup wine vinegar*
6 *slices salt pork*
2 *tablespoons sweet butter*
Garnish: Chestnut Puree (*p. 292*)

1. In a large casserole place the venison, onions, carrots, garlic, bay leaves, thyme, peppercorns, and salt.
2. Pour in the wine, Brown Stock or consommé, and wine vinegar and cover tightly. Marinate in the refrigerator for 24 hours. Turn the meat 2 or 3 times.

3. Remove the meat and set aside. Bring the marinade to a boil. Reduce the heat and simmer for 30 minutes.

4. Strain the marinade of all the vegetables and spices and simmer the liquid until reduced to 2 cups. Set aside for basting the roast.

5. Arrange the salt pork over the meat and roast in an uncovered roasting pan in a preheated 425° oven for 25 minutes. Baste with the fat from the salt pork during that period. Discard the fat and pork.

6. Reduce the heat to 350° and roast for approximately 1¼ to 1½ hours, basting the meat every 10 minutes with the marinade. Transfer meat to a hot platter.

7. Degrease the sauce if necessary. Swirl the butter in it and serve along with the venison. Be sure to taste the sauce and correct the seasoning if necessary, as it should be fairly spicy. This and all venison dishes are especially good served with Chestnut Puree.

Chevreuil en Casserole
Venison Pie

SERVES 6.

4 *pounds shoulder of venison, cut into 2-inch cubes*
¼ *teaspoon thyme*
2 *bay leaves, broken into small pieces*
1 *teaspoon salt*
½ *cup brandy*
3 *tablespoons vegetable oil*
8 *sprigs fresh parsley*
3 *cups red Burgundy wine*
6 *carrots, sliced*
6 *small white onions, sliced*
8 *peppercorns*
2 *cups Brown Stock (p. 4) or canned beef consommé*
1 *cup flour*
8 *strips thick bacon, cooked in boiling water for a few minutes and cut in pieces*
2 *tablespoons Tomato Puree (p. 149) or canned tomato puree*
2 *cloves garlic, minced*
1 *recipe Basic Short Paste (p. 362)*

1 *egg yolk*
2 *tablespoons heavy cream*

1. Place the cubes of venison on the bottom of a large covered casserole. Sprinkle with the thyme, bay leaves, and salt. Pour on the brandy, vegetable oil, and parsley. Stir and mix well. Add the wine, carrots, onions, and peppercorns and let marinate overnight in the refrigerator.

2. Take the venison and marinade out of the refrigerator. Remove the meat and strain the liquid. Put back the sliced vegetables and the spices. Add the Brown Stock or consommé and simmer the marinade for 1 hour, or until the liquid is reduced to about ⅔ of its original quantity.

3. When the marinade is finished cooking, strain it through a fine sieve and discard the vegetables and spices.

4. Dry the pieces of venison on paper towels while the marinade is cooking and roll the pieces in the flour until they are well coated. Shake off the excess flour.

5. Place a layer of blanched bacon on the bottom of the casserole, then a layer of meat. Repeat until all the bacon and meat are in the dish. Pour on the hot marinade—you should have enough liquid to cover the meat and bacon. Add the Tomato Puree and the garlic.

6. Cover tightly and put the casserole into a preheated 300° oven and simmer for about 2 to 2½ hours. Regulate the oven heat throughout so that the liquid just simmers, never boils. Skim the fat from the stock. Cool.

7. Transfer the stew to a deep baking dish and cover with a sheet of pastry dough made according to the recipe on p. 363, crimping the edges to fit the baking dish like a cover. Make a few slits in the top and brush with a mixture of the egg yolk and cream.

8. Set the baking dish in a preheated 400° oven for 10 minutes. Reduce the heat to 325° and bake for 20 to 30 minutes more, or until the crust is golden brown. Serve.

Civet de Lièvre
Rabbit Ragout

When you buy a live rabbit at a French market, it is quite common to reserve the blood, as it adds great zest to the sauce for whatever rabbit dish you are making. When you buy a hare in a market here, it is clean and ready to cook and, of course, without the blood. Although the result is not exactly the same, you can still make an excellent dish.

SERVES 8.

1 4- to 5-pound rabbit or hare, with liver reserved
3 cups dry red wine
½ cup rendered fat from salt pork
3 tablespoons flour
⅓ cup brandy
2 cups water
1 tablespoon Tomato Puree (p. 149) or canned tomato puree
2 sprigs fresh parsley
1 stalk celery
2 cloves garlic
1 teaspoon salt
¼ teaspoon freshly ground black pepper
24 small white onions
¾ pound small white fresh mushrooms
Liver of rabbit, cut into small pieces
½ cup heavy cream

1. Cut the rabbit into serving pieces and marinate in the wine for 2 days. Set aside the reserved liver.

2. Drain the rabbit pieces and dry them well. Reserve the marinade.

3. In a large, heavy casserole on top of the stove heat ¼ cup of the rendered salt pork fat. Sprinkle the flour all over the pieces of rabbit and brown the rabbit on all sides, being careful not to burn the flour.

4. Pour the brandy over the rabbit pieces and ignite, shaking the casserole so that the flames reach all the pieces of rabbit.

5. When the brandy is finished burning, add the wine marinade, water, Tomato Puree, parsley, celery, garlic, salt, and pepper. Cover. Bring to a boil and simmer for 30 minutes.

6. Meanwhile, brown the onions in the remaining pork fat and add to the rabbit. Continue to simmer for 40 minutes more.

7. Clean the mushrooms and add them to the rabbit and simmer 20 minutes or longer.

8. When the rabbit is tender, add the pieces of liver. Remove the

parsley. Stir in the cream and simmer for another 5 minutes. Correct the seasoning and serve.

Choucroute Braisée
Braised Sauerkraut for Game

SERVES 6.

3 *pounds fresh sauerkraut (approximately 2 quarts)*
6 *small white onions, sliced*
3 *carrots, finely sliced*
¾ *pound thick slices of bacon, blanched in boiling water*
    and cut into ½-inch pieces
6 *tablespoons sweet butter*
6 *sprigs fresh parsley*
2 *bay leaves*
12 *peppercorns*
1½ *cups Alsatian dry white wine*
⅓ *cup gin*
3 *cups White Stock (p. 6) or canned chicken consommé*
Salt and freshly ground black pepper

1. Wash the sauerkraut in cold water. Change the water 3 or 4 times to remove the brine. Drain and squeeze out as much of the water as possible.

2. In a large casserole, sauté the onions, carrots, and blanched bacon with the butter until the vegetables are nearly tender, but not browned.

3. Add the sauerkraut and stir. Cover and simmer for 15 minutes.

4. Add the parsley, bay leaves, peppercorns, wine, gin, and enough of the White Stock or consommé to cover the sauerkraut.

5. Simmer the covered casserole in a preheated 300° oven for 4 hours, or until all the liquid has been absorbed by the sauerkraut. Add more stock during the cooking if the sauerkraut becomes dry. Taste for seasoning.

NOTE: Prepared sauerkraut can be used, but fresh sauerkraut is much better.

CHAPTER 12

Organ Meats

Abats

Foie de Veau Sauté à la Moutarde
Foie de Veau Sauté au Vin Blanc

Bouchées à la Reine de Monblason

Cervelle de Veau au Beurre Noir

Rognons de Veau au Vin de Xérès
Rognons de Boeuf en Ragoût

Langue de Boeuf à la Piquant

Tripes à la Provençale

Foie de Veau
Calf's Liver

Liver is highly nutritious, particularly calf's liver which is often recommended as a help in curing anemia. Baby beef liver is quite often as tender as calf's liver, but steer liver has a stronger flavor and needs longer cooking. Lamb and pork liver are not as delicate as calf's liver, but the cooking procedure is the same.

It is important that the liver be cooked quickly over high heat so that a crust formed on the outside will keep the juices inside. When done, the liver should be slightly pink in the center. I prefer the slices to be about ½ inch thick, and the skin or membrane removed all around. In France, the butchers do this for you. Here they do not, but be sure to do it yourself, for the liver often curls in the skillet if the skin is left on.

The sauce you serve with sautéed calf's liver must be prepared in advance, since the liver takes so little time to cook. Some of the sauces that go particularly well with calf's liver are Tomato Sauce Provençale (p. 12), Sauce Robert (p. 13), Brown Mushroom Sauce (p. 14), and Mustard Sauce (p. 258). Just before you pour the sauce over the liver, be sure you add a few tablespoons of Brown Stock (p. 4) or canned beef consommé to the skillet in which the liver was satuéed. Boil it up quickly to incorporate the bits clinging to the pan and add that liquid to the sauce. This should be done with whichever sauce you are using as it adds considerable flavor.

Foie de Veau Sauté à la Moutarde
Sautéed Calf's Liver à la Moutarde

SERVES 6.

6 slices calf's liver, ½ inch thick
Salt and freshly ground black pepper
Flour
3 tablespoons sweet butter
1½ tablespoons vegetable oil
¼ cup Brown Stock (p. 4) or canned beef consommé
Garnishes: chopped fresh parsley and Mustard Sauce (see
    below) or other sauce of your choice (see p. 257)

1. Remove the skin of the liver. Sprinkle lightly with some salt and pepper and dredge in flour. Pat the slices gently to make the flour stick to the liver and shake off the excess.

2. Heat the butter and oil in a large skillet. When they are quite hot, but not burning, put the slices of liver in and sauté them very quickly on both sides until they are nicely browned. It should take about 3 to 4 minutes on the first side, and 2 minutes on the other side. Do not use a fork to turn the liver, as the juices will escape. A spatula is much better. When cooked, transfer the liver to a hot platter.

3. Have the sauce ready. Before pouring the sauce over the liver, add the Brown Stock or consommé to the pan used for sautéeing the liver. Bring it to a boil and stir it into the sauce. Taste for seasoning and pour over the liver. Serve immediately, garnished with parsley.

Mustard Sauce

½ cup Brown Stock (p. 4) or canned beef consommé
½ cup dry white wine, or dry vermouth
¾ cup heavy cream
2 tablespoons sweet butter

1 *tablespoon Dijon mustard*
Salt and freshly ground black pepper

1. Simmer the Brown Stock or consommé and wine or vermouth together until the liquid is reduced to only ½ cup.

2. Add the heavy cream and cook until the sauce has thickened.

3. Remove from the heat and swirl in the butter and mustard. Taste for seasoning.

NOTE: If you wish to serve the sautéed liver without a sauce, just add the Brown Stock or consommé to the pan the liver was sautéed in. Boil it up quickly, stirring to incorporate any bits clinging to the pan, and strain it over the liver on the serving platter. Garnish with chopped parsley.

Foie de Veau Sauté au Vin Blanc
Calf's Liver with White Wine

SERVES 6.

½ *cup Brown Stock (p. 4) or canned beef consommé*
½ *cup white wine*
6 *slices calf's liver, ½ inch thick*
Salt and freshly ground black pepper
2 *tablespoons flour*
8 *tablespoons sweet butter*
3 *shallots, minced*
1 *clove garlic, minced*
3 *sprigs fresh parsley, minced*
Extra chopped fresh parsley for garnish

1. Simmer the Brown Stock or consommé and wine together until the liquid is reduced to ½ cup.

2. Remove the skin or membrane of the liver. Sprinkle lightly with some salt and pepper and dredge in flour. Pat the slices gently with your fingers to make the flour stick to the liver and shake off the excess.

3. In a large skillet, melt 6 tablespoons of the butter. When bubbling, put the slices of liver in and sauté them very quickly on both sides until they are nicely browned. Remove to a warm platter and keep warm in a preheated 200° oven.

4. Meanwhile, in the same skillet, brown the shallots lightly. Add the garlic and parsley. Stir and add the reduced stock-wine mixture.

5. Strain the sauce into a saucepan and swirl in the remaining 2 tablespoons of butter. Taste for seasoning.

6. Pour the sauce over the liver slices. Sprinkle with parsley and serve.

Bouchées à la Reine de Monblason
Sweetbreads in Patty Shells Monblason

Sweetbreads are the delicate thymus glands of a calf. The flesh of the sweetbread is white and rather soft. It is considered to be one of the most delicate of all meat products and is therefore fairly expensive.

Unfortunately, most people shrink at the mere mention of sweetbreads. At my inn, I would instruct the waitresses not to mention the word, but just to say it was a new recipe from the boss, and the secret would be revealed to them at the end of the meal. No, I never got into trouble. From those who had never tasted sweetbreads the reaction was always a good one: "Never knew sweetbreads could taste that good." It proves once more that one should not be critical of a product unless he has tasted it first.

For this recipe, I recommend that you buy patty shells in a French pastry shop or use a good brand of frozen pastry shells.

SERVES 8.

3 *pairs sweetbreads, fresh or frozen*
Juice of 1 *lemon*
1 *cup dry white wine*
2 *cups White Stock* (*p.* 6) *or canned chicken consommé*
1 *bay leaf*
½ *teaspoon thyme*
6 *sprigs fresh parsley*
1 *pound fresh mushrooms, sliced*
8 *tablespoons sweet butter*
5 *tablespoons flour*
3 *tablespoons cognac*
1 *cup heavy cream*

2 *black truffles, sliced*
Salt and freshly ground black pepper
8 *patty shells*
Garnishes: green peas and boiled white rice

1. Poach the sweetbreads in a saucepan of boiling water (enough to cover the sweetbreads) to which you have added the lemon juice. Cook for 10 minutes, or longer if the sweetbreads are frozen. The centers should be a little soft. Drain and cool.

2. Simmer the wine and White Stock or consommé together with the bay leaf, thyme, and parsley until the liquid is reduced to 1½ cups. Strain and set aside.

SWEETBREADS·

3. Sauté the mushrooms in 2 tablespoons of the butter until all their liquid has evaporated.

4. Remove the outside skin and membraneous parts of the sweetbreads and slice them in halves lengthwise.

5. In a large skillet, melt 2 tablespoons of the butter and sauté the halved sweetbreads until they are lightly browned. Remove from the stove and cool. Take them out of the pan.

6. Pour a little of the wine-stock mixture into the skillet the sweetbreads were sautéed in and boil it up quickly to collect the coagulated juices and butter from the sweetbreads. Pour it back into the saucepan with the rest of the liquid.

7. In a saucepan, melt the remaining 4 tablespoons of the butter and blend in the flour. Stir and cook until the mixture is slightly brown.

8. Add the cognac and stir for 1 minute.

9. Slowly pour in the wine-stock mixture until you have a smooth sauce.

10. Add the cream, sautéed mushrooms, and truffles.

11. Dice the sweetbreads in 1-inch cubes and add them to the sauce. Simmer for 5 minutes. Taste for seasonings. If the sauce is too thick, add more cream.

12. Put the patty shells into a hot oven for about 3 minutes to heat them. Then fill up the hot shells with the hot sweetbread mixture. Top with an extra 1 to 2 tablespoons of sweetbreads and sauce. Set the covers of the patty shells on top. Serve with peas and plain rice.

Cervelle de Veau au Beurre Noir
Calf's Brains with Browned Butter

SERVES 4.

1 to 1½ pounds calf's brains
1 teaspoon salt
2 tablespoons lemon juice
11 tablespoons sweet butter
2 tablespoons chopped fresh parsley
¼ cup wine vinegar
Salt and freshly ground black pepper to taste
Flour
½ tablespoon vegetable oil
Garnishes: capers and chopped fresh parsley

1. Soak the brains in cold water for 1 hour and trim them.

2. Place the brains in a saucepan and cover with boiling water. Add the 1 teaspoon salt and the lemon juice. Simmer gently, without letting the water come to a boil again, for about 20 minutes. Let the brains cool in the cooking liquid for about ½ hour. Drain.

3. Clarify ½ cup of the butter to eliminate specks in the sauce. Cook the butter over moderately low heat until foam starts to appear on the surface. Skim the foam. Pour the yellow part of the butter into

another saucepan and discard the milky sediment at the bottom of the saucepan.

4. Return the butter to the stove over low heat and as soon as it starts to turn light brown, remove it from the stove and stir in the 2 tablespoons of parsley.

CALVES BRAINS.

5. Reduce the wine vinegar to 1 tablespoon by simmering and stir this reduced vinegar into the buttered sauce. Correct the seasoning and keep warm in the top of a double boiler until the brains are sautéed.

6. Dip the brains lightly into the flour and shake off the excess.

7. In a skillet, melt 3 tablespoons of the butter with the oil. As soon as the butter foams, brown the brains lightly, approximately 4 to 5 minutes on each side.

8. Place them on a hot platter and pour the hot brown butter sauce over them. Sprinkle with some capers or a little more fresh chopped parsley.

Rognons de Veau au Vin de Xérès
Calf's Kidneys with Sherry

Kidneys which come from young animals are generally more tender than those coming from old animals, and their flavor is more delicate. Calf's kidneys get first rating for quality, then lamb, beef, and pork.

SERVES 6.

½ pound fresh mushrooms, sliced
7 tablespoons sweet butter
3 calf's kidneys
Salt and freshly ground black pepper
1 cup Brown Stock (p. 4) or canned beef consommé
½ cup cream sherry
3 shallots, minced
2 cloves garlic, minced
¼ cup chopped fresh parsley
2 tablespoons cognac
2 tablespoons flour
Garnishes: chopped fresh parsley and rice or mashed or
        boiled new potatoes

1. Sauté the mushrooms in 3 tablespoons butter until their liquid has evaporated. Set aside.
2. Remove the membranes from the kidneys. Cut the kidneys into thin slices and sprinkle lightly with some salt and pepper.
3. In a saucepan add the Brown Stock or consommé to the sherry and simmer them together for 10 minutes. Set aside.
4. In a skillet, sauté the sliced kidneys in 4 more tablespoons butter until lightly browned. Add the kidneys to the sautéed mushrooms and set aside.
5. Working quickly, sauté the shallots, garlic, and parsley in the same skillet for about 2 minutes. Add the cognac and stir 1 minute longer.
6. Add the flour and stir constantly for 2 minutes. Now stir in the stock-sherry mixture, cooking until the sauce is smooth and thickened. If it is too thick, add a bit more stock.
7. Strain the sauce through a fine sieve into the saucepan with the

kidneys and mushrooms. Stir over moderate heat and taste for additional seasoning.

8. Serve on a platter and sprinkle with chopped parsley. You can garnish the platter with plain rice, mashed potatoes, or boiled new potatoes.

Rognons de Boeuf en Ragoût
Beef Kidney Ragout

SERVES 4 TO 5.

1 *young beef kidney*
½ *cup wine vinegar*
¾ *cup dry red wine*
1¼ *cups Brown Stock (p. 4) or canned beef consommé*
Salt and freshly ground black pepper
Flour for dredging kidney slices
5 *tablespoons sweet butter*
1 *tablespoon vegetable oil*
2 *small white onions, sliced*
2 *cloves garlic, minced*
1 *tablespoon flour*
1 *bay leaf*
½ *pound fresh mushrooms, sliced*
½ *teaspoon thyme*
Garnishes: buttered noodles, white rice, or croutons and
      1 *tablespoon chopped fresh parsley*

1. Remove the membrane from the kidney and soak the kidney in the wine vinegar, with cold water added to cover, for 3 hours.

2. Meanwhile, simmer the Brown Stock or consommé and wine together until it is reduced to 1 cup.

3. Drain the kidney. Wipe it dry and cut into thin slices. Sprinkle the slices lightly with some salt and pepper and dredge them in flour.

4. Heat 3 tablespoons of the butter and the oil together in a large skillet and brown the kidney slices on both sides. Transfer the slices to a baking casserole or covered baking dish.

5. In the same skillet, sauté the onions and garlic until slightly cooked, adding more butter if necessary.

6. Stir in the extra tablespoon of flour, cooking for a few minutes until it takes on a light golden color.

7. Add the cup of reduced wine-stock liquid and the bay leaf and pour the entire mixture over the kidney slices.

8. Cover and bake in a preheated 350° oven for 20 minutes.

9. Sauté the mushrooms in the remaining 2 tablespoons of butter until their liquid has evaporated.

10. Add the sautéed mushrooms and thyme to the kidney slices and cook 10 minutes longer.

11. Taste the sauce and correct the seasoning if necessary. Serve on a bed of buttered noodles or plain boiled rice, or on individual bread croutons. Sprinkle the parsley on top and serve.

Langue de Boeuf à la Piquant
Smoked Beef Tongue with Piquant Sauce

SERVES 5.

Piquant Sauce:
¾ *cup ketchup*
½ *cup water*
½ *cup dark corn syrup*
1 *8-ounce can tomato sauce*
½ *cup wine vinegar*
½ *cup light brown sugar*
1 *teaspoon chili powder*
1½ *tablespoons cornstarch*
6 *tablespoons Cointreau or other orange liqueur*

1 *smoked beef tongue*
Chopped fresh parsley for garnish
Garnishes: creamed spinach, boiled new potatoes

1. Combine the ketchup, water, corn syrup, tomato sauce, wine vinegar, brown sugar, and chili powder. Cook over low heat for 10 minutes. Blend the cornstarch with 4 tablespoons of the mixture and add it to the rest of the sauce. Cook the sauce slowly and stir until it

is slightly thickened. Then add the Cointreau and stir. Simmer gently for 20 minutes and set aside.

2. Some people soak the tongue overnight. I do not. I simply put the tongue in a large kettle, then cover with cold water and bring it to a boil and simmer for 1 hour. This first operation gets rid of the surplus salt brine and strong flavor used in smoking.

3. Remove the tongue. Discard the water and replace the tongue in the kettle.

4. Cover again with fresh water. Bring to a boil and simmer for 1 to 1½ hours more until you are able to remove the skin.

5. When cool enough to work with, remove the root portion, cartilage, fat, and gristle. Slice off 1 inch from the tip and peel off the skin.

6. Place the tongue in a Pyrex baking dish and cover with all the sauce. Cover the dish and place in a preheated 300° oven. Let it just simmer, never boil, for 1½ hours. Turn and baste the tongue every 15 minutes. It is ready when you can pierce it easily with a fork. If you overcook it, it will become mushy. It should be quite tender but firm.

7. Slice the tongue and set on a platter with the sauce over it. Garnish with creamed spinach and boiled small new potatoes. Sprinkle with a little parsley.

Tripes à la Provençale
Tripe Provençale

The secret of this inexpensive dish is slow cooking and the simmering of the vegetables in butter. The tripe can be rewarmed many times. In fact, the dish tastes even better the next day.

3 *pounds honeycomb tripe, cut into 1-inch cubes*
6 *large yellow onions, sliced*
4 *tablespoons sweet butter*
3 *green peppers, sliced*
1 *1-pound can stewed tomatoes*
2 *cups Brown Stock (p. 4) or canned beef consommé*
½ *cup Tomato Puree (p. 149) or canned tomato puree*
Salt and freshly ground black pepper to taste

1. Wash the tripe. Put it in a large pan and cover with water.

2. Bring the water to a boil and let the tripe simmer for 10 minutes. Drain and set aside to cool.

3. Sauté the onions slowly in the butter until they are tender and the liquid has evaporated.

4. Add the green peppers and cook, covered, until they are tender.

5. Add the can of tomatoes, Brown Stock or consommé, Tomato Puree, and tripe. Cook slowly in a covered pot for 3 to 4 hours, or until the tripe is tender. Season with some salt and pepper.

CHAPTER 13

Rice and
Pasta

Riz et Pâtes Alimentaires

Macaroni au Gratin
Macaroni aux Foies de Volaille

Nouilles aux Foies de Volaille à la Crème
Soufflé de Nouilles au Jambon à la Virion

Spaghetti à la Virion

Riz au Safran
Paella à la Française
Wild Rice à la Française

Pasta is high in food value. Macaroni, spaghetti, vermicelli, and all the countless other varieties of pasta are made of dried flour prepared mostly from durum wheat. The flavor of the pasta is bland, but when sauces, cheeses, and seasonings are added along with the various meats, poultry, and fish, you get a great variety of dishes with high nutritional value.

Macaroni au Gratin
Macaroni au Gratin

This dish is a complete meal in itself, but can be made even more so by the addition of shredded boiled ham. It can be prepared in advance and refrigerated until about half an hour before serving time. If the recipe is too large for one meal, divide it between two baking dishes before baking and freeze one of them. When you wish to use it, just defrost it and bake and broil as directed below.

SERVES 8.

5 *quarts boiling water*
3 *tablespoons salt*

16 *ounces semolina macaroni*
6 *tablespoons sweet butter*
3 *cups grated Swiss Gruyère cheese*
1 *cup light cream*
1 *cup boiled ham, shredded (optional)*
Salt and freshly ground black pepper

1. Bring the water and salt to a fast boil. Add the macaroni. Stir a few times so that the macaroni does not stick to the bottom of the pan. Cook about 25 minutes, or until the pasta is tender, but not mushy. Drain thoroughly, but do not rinse.

2. Return the macaroni to the pan. Add the butter and mix well.

3. Stir in ½ the cheese. Be certain the cheese is entirely mixed with the macaroni.

4. Stir in the cream, the ham, if you are using it, and salt and pepper to taste.

5. Put the mixture into a large, shallow Pyrex baking dish, or 2 or 3 smaller ones. Spread the rest of the grated cheese evenly on top.

6. Bake in a preheated 350° oven for 10 minutes. Then place under the broiler for 5 more minutes, or until a golden crust is formed.

Macaroni aux Foies de Volaille
Macaroni with Chicken Livers

SERVES 4.

1 *pound chicken livers*
7 *tablespoons sweet butter*
½ *pound fresh mushrooms, sliced*
1½ *cups Brown Sauce (p. 12)*
¼ *cup cream sherry*
2 *cloves garlic, minced*
Salt and freshly ground black pepper
1 *pound macaroni*
5 *to 6 quarts boiling salted water*
½ *cup grated Swiss Gruyère cheese*
2 *tablespoons heavy cream*
1 *tablespoon chopped fresh parsley*

1. Sauté the livers in 2 tablespoons of the butter until they have lost their red color. Set aside.

2. Sauté the mushrooms in 2 tablespoons of the butter until cooked, but not browned. Set aside.

3. Prepare the Brown Sauce as directed on p. 12.

4. Add the sherry to the Brown Sauce. Simmer for 10 minutes.

5. Combine the sauce, livers, mushrooms, and garlic. Taste for seasoning. Set aside.

6. Cook the macaroni in boiling salted water until tender. Drain.

7. Stir in 3 tablespoons of the butter, the cheese, and cream. Mix well.

8. Set on a platter and top with the chicken livers. Sprinkle with the parsley.

Nouilles aux Foies de Volaille à la Crème
Noodles with Chicken Livers

SERVES 4 TO 6.

½ pound fresh mushrooms, sliced
8 tablespoons sweet butter
3 shallots, minced
1 pound chicken livers
2 tablespoons cognac
½ cup White Stock (p. 6) or canned chicken consommé
½ cup heavy cream
⅛ teaspoon thyme
1 tablespoon chopped fresh chervil
1 tablespoon chopped fresh parsley
Salt and freshly ground black pepper
8 ounces noodles
3 to 4 quarts boiling salted water
½ cup grated Swiss Gruyère cheese

1. Sauté the mushrooms in 4 tablespoons of the butter until their liquid has evaporated. Remove from skillet and set aside.

2. In the same skillet, sauté the minced shallots until transparent, but not browned.

3. Cut the livers in halves. Add them to the shallots in the skillet and cook quickly.

4. Put back the mushrooms. Add the cognac and stir.

5. Add the White Stock or consommé and reduce by simmering to ½ its quantity.

6. Add the cream, thyme, chervil, and parsley and simmer for 5 minutes. Taste for seasoning.

7. Cook the noodles in a large saucepan in boiling salted water.

8. When the noodles are tender, but not mushy, drain them and add 4 tablespoons of the butter. Stir. Add the cheese.

9. Set the noodles on a warm platter. Place the livers on top of the noodles and serve.

Soufflé de Nouilles au Jambon à la Virion
Noodle Soufflé with Ham à la Virion

This can be served as a luncheon dish, along with a salad, and a fresh-fruit cup for dessert. This recipe is very similar to a soufflé, except it lacks flour. You can either serve it like a soufflé right from the baking dish or reverse it onto a platter like a golden pudding. If you wish, you can substitute chicken, cooked sausages, or tongue, finely chopped, for the boiled ham.

SERVES 6.

8 *ounces egg noodles*
3 *to* 4 *quarts boiling salted water*
4 *tablespoons sweet butter*
1¼ *cups grated Swiss Gruyère cheese*
1 *cup finely chopped boiled Polish ham*
4 *egg yolks*
1½ *cups light cream*
Salt and freshly ground black pepper (*optional*)
Pinch of nutmeg (*optional*)
6 *egg whites*

1. Cook the noodles in boiling salted water until tender. Drain.

2. Stir in the butter, 1 cup of the cheese, and the ham.

3. Beat the egg yolks with the cream and add the mixture to the noodles. Stir and taste for seasoning, adding the salt, pepper, and nutmeg if you wish. Make sure the noodle mixture is well seasoned, as the egg whites will absorb some of the seasoning.

NOODLE SOUFFLÉ
WITH HAM.

4. Beat the egg whites until stiff but not dry.

5. Fold them into the noodles and transfer the mixture to a well-buttered 2½-quart soufflé dish or Pyrex baking dish of the same capacity. Sprinkle the top with the extra ¼ cup of cheese.

6. Bake in a preheated 400° oven for 10 minutes. Reduce the heat to 350° and continue baking for another 25 minutes, or until done.

Spaghetti à la Virion
Spaghetti à la Virion

Although this was originally an Italian dish, it has been prepared in French kitchens for many years. Here is my French version of an old Italian recipe.

SERVES 6 TO 8.

Meatballs:
¾ *pound ground veal*
¾ *pound ground pork*
½ *pound ground beef chuck*

1 *cup bread crumbs*
2 *eggs, lightly beaten*
½ *cup chopped fresh parsley*
2 *cloves garlic, minced*
¾ *cup Brown Stock (p. 4) or canned beef consommé*
1 *teaspoon salt*
¾ *teaspoon freshly ground black pepper*
½ *cup vegetable oil*
½ *cup flour*

Sauce:
4 *to 5 shallots, minced, or 3 small white onions, minced*
8 *tomatoes, peeled and chopped (out of season use*
    2 1-pound cans stewed tomatoes)
2 *teaspoons basil*
1 *teaspoon salt*
¼ *teaspoon freshly ground black pepper*
½ *cup tomato paste*

Spaghetti:
2 *pounds spaghetti*
6 *quarts boiling salted water*
6 *tablespoons sweet butter*
1 *cup grated Swiss Gruyère cheese*

1. Combine the veal, pork, beef, bread crumbs, eggs, parsley, garlic, Brown Stock or consommé, salt, and pepper. Mix thoroughly and shape into approximately 20 meatballs.

2. Heat the oil in a large frying pan. Dredge the meatballs in the flour and brown on all sides. Remove from the pan.

3. In the same oil, sauté the shallots or onions until lightly browned.

4. Add the tomatoes, basil, salt, and pepper and simmer for 45 minutes.

5. Add the tomato paste and stir to blend.

6. Add the meatballs and simmer 30 minutes longer.

7. Meanwhile, cook the spaghetti in boiling salted water until tender, approximately 10 minutes. Do not overcook, as the spaghetti should not be mushy. Drain thoroughly.

8. Stir in the butter and mix well.

9. Place the spaghetti on a platter. Arrange the meatballs on top. Pour the sauce over and sprinkle with the cheese.

Riz au Safran
Saffron Rice

Saffron rice should always have a fairly dry consistency, so be sure that all the liquid is absorbed by the rice during the cooking.

MAKES 6 TO 8 CUPS.

6 *tablespoons sweet butter*
2 *cups uncooked converted long-grain rice*
4 *shallots, minced*
3½ *cups White Stock (p. 6) or canned chicken consommé*
½ *teaspoon saffron*
Salt and freshly ground black pepper

1. In a large saucepan, melt 4 tablespoons of the butter and simmer the rice for 10 minutes. Stir often, as the rice should be transparent, not brown.
2. In another saucepan, sauté the shallots in 2 tablespoons of the butter and cook until they are tender, but not brown.
3. Add the White Stock or consommé and bring to a boil.
4. Add ½ of the liquid to the rice along with the saffron. Stir; cover and simmer.
5. When the liquid is absorbed, add the remaining liquid and continue the simmering until the rice is tender and the grains separate. During the cooking, stir often so that the saffron is well mixed with the rice. Taste for seasoning and serve.

Paella à la Française
Paella à la Française

There is no true paella any more than there is a true bouillabaisse, and anyone can bring to this dish his own ingredients, imagination, and talent. You can add crabmeat, lobster, clams, or scallops. Here is one variation using chicken, shrimp, and vegetables.

SERVES 8.

6 *shallots, minced*
4 *tablespoons sweet butter*
1 *pound fresh mushrooms, sliced*
1 *8-ounce bottle clam juice*
24 *large frozen or fresh shrimp, shelled and deveined*
8 *cups Saffron Rice (p. 277)*
1 *cup cubed, cooked chicken*
1½ *cups cooked green peas*
½ *cup chopped fresh parsley*
1 *clove garlic, minced*
Salt and freshly ground black pepper

1. Sauté the shallots in 2 tablespoons of the butter until transparent, but not browned. Set aside.
2. Sauté the sliced mushrooms in 2 tablespoons of the butter until all their liquid has evaporated. Set aside.
3. Bring the clam juice to a boil and add the frozen shrimp. Cook until they have just defrosted. If you are using fresh shrimp, add them to the clam juice. When the clam juice returns to the boil, remove from the stove and let the shrimp stand in the juice for 1 more minute. Then remove them and slice them in halves lengthwise.
4. Add the shallots, mushrooms, Saffron Rice, chicken, peas, parsley, and garlic to the shrimp and taste for seasoning.
5. Bake, covered, in a 4-quart casserole in a preheated 350° oven for 15 minutes. Stir occasionally and serve hot.

Wild Rice à la Française
Wild Rice à la Française

Wild rice is not a French product and is very rarely served in France, but in the United States there is a great demand for it. Actually it is not rice at all, but a grain which grows primarily around the lakes of Minnesota. Its relative scarcity causes the price to be quite high. I object to wild rice being cooked in plain boiling salted water. The flavor has to be improved by other ingredients and seasonings added to the water. Here is my French recipe for a non-French food.

MAKES 8 CUPS.

2 *cups uncooked wild rice*
2 *tablespoons salt*
4 *quarts boiling water*
2 *carrots, minced*
2 *small white onions, minced*
1 *stalk celery, minced*
6 *tablespoons sweet butter*
2 *bay leaves*
½ *teaspoon thyme*
2½ *cups Brown Stock (p. 4) or canned beef consommé*
Salt and freshly ground black pepper to taste

1. Boil the wild rice in the salted water for 10 minutes, uncovered. Drain.

2. Sauté the carrots, onions, and celery in the butter in a large saucepan until they are tender, but not brown.

3. Add the wild rice. Stir and cook over moderate heat until all the butter has been absorbed. Transfer the rice into a 3-quart Pyrex baking dish.

4. Add the bay leaves, thyme, and 2 cups of heated Brown Stock or consommé.

5. Cover and simmer in a preheated 300° oven until the rice is tender, approximately 1 to 1½ hours. If you need more liquid during the cooking time, add the remaining ½ cup of stock. Season with salt and pepper. When cooked, the rice should be almost dry and the grains separate. If it is overcooked, it will be mushy. Before serving, discard the bay leaves. Wild rice is a nice garnish for duck and game recipes.

CHAPTER 14

Vegetables

Légumes

Artichauts Entiers Bouillis

Asperges Bouillies

❋

Choux de Bruxelles au Gratin

❋

Carottes au Beurre
Carottes Glacées

❋

Chou-fleur Bouilli
Chou-fleur au Gratin

❋

Céleris Braisés au Vin Blanc
Céleris au Gratin
Céleri-rave

❋

Purée de Marrons

❋

Maïs à la Béchamel

❋

Aubergines Monblason

❋

Endives Braisées

❋

Haricots Verts au Beurre Maître d'Hôtel
Haricots Verts au Gratin

Piments Doux Farcis

❊

Lentilles à la Lorraine

❊

Poireaux Braisés

❊

Laitues de Boston Braisées

❊

Gombos à la Créole

❊

Oignons à la Crème
Oignons Glacés

❊

Petits Pois à la Française

❊

Pommes de Terre à la Duchesse
Pommes de Terre Farcies
Galette de Pommes de Terre comme à la Campagne

❊

Ratatouille à la Provençale

❊

Épinards à la Crème
Épinards au Gratin

❊

Pâtissons Jaunes Farcis au Gratin

❊

Tomates à l'Ail
Tomates Farcies à la Duchesse
Tomates Farcies aux Viandes

The infinite number of dishes a cook can prepare is due in large part to vegetables, herbs, and condiments, as they provide such a large range of flavors. Off season, when you have to use certain frozen vegetables, you may have a sad experience, as some vegetables do not freeze and defrost as easily as others. For example, asparagus, string beans, carrots, and onions lose some of their goodness after defrosting. For this reason, try to use fresh vegetables in season whenever possible.

Vegetables can be classified as:

1. *Roots, Tubers, and Bulbs:* potatoes, yams, carrots, beets, celeriac, etc.

2. *Fruits:* tomatoes, squash, pumpkins, etc.

3. *Flowers:* artichokes, cauliflowers, etc.

4. *Fungus:* mushrooms, truffles, etc.

Artichauts Entiers Bouillis
Whole Boiled Artichokes

The artichoke lends itself to many delicious culinary preparations. It is cultivated all over France and in certain sections of California. Unfortunately, the average American cook hardly ever buys artichokes. If their lack of popularity is due to a lack of information on how to prepare them, I will try to help, as I believe it is one of the tastiest of vegetables.

SERVES 8.

8 *large artichokes*
1 *tablespoon salt*
½ *cup lemon juice*
2 *cups Hollandaise Sauce* (*p.* 16), *Mousseline Sauce* (*p.* 17),
    French Dressing (*p.* 21), *or sweet butter, melted*

1. Cut the stalks off the artichokes and take off the outer leaves. Trim across the tips.
2. In a large kettle, put enough water to cover the artichokes and bring them to a boil. Add the salt, lemon juice, and artichokes.
3. Cover and simmer until the outer leaves pull off easily, about 45 minutes. If you intend to serve the artichokes hot, prepare a Hollandaise Sauce, Mousseline Sauce, or simply some melted sweet butter to accompany them. Served cold with French Dressing, they make a nice appetizer.
NOTE: The artichoke is eaten by picking off the leaves, 1 at a time, and dipping the soft pulpy part at the bottom into the sauce and biting off just part of the leaf. The fuzzy portion inside the artichoke should be discarded, as it is unpleasant to eat and will irritate your throat. The bottom of the artichoke is the most delicious part and can be dipped into the sauce and eaten completely.

Asperges Bouillies
Boiled Asparagus

Asparagus can be reheated in butter and served with Hollandaise Sauce (p. 16), Mousseline Sauce (p. 17), or Maître d'Hôtel Butter (p. 22). Cold asparagus is excellent with Vinaigrette Sauce (p. 20), Mustard Sauce (p. 258), Mayonnaise Sauce (p. 18), or Ravigote Sauce (p. 21). If you are going to serve only the asparagus tips, reserve the butts for a soup.

1. Cut off a small section of the butt and peel the tough outer skin.

2. Tie the asparagus in bundles and plunge them into a large kettle of boiling salted water.

3. Boil slowly until barely tender, approximately 10 minutes. Drain. Now you can reheat them in butter as described above, or chill them to use as a salad or appetizer.

NOTE: Off season, when you have to use frozen asparagus, you will have a sad experience, because they do not freeze well. They become very soft and lose some of their juices in thawing and cooking. My suggestion is to cook them quickly by plunging them while still frozen into rapidly boiling salted water. As soon as the water boils again, drain the asparagus and leave them in the colander until all the water is gone. When nearly ready to serve, simmer them slowly in a little butter in a covered pot until ready, about 10 minutes. Check them often for tenderness and do not overcook.

Choux de Bruxelles au Gratin
Brussels Sprouts au Gratin

SERVES 6.

2 *pounds brussels sprouts*
2 *quarts boiling water*
1 *tablespoon salt*
3 *cups Mornay Sauce (p. 11)*
1 *cup grated Swiss Gruyère cheese*
2 *tablespoons sweet butter*
Salt and freshly ground black pepper

1. Wash and trim brussels sprouts and remove all the wilted leaves.

2. Bring the water to a boil. Add the 1 tablespoon of salt and the brussels sprouts.

3. Bring the water back to a boil and cook, uncovered, for 6 minutes.

4. Cover and cook for 10 to 15 minutes longer, or until the sprouts are barely tender. Drain off the water.

5. When the sprouts are well drained, place them in a shallow

baking dish. Pour the Mornay Sauce over them. Sprinkle with the cheese. Dot with the butter and add some salt and pepper.

6. Set the dish in a preheated 375° oven and bake for 10 minutes.

7. Turn on the broiler and brown the top lightly. Serve immediately.

Carottes au Beurre
Carrots with Butter

Late in the spring sweet baby carrots are a pleasure to prepare. You do not have to peel them, just wash them with a brush and they are ready for cooking.

SERVES 6.

2 *cups water*
1 *tablespoon sugar*
1 *teaspoon salt*
2 *bunches baby carrots*
Salt and freshly ground black pepper to taste
3 *tablespoons sweet butter*
2 *tablespoons chopped fresh parsley*

1. Bring the water, sugar, and salt to a boil in a saucepan and add the baby carrots.

2. Boil slowly until the carrots start to get tender.

3. Uncover the pan and cook longer until the liquid has evaporated. Season with additional salt and pepper.

4. Add the butter and parsley. Stir and serve.

Carottes Glacées
Glazed Carrots

SERVES 6.

2 *pounds carrots, peeled and cut into* 1¾-*inch lengths*
6 *tablespoons sweet butter*

2 cups *White Stock* (*p. 6*) *or canned chicken consommé*
2 *tablespoons sugar*
Salt and freshly ground black pepper
2 *tablespoons chopped fresh parsley*

1. Simmer the carrots in a covered saucepan with the butter, White Stock or consommé, and sugar.
2. When the carrots are tender, uncover the pan and continue the simmering until the liquid has been reduced to a syrupy glaze.
3. Taste for seasoning. Put into a serving dish and sprinkle the parsley on top.

Chou-fleur Bouilli
Boiled Cauliflower

SERVES 4 TO 6.

1 *head cauliflower*
2 *quarts boiling water*
1 *tablespoon salt*
1 *cup milk*
1 *cup Béchamel Sauce* (*p. 9*), *Mornay Sauce* (*p. 11*),
   or Hollandaise Sauce (*p. 16*)

1. Wash the cauliflower and divide it into flowerets.
2. Put the pieces into the boiling water with the salt and milk. Let it boil slowly, uncovered, for about 10 to 15 minutes, or until tender. The cauliflower should be served cooked through, but still firm and a little crunchy.
3. Strain and serve with Béchamel Sauce, Mornay Sauce, or Hollandaise Sauce.

Chou-fleur au Gratin
Cauliflower au Gratin

Buy a nice white head of cauliflower with fresh green leaves. Cut off the stem and cut out the stalk up through the center of the cauliflower. The stalk is usually too tough to cook.

SERVES 6.

1 *head cauliflower*
2 *quarts boiling water*
3 *cups milk*
1 *tablespoon salt*
4 *tablespoons sweet butter*
4 *tablespoons flour*
1 *cup grated Swiss Gruyère cheese*
Salt and freshly ground black pepper
Extra butter for topping

1. Wash the cored cauliflower and divide it into flowerets.

2. Put the pieces into a saucepan with the boiling water, 1 cup of the milk, and the salt. Let it boil slowly, uncovered, for about 10 minutes. Taste for tenderness. The flowerets should be cooked but still firm and a little crunchy, particularly at the core.

3. Drain well and place the cauliflower pieces in a flat, shallow, oblong baking dish.

4. Melt the butter and stir in the flour, stirring for about 3 minutes until golden. Gradually add 2 cups of the milk, stirring until it is a smooth, thick white sauce.

5. Add ½ cup of the cheese to the sauce. Season to taste with some salt and pepper.

6. Pour the white sauce over the cauliflower and sprinkle the rest of the cheese on top. Dot with butter.

7. Set under a moderately hot broiler for 10 minutes, or until it is nicely browned. Serve hot.

Céleris Braisés au Vin Blanc
Braised Celery with White Wine

This recipe requires very long, slow cooking to allow the braising sauce to blend with the flavor of the celery.

SERVES 6 TO 8.

8 *bunches fresh celery, trimmed to a length of 7 to 8 inches*
6 *quarts water*

3 *tablespoons salt*
4 *small white onions, chopped*
3 *small carrots, sliced thin*
6 *tablespoons sweet butter*
8 *to* 10 *slices bacon*
3 *cups Brown Stock* (*p.* 4) *or canned beef consommé*
⅔ *cup dry white wine*
5 *sprigs fresh parsley*
1 *bay leaf*
¼ *teaspoon thyme*
Superfine sugar (*optional*)
Salt and freshly ground black pepper (*optional*)
Chopped fresh parsley

1. Be certain that you are using only the tender parts of the celery by cutting off the tops and trimming the roots. Also, remove the outer green stems. Wash the celery bunches thoroughly to remove any grit remaining between the stems. Then tie the bunches of celery with white string to hold them together during braising.

2. Bring the water to a rapid boil. Add the salt and celery. Bring the water back to a boil, then reduce the heat so that the celery simmers slowly for 12 minutes.

3. Drain. Plunge the celery into cold water and extract all the water as gently as possible by pressing the bunches in a towel.

4. Sauté the onions and carrots in 3 tablespoons of the butter until tender. Do not burn them. Set aside.

5. Blanch the bacon in boiling water for 8 minutes. Drain. Add to the onions and carrots.

6. Simmer the Brown Stock or consommé, wine, parsley, bay leaf, and thyme until the liquid is reduced to 2½ cups. Strain the liquid into the vegetables and bacon. Simmer together, covered, for another 5 minutes.

7. Place the celery bunches in 1 layer in a baking dish or casserole. Pour the sauce, vegetables, and bacon evenly on top.

8. Cover and bake in a preheated 350° oven for 1 hour.

9. Uncover and continue braising the celery in the oven for 1 more hour, basting with the sauce every 10 minutes. The celery should be slightly browned and tender.

10. About 10 minutes before taking the celery out of the oven, taste the sauce. If you find it a little bitter, sprinkle some superfine sugar on the celery. Then broil with the oven door open for a few seconds.

Baste the celery with the sauce and take it out. Some celery does not require the sugar. Your taste buds will tell you.

11. Strain the liquid and keep the celery warm. Simmer the liquid in a saucepan until it is reduced to 1 cup and swirl in the remaining 3 tablespoons of the butter. The sauce should have the consistency of a syrup. Correct seasoning if necessary.

12. Slice the bunches of celery in halves lengthwise. Arrange them on a platter. Pour on the sauce and sprinkle with parsley. Serve hot.

Céleris au Gratin
Baked Celery au Gratin

SERVES 6 TO 8.

8 *bunches fresh celery*
6 *quarts boiling water*
3 *tablespoons salt*
2 *cups Béchamel Sauce (p. 9) or Mornay Sauce (p. 11)*
½ *cup grated Swiss Gruyère cheese*

1. Clean the celery and blanch it for 20 minutes in the boiling water, to which the salt has been added, as described in the recipe on pp. 289–290. Drain as directed.

2. Place the celery in a baking dish. Pour on the Béchamel Sauce or Mornay Sauce and sprinkle the cheese on top.

3. Bake for 40 minutes in a preheated 350° oven, until nicely browned on top.

Céleri-rave
Celeriac

Celeriac is a large edible root of the celery family. It can be served either raw or cooked. As an appetizer, or as part of an *hors d'oeuvres variés,* it can be sliced raw into thin strips and served with Mayonnaise Sauce (p. 18) or French Dressing (p. 21). To serve as a hot vegetable, trim the leaves and roots. Then slice or dice the celeriac and cook it in boiling salted water for about 20 minutes, or until it is tender. Drain

CELERIAC.

and serve it with Béchamel Sauce (p. 9), Hollandaise Sauce (p. 16), or just melted sweet butter. Add salt and freshly ground black pepper to taste.

Purée de Marrons
Chestnut Puree

This puree is usually served as a side dish with fowl, venison, and all types of wild game.

SERVES 6.

2 *pounds chestnuts, peeled, or a 1-pound 5-ounce can*
    imported whole chestnuts
3 *ribs celery, diced*
2 *cups White Stock (p. 6) or canned chicken consommé*
3 *tablespoons sweet butter*
¼ *cup heavy cream*
Salt and freshly ground black pepper to taste

1. Cook the chestnuts and celery in the White Stock or consommé until tender, usually about 20 minutes. If using canned chestnuts, cook

the celery in the White Stock until almost tender, about 15 minutes, then add the chestnuts for about 5 minutes.

2. Drain and put the chestnuts and celery through a sieve or in a blender, adding only enough of the stock to make a smooth, thick consistency.

3. Add the butter and cream. Taste for seasoning. Serve hot.

Maïs à la Béchamel
Fresh Corn with Béchamel Sauce

SERVES 6.

10 *to* 12 *ears of fresh corn on the cob*
1 *teaspoon salt*
1 *quart boiling water*
3 *tablespoons sweet butter*
1 *cup Béchamel Sauce* (*p.* 9)
Salt and freshly ground black pepper

1. Add the corn on the cob and salt to the boiling water and boil for 5 to 6 minutes.

2. Remove the ears from the water and let cool. When cool enough to handle, remove the kernels with a sharp knife. You should have 2 cups of kernels.

3. Put the kernels in a saucepan and melt the butter with them.

4. In another saucepan, make the Béchamel Sauce.

5. Simmer the corn and butter for 1 to 2 minutes and then combine with the Béchamel Sauce. Add salt and pepper to taste.

Aubergines Monblason
Eggplant Monblason

SERVES 6 TO 8.

3 *large eggplants*
Salt and freshly ground black pepper

1 *cup sweet butter, more if needed*
8 *large yellow onions, sliced*
2 *1-pound cans stewed tomatoes*
1 *large bouquet fresh parsley* (6 *to* 8 *sprigs*)
3 *cloves garlic, minced*
1 *cup grated Swiss Gruyère cheese*

1. Get some nice unbruised eggplants. Cut them crosswise into 1-inch slices. Peel them and season them on both sides with some salt and pepper. Place them side by side in a large roasting pan.

2. Top each slice with 1 tablespoon of the butter and bake in a preheated 300° oven until the slices are cooked and soft to the touch. They will absorb all the butter. Add more butter whenever needed if the eggplant seems too dry. This baking will take approximately 1½ hours.

3. Sauté the onions slowly in 3 tablespoons of the butter until all their liquid has evaporated and the onions are soft and transparent, but not browned.

4. Simmer the stewed tomatoes slowly until their surplus liquid has cooked away.

5. Mince the parsley very fine. Mix the onions, tomatoes, parsley, and garlic together. Season with some salt and pepper to taste. Raise the oven heat to 350°.

6. Spread ½ of the sauce in 2 shallow Pyrex baking dishes. Place the sliced eggplant on top and cover with the rest of the sauce. On top of this, spread the cheese and dot with little pieces of butter. When ready to serve, put the dishes in a 350° oven for 15 minutes. Then turn on the broiler and place them under the broiler to make the top golden brown and crisp. Serve immediately.

Endives Braisée
Braised Endives

Endives are especially nice as a garnish for roast veal, but they go well with many other main courses. The usual portion is two endives per person. If you cannot get fresh ones and wish to use the imported canned endives from Belgium, just drain the juice from the can and begin the braising. Omit the blanching as they are already cooked.

SERVES 4.

8 *endives, fresh*
2 *quarts boiling water*
1 *tablespoon salt*
4 *tablespoons sweet butter, melted*
1 *teaspoon lemon juice*
1 *cup Brown Stock (p. 4) or canned beef consommé*

1. Cut the base of the endives and pull off any withered leaves.
2. Drop the endives into boiling salted water for 15 minutes. Drain and dry thoroughly.
3. Lay the endives in a shallow Pyrex baking dish in 1 layer. Pour the butter and lemon juice over them. Bake in a preheated 325° oven for 10 minutes.
4. Pour ½ cup of the Brown Stock or consommé over them and continue baking until the stock has evaporated.
5. Add the rest of the stock. Turn the endives and braise and brown them to a golden color. Serve. Total baking time should be 1 to 1½ hours.

Haricots Verts
Green String Beans

This is a vegetable which goes with practically every type of meat. I remember in my youth going to the vegetable garden an hour before dinner time to pick some of the small young string beans from the vines. They were then cooked slowly, simmered in a little water with some butter. In a matter of minutes they were ready for the table. The water had evaporated and the beans were tender, tasty, and just barely wet with butter. Sometimes a couple of sliced onions, sautéed in butter, would be added for flavor.

Haricots Verts au Beurre Maître d'Hôtel
Green String Beans with Maître d'Hotel Butter

SERVES 6.

2 *pounds fresh green string beans*
3 *quarts boiling water*
1½ *tablespoons salt*
4 *tablespoons sweet butter*
1 *tablespoon lemon juice*
½ *cup chopped fresh parsley*
Salt and freshly ground black pepper

1. Wash the beans. Cut off the ends and pull off the strings if any.
2. Drop the beans into the boiling water to which the salt has been added. Stir. When the water comes to a boil again, boil slowly for 10 minutes or more. Test the beans for tenderness. They should be a little crunchy, but tender. Drain thoroughly in a colander.
3. Melt 2 tablespoons of the butter in a saucepan over moderately high heat. Add the beans and sauté slowly. When the moisture has evaporated, add the remaining 2 tablespoons of butter, the lemon juice, and the parsley. Taste for seasoning and serve hot.

Haricots Verts au Gratin
Green String Beans au Gratin

You can prepare this dish beforehand and wait until twenty minutes before serving time to do the broiling.

SERVES 6.

2 *pounds fresh green string beans*
3 *quarts boiling salted water*
2 *cups Béchamel Sauce (p. 9)*
1 *cup grated Swiss Gruyère cheese*
Salt and freshly ground black pepper to taste
Butter for topping

1. Wash the beans. Cut off the ends and remove strings if any.

2. Drop the beans into the boiling water. Stir. When the water comes to a boil again, boil slowly for 10 minutes or more. Test for tenderness. The beans should be a little crunchy, but tender. Drain thoroughly in a colander.

3. Make the Béchamel Sauce.

4. Add ½ cup of the cheese to the sauce.

5. Mix the beans with ½ of the sauce and place them in a shallow Pyrex baking dish.

6. Pour on the rest of the sauce. Sprinkle on the other ½ cup of cheese and dot with butter.

7. Set under the broiler for 10 to 15 minutes or more, or until the sauce is lightly browned on top. Serve immediately.

Piments Doux Farcis
Stuffed Green Peppers

SERVES 8.

8 *large green peppers*
3 *quarts boiling water*
1 *tablespoon salt*
3 *small white onions, chopped*
4 *tablespoons sweet butter*
1 *pound ground veal, beef, pork, or sausage or a*
   combination of any of these
2 *cloves garlic, minced*
2 *cups cooked rice*
⅔ *cup Brown Stock (p. 4) or canned beef consommé*
½ *cup bread crumbs plus some extra for topping*
¼ *cup chopped fresh parsley*
Salt and freshly ground black pepper to taste
2 *tablespoons sweet butter for topping*
3 *cups Tomato Sauce Provençale (p. 12)*

1. Cut a thin slice from the stem ends of the peppers and remove the seeds and pith.

2. Place the peppers in boiling water to cover, with the 1 table-

spoon of salt. Boil for 6 minutes. Remove the peppers carefully from the pan and invert them to drain.

3. Sauté the onions in the butter over moderate heat until they are slightly tender.

4. Add the meat and garlic. Simmer for 2 minutes, stirring constantly. Transfer to a mixing bowl.

5. Add the rice, Brown Stock or consommé, bread crumbs, parsley, and seasonings. Mix well and stuff the well-drained peppers with the mixture.

6. Sprinkle some more bread crumbs on top and dot with the extra butter.

7. Place the peppers in a baking pan and put into a preheated 350° oven. Pour the Tomato Sauce Provençale over them and baste often. The baking should take approximately 1 hour. The tops will be nicely browned. If the sauce is too thick, add a little more stock. Taste for seasoning before serving.

Lentilles à la Lorraine
Lentils à la Lorraine

SERVES 6.

2 *cups dried lentils*
4 *cups Brown Stock (p. 4) or canned beef consommé*
2 *carrots, quartered*
6 *medium-sized white onions*
3 *sprigs fresh parsley*
1 *bay leaf*
1 *Polish sausage, precooked and sliced, and/or 2½ pounds*
     precooked smoked ham, cubed
2 *small cloves of garlic, minced*
4 *tablespoons sweet butter*
Salt and freshly ground black pepper

1. Soak the lentils in enough cold water to cover for 2 hours. Drain.

2. In a large saucepan, put the lentils, Brown Stock or consommé, carrots, onions, parsley, and bay leaf. Bring to a boil and simmer slowly until the lentils are nearly tender. If necessary, add more stock.

3. Discard the bay leaf and parsley. Add the sausage or ham, or both, and the garlic. Simmer until the ham and sausage are heated through.

4. Swirl in the butter and add some salt and pepper to taste if necessary.

Poireaux Braisés
Braised Leeks

In braising the leeks, as in braising any other vegetables, use just the amount of liquid necessary. The leeks should be nicely moistened but not floating, when you bring them to the table.

SERVES 4 TO 6.

12 *medium-sized fresh leeks*
2 *quarts water*
1 *tablespoon salt*
½ *cup sweet butter, in small pieces*
1½ *cups White Stock (p. 6) or canned chicken consommé*

1. Cut off the root ends of the leeks. Discard the outside leaves and cut off a portion of the green tops. Slit the leeks about ¾ of the way up from the bottom in 2 crossing directions. In this way, you can clean out the sand from between the leaves. Wash thoroughly and let the water run over and between the leaves.

2. Put the water and salt in a skillet and bring to a boil. Plunge the leeks into it and cook for 5 minutes. Drain.

3. Place the leeks in a baking dish. Dot with the butter and add 1 cup of White Stock or consommé. Bake, uncovered, in a preheated 325° oven for 20 minutes. Turn the leeks over. Add the extra ½ cup of stock only if the leeks seem dry. Continue baking until they are lightly browned.

Laitues de Boston Braisées
Braised Boston Lettuce

SERVES 4.

4 *heads fresh Boston lettuce*
Boiling water to cover, slightly salted
5 *tablespoons sweet butter*
4 *baby carrots*
4 *tiny white onions*
1 *cup Brown Stock (p. 4) or canned beef consommé*
¼ *cup dry vermouth*
4 *slices bacon*
6 *sprigs fresh parsley, tied together*
Salt and freshly ground black pepper
Garnish: chopped fresh parsley

1. Wash the heads of lettuce thoroughly after removing the outside leaves. Plunge them into the boiling salted water. When they are wilted, take them out and drain all the water. Slice the heads in two and set aside.

2. Melt 3 tablespoons of the butter in a saucepan and add the carrots and onions. Cover and sauté the vegetables until tender, but do not brown. Add the Brown Stock or consommé and the vermouth and cook for 2 more minutes uncovered.

3. Drop the bacon slices into boiling water for a few minutes. Drain and cut them into small pieces.

4. In a casserole, place the lettuce and the vegetables with the liquid, bacon, and parsley sprigs and simmer in a preheated 300° oven for 1¼ hours. Place the lettuce and vegetables in a serving dish and keep warm.

5. Quickly boil down the liquid to about ⅓ cup. Swirl in the remaining butter. Taste for seasoning and pour the liquid over the lettuce. Sprinkle with chopped parsley.

Gombos
Okra

Okra pods can be used as a simple vegetable, as a garnish for consommé or bouillon, or in Creole dishes. They have a gelatinous texture and are considered by some to be a good body lubricant. I used to raise them in my vegetable garden. They can be bought in the market during their season and are available frozen all year round.

To Cook Okra: Plunge the okra into salted boiling water until they are tender, but not too soft, approximately 10 minutes. Drain.

Consommé with Okra: After the cooked okra has cooled, cut off little pieces from the stem and tip ends. Slice the okra pods into ¼-inch pieces. Add them to some consommé with chopped fresh chervil or parsley. Heat and serve.

Gombos à la Créole
Okra à la Creole

SERVES 4.

4 *small white onions, diced*
1 *green pepper, sliced*
4 *tablespoons sweet butter*
2 *cups sliced okra*
4 *fresh tomatoes*
1 *teaspoon chopped fresh or* ½ *teaspoon dried basil*
Salt and freshly ground black pepper
¼ *cup Brown Stock (p. 4) or canned beef*
   consommé (optional)

1. Sauté the onions and green pepper in butter and cook slowly until they are soft, but not browned.

2. Add the okra and simmer slowly for about 5 minutes, stirring constantly.

3. Blanch, peel, and chop the tomatoes.

4. Add the tomatoes, basil, and a little salt and pepper and continue simmering for 25 minutes.

5. Add the Brown Stock or consommé if necessary so the dish will have a moist consistency. Serve over rice, or as an accompaniment to broiled meats.

Oignons à la Crème
Creamed Onions

This vegetable is especially nice as an accompaniment for turkey on Thanksgiving Day or a goose at Christmastime. Creamed onions go well with all types of fowl and game.

SERVES 6 TO 8.

24 *small white onions*
1 *cup White Stock (p. 6) or canned chicken consommé*
¼ *teaspoon thyme*
2 *cups Béchamel Sauce (p. 9)*
¼ *cup grated Swiss Gruyère cheese (optional)*
Salt and freshly ground black pepper
Chopped fresh parsley

1. Place the unpeeled onions in boiling water and cook them for 5 minutes. Drain and cool. Remove the skins.
2. Put the onions into a saucepan with the White Stock or consommé and thyme and simmer until they are tender.
3. Meanwhile, make the Béchamel Sauce. If you wish, you can add a little of the stock in which the onions are cooking, along with the cheese, and stir until blended. Season to taste with salt and pepper.
4. When the onions are tender, remove them from the stock. Place them in the Béchamel Sauce and simmer for 5 minutes. Correct the seasoning and serve with parsley.

Oignons Glacés
Glazed Onions

SERVES 6.

24 *small white onions, unpeeled*
4 *tablespoons sweet butter*

1 *cup White Stock (p. 6) or canned chicken consommé*
1½ *tablespoons sugar*
Salt

1. Place the unpeeled onions in a pot of rapidly boiling water and cook for 15 minutes, long enough to be able to easily remove the skins from the onions. Drain the onions and cool them. Then remove the skins.

2. Place the peeled onions in a pan with the butter, ½ cup White Stock or consommé, and the sugar. Simmer, uncovered, until the onions are tender and glazed, adding more stock if necessary. The onions should be a light golden brown. Add salt to taste.

Petits Pois à la Française
Green Peas à la Française

SERVES 4 TO 6.

1 *cup salted water*
8 *tiny white onions*
1 *head Boston lettuce*
2 *pounds fresh peas*
3 *sprigs fresh parsley, tied*
2 *tablespoons sweet butter*
Salt and freshly ground black pepper (*optional*)
Sugar (*optional*)

1. Bring the salted water to a boil and cook the white onions until tender.

2. Wash the lettuce well and discard the outside leaves.

3. Add the lettuce to the onions and cook until it gets wilted.

4. Shell the peas and add them along with the parsley. Cook until tender.

5. Simmer until the liquid is reduced to about 1 tablespoon and then add the butter.

6. Discard the parsley and taste for seasoning. Add the salt, pepper, and a little sugar if necessary.

NOTE: If you wish to make this dish in the off season when fresh peas are not available and Boston lettuce is not in the market, you can substitute 2 cups of frozen tiny peas and escarole lettuce.

Pommes de Terre à la Duchesse
Duchess Potatoes

These are mashed potatoes mixed with beaten eggs, usually served as a border for decorating meat or fish platters, or creamed dishes. You put the potato mixture through a pastry bag while it is still hot. That way it is easy to form a pattern. Then the potato border is brushed with a mixture of beaten egg and a little cream and browned lightly in the oven or under a broiler.

SERVES 6.

2 *pounds potatoes*
1 *teaspoon salt*
4 *tablespoons sweet butter*
½ *teaspoon ground or freshly grated nutmeg*
2 *whole eggs, beaten*
¼ *cup heavy cream*
Salt and freshly ground black pepper to taste
1 *egg yolk, beaten*
2 *tablespoons light or heavy cream*

1. Peel the potatoes and cut into quarters. Place them in boiling water with 1 teaspoon of salt. Cover and cook them until they are soft, but still holding their shape. Drain.

2. Put the potatoes through a sieve, potato ricer, or food mill.

3. Add the butter, mashing until smooth.

4. Add the nutmeg, the beaten whole eggs, the ¼ cup heavy cream, salt, and pepper. Whip until fluffy.

5. Pipe the mixture through a pastry bag onto a flat baking dish or ramekin, making any design you wish around your meat, fish, or creamed dish.

6. Brush the potatoes with the beaten egg yolk mixed with the 2 tablespoons of cream.

7. Bake in a preheated 425° oven until lightly browned, or place under the broiler flame until browned.

Pommes de Terre Farcies
Stuffed Baked Potatoes

SERVES 6 TO 12.

6 *Idaho baking potatoes*
5 *tablespoons sweet butter*
3 *tablespoons heavy cream*
1½ *cups grated Swiss Gruyère cheese*
½ *cup finely minced cooked ham*
1 *teaspoon salt*
½ *teaspoon freshly ground black pepper*

1. Wash the potatoes and scrub with a vegetable brush. Bake in a preheated 400° oven until they are soft.

2. Cut in half lengthwise. Scoop out the insides and mash together with 3 tablespoons of the butter, cream, 1 cup of the cheese, and the ham. Season to taste.

3. Refill the potato shells. Sprinkle with the remaining ½ cup cheese. Dot with butter and set the shells on a baking sheet. Cover and set aside until shortly before dinner.

4. When you are ready to eat, place the potatoes in a preheated 400° oven for 15 minutes and then under the broiler for 5 to 10 minutes until nicely browned.

Galette de Pommes de Terre comme à la Campagne
Country-Style Potato Cake

SERVES 6.

6 *yellow California potatoes or 6 Idaho baking potatoes*
Salt and freshly ground black pepper
Garlic salt (optional)
6 *tablespoons sweet butter*

1. Slice the potatoes very thin or shred them in julienne strips. This should be done just before you cook them to prevent them from turning black. Do not put the potatoes in water, as the starch must remain on the potatoes to make them adhere to each other.

2. Season them with some salt, pepper, and garlic salt if you wish.

3. Heat the butter in a skillet. When it starts to foam, add the shredded potatoes. Press the potatoes down with a fork so that all the small shredded pieces stick together and form a flat cake (*galette*).

4. When ¾ cooked (slightly on the raw side but when the strips are beginning to stick to each other) and nicely browned on the bottom, turn the potato cake over with a large spatula and brown the other side. When the cake is browned on both sides, you can slice it in wedges like a pie and arrange the slices on a platter with your meat and other vegetables.

NOTE: Potato Cake can also be baked in a preheated 350° oven for 35 to 45 minutes, or until browned on both sides.

Ratatouille à la Provençale
Eggplant, Zucchini, and Tomato Casserole

In the South of France, they use olive oil exclusively for this dish. I prefer the flavor of sweet butter. Just be careful not to let any of the vegetables get scorched when you fry them, as that would lend a bitter taste to the ratatouille.

SERVES 4.

1 ¾-*pound eggplant*
¾ *pound zucchini*
1 *tablespoon salt*
3 *cups canned, stewed tomatoes*
1 *to 2 teaspoons sugar* (*optional*)
6 *small white onions, sliced*
2 *green peppers, minced*
11 *tablespoons sweet butter or 7 tablespoons olive oil*
3 *cloves garlic, minced*
1 *cup chopped fresh parsley*
1 *teaspoon salt*
½ *teaspoon freshly ground black pepper*

1. Peel the eggplant. Slice it ⅜ inch thick and cut the slices into strips 1½ inches wide.

2. Wash the zucchini. Slice off both ends and slice the zucchini into ⅜-inch pieces.

3. Put the zucchini and eggplant in a bowl. Sprinkle with the salt and mix together. Let them stand until you are ready with the other ingredients.

4. Simmer the stewed tomatoes in a saucepan until most of the liquid has cooked away and it becomes a puree. If the taste is too acidic, add a little sugar.

5. Sauté the onions and green peppers in 3 tablespoons of the butter or 2 tablespoons oil until tender, but not browned.

6. In a large skillet, sauté the eggplant and zucchini in 8 tablespoons of the butter or 5 tablespoons oil and brown lightly. Take the vegetables out of the skillet and set aside.

7. In the same skillet put the tomatoes, onions, peppers, garlic, and parsley and cook together for 2 minutes. Season with the salt and pepper.

8. In a casserole, place a layer of the tomato mixture, then ½ of the eggplant and zucchini, another layer of tomatoes, the rest of the vegetables, and the rest of the tomatoes. Simmer the casserole in a preheated 300° oven for 45 minutes or until tender. Taste for additional seasoning.

Épinards à la Crème
Creamed Spinach

SERVES 4.

3 *cups washed, chopped, and drained fresh spinach*
5 *tablespoons sweet butter*
Salt and freshly ground black pepper to taste
¼ *cup Brown Stock (p. 4) or canned beef consommé*
2 *tablespoons flour*
1 *cup heavy cream, heated*
¼ *teaspoon freshly grated or ground nutmeg*

1. Spinach cooks quickly and should be cooked without any liquid. Simply sauté the chopped spinach with 2 tablespoons of the butter and cook until the spinach is limp and the excess moisture is cooked away.

Add the necessary salt and pepper. If using frozen spinach, cook according to package directions and drain.

2. When the spinach has cooled a bit, put it through a blender with the Brown Stock or consommé to make a puree.

3. Melt the remaining 3 tablespoons of butter and add the flour, stirring until golden. Gradually add the cream, stirring constantly until you have a smooth, thick white sauce.

4. Stir in the spinach and nutmeg and taste again for additional seasoning.

5. Simmer for 5 minutes. Be careful not to let the spinach stick to the bottom of the pan. Serve hot.

Épinards au Gratin
Spinach au Gratin

SERVES 4.

1 *recipe Creamed Spinach* (*p.* 307), *substituting* 1 *cup grated
    Swiss Gruyère cheese for the nutmeg and adding
    1 extra tablespoon sweet butter*

1. Prepare Creamed Spinach as indicated on pp. 307–308 until the white sauce is made.

2. Add ½ cup of the cheese in place of the nutmeg to the white sauce and then combine the sauce with the cooked spinach.

3. Arrange the spinach mixture in a shallow baking dish and sprinkle the top with the rest of the cheese. Dot the top with the tablespoon of butter.

4. Set under a preheated broiler for 10 to 15 minutes, or until the top is lightly browned.

Pâtissons Jaunes Farcis au Gratin
Yellow Squash au Gratin

SERVES 8.

4 *medium-sized yellow squash
Salt and freshly ground black pepper*

3 *or 4 medium-sized white onions, finely chopped*
6 *tablespoons sweet butter*
1 *large clove garlic, minced*
5 *slices white bread, made into bread crumbs*
½ *teaspoon Worcestershire sauce*
3 *canned pimentos, sliced*
¾ *cup Parmesan cheese*
½ *teaspoon salt*
¼ *teaspoon cayenne pepper*

1. Boil the squash in salted water until tender. Let them cool.
2. Cut the squash in half lengthwise and scoop out the seeds. Place the squash in a shallow baking dish and sprinkle with salt and pepper.
3. Sauté the onions in the butter until tender and transparent, but not browned.
4. Add the garlic, bread crumbs, Worcestershire sauce, pimentos, and cheese. Mix together and season with the ½ teaspoon salt and the cayenne pepper.
5. Fill the centers of the squash and bake in a preheated 400° oven for 20 minutes. Then place under the broiler for a few minutes until slightly browned on top.

Tomates à l'Ail
Garlic Tomatoes

SERVES 6.

6 *large-sized tomatoes*
4 *tablespoons sweet butter*
1 *teaspoon garlic salt*
1 *teaspoon freshly ground black pepper*
1 *teaspoon sugar*
2 *tablespoons chopped fresh parsley*
2 *cloves garlic, minced* (*optional*)

1. Cut a thin slice off the top of each tomato.
2. Melt the butter in a baking dish large enough to hold all of the tomatoes and place the tomatoes in the dish side by side.

3. Sprinkle each tomato with the garlic salt, pepper, and sugar.

4. Bake, uncovered, in a preheated 300° oven for 1½ hours.

5. A few minutes before serving, place under the broiler until just slightly browned. Place on platter and sprinkle with parsley.

6. For those who like more garlic flavor, mix the chopped parsley with the cloves of garlic and sprinkle the mixture on top of the tomatoes just before serving.

Tomates Farcies à la Duchesse
Tomatoes Stuffed with Duchess Potatoes

These tomatoes make a beautiful and delicious garnish on a meat or fish platter.

SERVES 8.

8 *large tomatoes*
Salt and freshly ground black pepper
1 *recipe Duchess Potatoes* (*p.* 304)
½ *cup grated Swiss Gruyère or Parmesan cheese*
2 *tablespoons sweet butter*

1. Wash the tomatoes and cut them in half. Scoop out the centers and sprinkle the insides lightly with some salt and pepper. Turn them over on a tray to drain for a few minutes.

TOMATOES STUFFED
WITH DUCHESSE POTATOES.

2. Fill the tomatoes with the Duchess Potatoes mixture, using a pastry bag or a spoon and heaping them over the top.

3. Sprinkle the tops with the cheese and brush with melted butter.

4. Place the tomatoes in a shallow baking dish and bake in a preheated 425° oven until the tops are nicely browned, approximately 20 minutes.

Tomates Farcies aux Viandes
Tomatoes Stuffed with Meat

SERVES 6.

6 *large tomatoes*
Salt and freshly ground black pepper
1½ *to 2 cups finely ground, cooked beef, veal, or lamb*
2 *small white onions, minced and lightly sautéed in sweet butter*
1 *cup soft bread crumbs*
5 *tablespoons chopped fresh parsley*
2 *cloves garlic, minced*
½ *cup Brown Stock* (p. 4) *or canned beef consommé*
⅔ *cup grated Swiss Gruyère cheese*
3 *tablespoons sweet butter*
Garnishes: Duchess Potatoes (p. 304) *and Tomato-Stock Sauce* (*optional*) (*below*)

Tomato-Stock Sauce:
Reserved tomato pulp
⅓ *cup Brown Stock* (p. 4) *or canned beef consommé*
2 *tablespoons sweet butter*

1. Wash the tomatoes. Cut them in halves and scoop out the centers carefully. Reserve the scooped-out tomato pulp. Sprinkle the insides lightly with some salt and pepper. Turn them over on a tray to drain for a few minutes.

2. In a mixing bowl, place the meat, onions, ½ cup of the bread crumbs, 3 tablespoons of the parsley, the garlic, and the Brown Stock or consommé. Mix well and season with some salt and pepper.

3. Fill the tomatoes with this mixture.

4. Sprinkle the remaining ½ cup of bread crumbs on top and then the grated cheese. Dot with butter.

5. Place the tomatoes in a shallow baking dish. Make the sauce by blending the pulp, stock, and butter. Spoon this sauce around the stuffed tomatoes in the baking dish. This is optional but adds to the flavor of the dish.

6. Bake the tomatoes in a preheated 350° oven for about 1 hour. Serve the tomatoes with the remaining 2 tablespoons of parsley sprinkled on top of them, and the Tomato-Stock Sauce spooned around them. You can also place Duchess Potatoes around the tomatoes on the serving platter and put it all under the broiler for 10 minutes before serving.

CHAPTER 15

Salads

Salades

Salade de Pissenlit au Bacon
Salade d'Endive aux Betteraves Rouges
Salade d'Épinards

Salade de Chou-fleur
Salade de Haricots Verts à la Vinaigrette
Salade de Légumes
Salade de Pommes de Terre (Chaude)
Salade de Pommes de Terre (Froide)
Salade Niçoise

Salade à la Mimosa
Salade d'Oeufs à la Russe

French salads are made with fresh raw greens, various types of vegetables, or a combination of other foods. There are a great number of leafy greens that can be used for salads: iceberg, Boston, Bibb, and Romaine lettuce, field and salad lettuce, endives, escarole, chicory, and dandelion greens. Some salads are made with vegetables like tomatoes, cucumbers, celeriac, green beans, carrots, cabbage, leeks, radishes, artichokes, spinach, shell beans, potatoes, and lentils.

Combination salads are numerous. Cooked meats like beef, chicken, veal, and tongue can be used with different salad recipes. Fish and seafood, like crabmeat, shrimp, lobster, tuna, or salmon, also make delicious salads when properly prepared. These combination salads can be served either as appetizers or main courses, depending on the occasion.

Green salads should always be washed thoroughly and carefully drained, as they must be absolutely dry before being mixed with the salad dressing and seasonings. The dressings most widely used with greens and vegetables are vinaigrette and French dressing, mayonnaise, remoulade sauce, and mustard sauce. Olive oil is best to use for salad dressings but can be replaced by a vegetable oil or a nut-based oil. It is very important to use good brands of salad oil and wine vinegar in order to make an excellent dressing. I do not believe that lemon juice can replace a good vinegar. If you are not making your own mayonnaise, be sure to use a good brand of that, too.

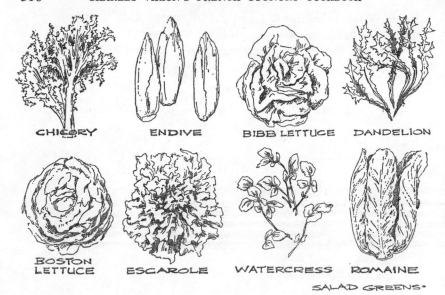

SALAD GREENS.

For simple green salads, aromatic herbs can be added in season. Their delicate flavors will enhance the taste of the greens and the dressing. The most frequently used herbs are parsley, chervil, chives, tarragon, and savory.

Salade de Pissenlit au Bacon
Dandelion Salad with Bacon

Early in the spring, before the dandelions start blooming, many people in rural districts go into the fields to pick dandelion leaves. In that season, they are a tender delicacy. Later, when the dandelions bloom and the leaves turn a darker green, they become bitter and tough. If you live in a big city, you can find the tender young dandelion leaves in Italian produce markets in the springtime.

SERVES 4.

1 *pound fresh dandelion greens*
8 *slices bacon, cooked and diced*
⅓ *cup French Dressing (p. 21)*
½ *to 1 teaspoon salt*
½ *teaspoon freshly ground black pepper*

1. Cut the roots off the dandelion greens and discard any damaged

leaves. Wash a few times under cold running water to remove all the grit. Shake in a towel or salad shaker to get rid of all the water.

2. Mix the dandelion greens, bacon, French Dressing, and seasonings in a salad bowl and serve.

Salade d'Endive aux Betteraves Rouges
Endive and Beet Salad

SERVES 8 TO 10.

1 *cup shredded beets, cooked or canned*
½ *cup wine vinegar*
2 *tablespoons sugar*
1 *pound fresh Belgian endives*
⅓ *cup Vinaigrette Sauce* (*p.* 20)

1. Marinate the shredded beets in the wine vinegar and sugar for 2 hours.
2. Slice the endives in half and separate the leaves.
3. Drain the beets.
4. Toss together the beets, endives, and the Sauce Vinaigrette. Mix well and serve.

Salade d'Épinards
Spinach Salad

SERVES 4.

1 *pound fresh spinach*
⅓ *cup Vinaigrette Sauce* (*p.* 20)
3 *hard-boiled eggs*
1 *avocado, diced* (*optional*)
2 *large tomatoes, cut into wedges*
2 *small white onions, thinly sliced*

1. Wash the spinach thoroughly to remove the grit. Cut off the stems and slice the leaves into strips. Squeeze out the moisture.
2. Put the spinach in a salad bowl and mix with the Vinaigrette Sauce.

3. Slice the hard-boiled eggs and arrange them on top. Add the avocado if you wish.

4. Garnish with tomato wedges and thinly sliced white onions.

ALTERNATE METHOD: After washing the spinach and removing the stems, plunge the spinach into slightly salted boiling water for 5 or 6 seconds. Remove and quickly drop into cold water. Drain thoroughly and dry in a towel. Then proceed with step 2 in the above recipe.

Salade de Chou-fleur
Cauliflower Salad

SERVES 6.

1 *head cauliflower, boiled in milk and salted water* (p. 288)
¾ *cup French Dressing* (p. 21)
½ *teaspoon salt*
½ *teaspoon freshly ground black pepper*
2 *tablespoons chopped fresh chervil or parsley, or mixture*
   of both
Boston or Bibb lettuce leaves

1. Cook the cauliflower in milk and salted water as directed on p. 288. Drain well and cool.

2. Mix the cooled cauliflower with ¾ cup French Dressing. Season with extra salt and pepper if necessary.

3. Sprinkle with the chervil or parsley and serve on lettuce leaves.

Salade de Haricots Verts à la Vinaigrette
Green String Bean Salad with Vinaigrette Sauce

SERVES 6.

2 *pounds fresh string beans, small and tender*
4 *white onions, sliced very thin*
Vinaigrette Sauce (p. 20) *to taste*
4 *medium-sized tomatoes, sliced*

1. Buy string beans that are fresh looking and firm. If they have

strings, pull them off. Wash the beans and cut off the ends. Blanch them in a large, uncovered kettle of boiling salted water until partly cooked. Strain.

2. Drop the beans into another kettle of boiling water and cook until just tender, but with a slight crunchiness. Drain to remove all traces of water.

3. When cold, toss together the beans, onions, and Vinaigrette Sauce to taste and let marinate for 1 hour.

4. Place the sliced tomatoes on a serving dish and set the string bean salad on top. Serve.

Salade de Légumes
Mixed Vegetable Salad

Peas, string beans, cauliflower, carrots, artichoke bottoms, potatoes, or beets cooked without butter are excellent when combined and mixed with mayonnaise or French dressing. The quantity of each vegetable may vary according to what you have on hand, and which vegetables you like the best. Suit your own taste. Here is one suggested combination.

SERVES 8.

3 *artichoke bottoms, cooked and sliced*
1 *cup cooked fresh peas*
1 *cup cooked and sliced fresh string beans*
1 *cup cooked and diced carrots*
1 *cup cooked and diced potatoes*
½ *cup cooked and shredded beets*
¾ *cup Mayonnaise Sauce (p. 18) or ½ cup French Dressing*
   (p. 21)
2 *hard-boiled eggs, sliced*
2 *tablespoons chopped fresh parsley*
½ *to 1 teaspoon salt*
½ *teaspoon freshly ground black pepper*

1. In a large salad bowl, combine all the cooked vegetables and add the Mayonnaise Sauce or French Dressing. Mix well.

2. Decorate the top of the salad with the slices of hard-boiled egg and sprinkle the parsley on top. Season with additional salt and pepper if necessary.

Salade de Pommes de Terre (Chaude)
Hot Potato Salad

This salad is really a luncheon dish and is delicious when served with hot garlic sausage.

SERVES 4.

6 to 8 medium-sized yellow potatoes
½ cup French Dressing (p. 21)
Salt and freshly ground black pepper
2 tablespoons chopped fresh parsley

1. Boil the potatoes until tender, but still firm. Cool and then peel them. Slice them ½ inch thick.
2. Mix the potatoes with the French Dressing immediately and sprinkle with some salt and pepper and the parsley on top. Serve warm.

Salade de Pommes de Terre (Froide)
Cold Potato Salad

Even for this cold salad, we add the dressing to the potatoes while they are still warm as they absorb the seasonings more easily that way.

SERVES 4.

6 to 8 medium-sized yellow potatoes
6 shallots, minced fine
1 tablespoon French celery seeds
1 cup Mayonnaise Sauce (p. 18)
3 tablespoons chopped fresh parsley
Salt and freshly ground black pepper

1. Cook the potatoes in boiling water until tender, but still firm. Cool slightly and peel off the skins.
2. Slice them ¼ inch thick and mix them with the shallots, celery seeds, Mayonnaise Sauce, and parsley while they are still warm.
3. Taste for seasoning. Serve when the potatoes are cold.

Salade Niçoise
Tomato and Tuna Fish Salad

This salad should be served as a luncheon dish, along with a cheese soufflé or perhaps a *pâte de campagne*. It is quite filling, so it should never accompany a full dinner menu.

SERVES 8.

3 *cups sliced cold boiled potatoes*
3 *cups cold cooked fresh string beans, sliced and cooked without butter*
½ *cup French Dressing (p. 21)*
Salt and pepper to taste
Romaine or Boston lettuce leaves
4 *fresh tomatoes, quartered*
4 *hard-boiled eggs, quartered*
16 *pitted ripe black olives*
1 *7-ounce can white tuna fish, broken into chunks*
12 *anchovy fillets*

1. Mix the potatoes, string beans, and the French Dressing, adding salt and pepper if necessary.
2. Line a salad bowl with leaves of Boston or Romaine lettuce. Place the potatoes and string beans on the leaves and decorate the salad with the tomatoes, eggs, olives, tuna, and anchovies.

Salade à la Mimosa
Mimosa Salad

SERVES 6.

2 *heads Boston lettuce*
6 *hard-boiled eggs*
½ *cup French Dressing (p. 21)*
2 *tablespoons chopped fresh chervil*

½ *to* 1 *teaspoon salt*
½ *teaspoon freshly ground black pepper*

1. Wash the lettuce thoroughly and drain well. Shake to get rid of the excess water.
2. Slice the eggs, approximately 6 slices to each egg.
3. Toss together the lettuce, eggs, French Dressing, and chervil. Season with the salt and pepper. Serve in a deep salad bowl.

Salade d'Oeufs à la Russe
Egg Salad à la Russe

SERVES 6.

1 *large head Boston lettuce*
6 *hard-boiled eggs, cut in halves lengthwise*
1¼ *cups Mayonnaise Sauce (p.* 18)
¼ *cup chili sauce*
1 *tablespoon finely chopped green olives*
1 *tablespoon finely chopped fresh chives*
1 *tablespoon finely chopped fresh parsley*
1 *tablespoon finely chopped shallots*
½ *teaspoon lemon juice*
Dash of Tabasco sauce
Garnish: watercress sprigs

1. Arrange the leaves of Boston lettuce on 6 salad plates with 2 egg halves on each.
2. Mix the Mayonnaise Sauce, chili sauce, olives, chives, parsley, shallots, lemon juice, and Tabasco sauce and spoon over the eggs.
3. Garnish with watercress sprigs.

CHAPTER 16

Desserts

Desserts

Bavarois aux Amandes
Bavarois aux Marrons et Cognac
Bavarois au Café et Cognac
Bavarois au Citron
Bavarois à l'Orange
Bavarois aux Fraises

Coeur à la Crème

Crème Brûlée
Crème Renversée au Caramel
Petits Pots de Crème au Chocolat
Pouding au Caramel et Tapioca

Glace au Cognac, Rhum, ou Kirsch
Glace au Grand Marnier
Glace au Thé Vert

Mousse au Chocolat Monblason

Oeufs à la Neige au Caramel
Profiteroles à la Crème Chantilly
Meringues Glacées aux Fraises

Gâteau de Riz au Caramel
Riz à la Neige

Soufflé Simple à la Vanille
Soufflé au Chocolat Monblason

Soufflé au Café
Soufflé au Citron
Soufflé aux Fruits Confits Monblason
Soufflé aux Prunes Mirabelles
Soufflé de Pruneaux à la Georges Balanchine

Gâteau de Crème au Chocolat
Gâteau de Fruits à l'Anniversaire
Gâteau Génois au Moka

Pâte Ordinaire
Pâte Sucrée
Tarte aux Pommes à l'Abricot
Tarte aux Pommes à la Vosgienne
Tarte au Citron avec Amandes
Tarte aux Pêches à l'Abricot
Tarte aux Prunes à l'Abricot
Tarte au Fromage Frais
Gâteau de Fromage à la Village

Crêpes Suzette
Crêpes aux Pêches Monblason
Gaufres à la Française

Macédoine de Fruits Rafraîchis au Kirsch
Macédoine de Fruits Rafraîchis au Champagne
Pommes Cuites au Miel
Pommes Cuites à la Grand-mère
Pommes Cuites Monblason
Charlotte de Pommes
Melon au Porto
Poires Belle Hélène

Once the initial hunger of your guests has been satisfied, you have to be careful that your attempt at a complete culinary success is not destroyed by that last sweet touch.

You should try to plan your dessert course according to what you served in the first part of the meal. If you have served rather heavy, rich food, stay away from desserts like plum pudding, which are filling themselves. A fruit tart, baked apple, or some fine sherbet would certainly be a better conclusion to such a meal. On the other hand, a light luncheon or dinner might be topped off with a chocolate mousse, a Bavarian cream, or a rich cake, and your guests will have sufficient appetite to savor them. Of course, any meal can be concluded with cheese or fruit.

Following is a variety of dessert recipes, some of them quite original and rarely served in restaurants. The mousses, Bavarian creams, pastries, and puddings can all be prepared well ahead of time, but others, such as the soufflés and Crepes Suzette, must have the final touch when your guests are at the table. Don't let these last-minute preparations worry you; just be relaxed and informal. A little informality at the end of a meal, like the ten-minute wait for the soufflé, or watching the hostess nervously flame the crepes, adds to the fun of the evening.

Using Liqueurs in Dessert Recipes

Grand Marnier, curaçao, rum, crème de menthe, kirsch, and cognac are the most frequently used liqueurs in dessert recipes. In certain dishes like Crepes Suzette, Baked Alaska, and Cherries Jubilee, the liqueurs need to be flamed. By doing this you get just the flavor of the liqueur, not the alcohol. For fruit salads that can be served as either appetizers or desserts, the liqueurs or wines are added to the recipe straight from the bottle.

Fromages
Cheese

I am a cheese lover. I recall one of my earliest cheese-eating experiences when I was about five years old and living on the outskirts of Paris. One day my parents invited some friends for dinner. My mother bought a magnificent Camembert, and let it stand as one should, on a serving table at room temperature. Attracted by the enticing aroma of the cheese, I got hold of the Camembert, and without the help of any bread ate the whole magnificent wheel of ambrosia. I disposed of the box and wrappings through the window. That was pure carelessness, for my father who was coming home saw the proof of my delinquency. I do not remember the spanking I received, but the taste of that wonderful Camembert is still with me, just as the love of cheese will stay with me as long as I can eat.

Happily for the gourmet, the memories of good meals linger a long time after the last bite. Unhappily, the opposite is also true. After a mediocre lunch or dinner I try my best to forget the mistakes of a careless chef by ordering some cheese, particularly if the wine I ordered is of excellent vintage. The wine, good cheese, and a piece of hard-crusted bread are enough to provide me with a certain pleasure and improve the impression of the meal.

There is an air of romance attached to the history of cheese. I like to read how certain cheeses were manufactured for the first time, even if the stories are not always completely true. I have heard about the shepherd who inadvertently was the first to discover Roquefort cheese after leaving a crust of bread with some cheese on it in a cave near the little town of Roquefort in France. When he returned to the cave some weeks later, he found that the poor cheese he had left in the cave had changed to a delicacy. The cave was the right place for that phenomenon. In 1968, I traveled hundreds of miles to visit the largest cheese factory at Roquefort, and I was not surprised to see how the factory was built into the mountain. I asked many questions about the fissures in the rock, the molds, the milk from ewes, and how they came to make a cheese so rare in flavor and so beautifully veined with blue.

Monks are clever at making excellent cheeses. One of them is Port-Salut, which has been so poorly duplicated by many manufacturers in other countries. If you travel through France, try some of the goat's cheese called Chèvre, the incomparable Brie, or if you go for a strong-flavored cheese, have a ripe Pont l'Évêque. Or take a chance on the Livarot. I love Muenster, Reblochon, Boursin, and Triple-Crème. For cooking, Swiss Gruyère cheese will do wonders for you in soufflés, sauces, au gratin dishes, or even plain with a hard roll as a sandwich.

Great assortments of French cheeses are imported into the United States. Unfortunately, some of them reach us too ripe or too dry because of poor handling or sitting too long in the store. In addition, government regulations forbid the importation of unpasteurized cheese. Pasteurization is detrimental to the taste of good cheese, but is indispensable for our health as a safeguard against germs. In some cases, additives or preservatives have been added to certain cheeses to prevent ammoniating and to keep them in the stores longer without spoiling.

Once you have selected a good cheese, you should inquire from the storekeeper how and when it should be served. As a general rule, cheese should not be frozen. Certain cheeses, like goat cheese, do not keep too long. Others take time before they reach their peak of flavor. For each type of cheese you serve, be sure to find out the correct age and temperature at which it should be eaten.

Bavarois
Bavarian Cream

A Bavarian cream is actually a flavored custard which contains gelatin to give it firmness and whipped cream and beaten egg whites to give it lightness. It can be chocolate, vanilla, lemon, orange, strawberry, chestnut, or almond, to name just a few flavors. If you have a keen taste for sweets and some imagination, you can make Bavarian creams in practically any flavor.

The basic technique is to cook the eggs and milk in the top of a double boiler until they have thickened into a soft custard. Then the flavoring and gelatin are added. The custard is refrigerated to set, *but it must not set too firmly, or it will get lumpy later.* Meanwhile, the egg whites must be beaten and the heavy cream whipped. When the custard is just the right consistency (and experience will help you judge this), you fold in the egg whites and whipped cream. Bavarian creams can be frozen and defrosted without impairing the taste or the texture.

The Bavarian-cream recipes that follow were developed for my guests at Monblason. They loved them. I hope you do too.

BAVARIAN CREAM.

Bavarois aux Amandes
Almond Bavarian Cream

SERVES 10 TO 12.

2 *tablespoons sweet butter for molds*
24 *ladyfingers*
½ *cup cold milk*
2 *envelopes unflavored gelatin*
6 *egg yolks*
2 *tablespoons sugar*
1 *pint milk, scalded*

1 8-*ounce can imported almond paste*
½ *cup hot milk*
1 *tablespoon vanilla extract*
6 *egg whites*
⅛ *teaspoon cream of tartar*
2 *tablespoons superfine sugar*
1½ *cups heavy cream, whipped*
Toasted slivered almonds for garnish

1. Grease 3 4-cup molds with the butter. Line them with lady-fingers and place them in the refrigerator.

2. Pour the ½ cup cold milk into a large bowl and sprinkle on the gelatin to soften.

3. Combine the egg yolks, sugar, and milk in the top of a double boiler and cook over simmering water until the mixture thickens enough to coat a spoon. This is called English Custard. Stir constantly and do not let it boil.

4. Blend the almond paste with the ½ cup hot milk. With a wire whisk, add the dissolved almond paste to the English Custard and blend until smooth.

5. Pour the hot almond mixture over the softened gelatin and stir to blend. Add the vanilla. Set in the refrigerator.

6. As soon as the mixture starts to set, beat the egg whites with the cream of tartar until stiff but not dry. When the whites are almost stiff, add the superfine sugar. Have the whipped cream ready.

7. Very gently, fold the whipped cream and the egg whites alternately into the almond custard, which is partly set.

8. Pour the mixture into the refrigerated molds and chill until firm. Unmold by dipping the molds quickly into hot water and turn out onto chilled serving platters. Garnish with toasted slivered almonds on top.

Bavarois aux Marrons et Cognac
Chestnut Bavarian Cream with Brandy

SERVES 10 TO 12.

2 *tablespoons sweet butter for molds*
24 *ladyfingers*
½ *cup cold water*

2 *envelopes unflavored gelatin*
6 *egg yolks*
2 *tablespoons sugar*
1 *pint of milk, scalded*
1-*pound* 1-*ounce can imported sweetened chestnut puree*
1 *teaspoon vanilla extract*
5 *tablespoons brandy, rum, or Grand Marnier*
6 *egg whites*
⅛ *teaspoon cream of tartar*
3 *tablespoons superfine sugar*
1½ *cups heavy cream, whipped*
Garnish: chestnuts in brandied syrup (*available in gourmet*
shops)

1. Grease 3 4-cup molds with the butter. Line them with ladyfingers and place them in the refrigerator.

2. Put the cold water into a large bowl and sprinkle the gelatin over it to soften.

3. Combine the egg yolks, sugar, and milk and cook in the top of a double boiler over simmering water until the mixture thickens enough to coat a spoon. This is called English Custard. Stir constantly and do not let it boil.

4. Blend the softened gelatin into the hot custard with a wire whisk.

5. Now, stir in the chestnut puree, vanilla, and brandy or other liquor and stir with the whisk to make the mixture completely smooth and free of lumps. Refrigerate.

6. As soon as the mixture starts to set, beat the egg whites with the cream of tartar until stiff but not dry. When the whites are almost stiff, add the superfine sugar. Have the whipped cream ready.

7. Very gently, fold the whipped cream and the egg whites alternately into the chestnut custard, which is partly set.

8. Pour the mixture into the refrigerated molds and chill until firm. Unmold by dipping the molds quickly into hot water and turn out onto chilled serving platters. Garnish with whole chestnuts in brandied syrup.

Bavarois au Café et Cognac
Coffee Brandy Bavarian Cream

SERVES 10 TO 12.

2 *tablespoons sweet butter for molds*
24 *ladyfingers*
1½ *envelopes unflavored gelatin*
½ *cup cold water*
6 *egg yolks*
¾ *cup sugar*
1 *tablespoon cornstarch*
1½ *cups boiling milk*
4 *tablespoons powdered instant coffee*
½ *cup brandy*
1 *tablespoon vanilla extract*
6 *egg whites*
⅛ *teaspoon cream of tartar*
3 *tablespoons superfine sugar*
1½ *cups heavy cream, whipped*
Garnish: toasted slivered almonds

1. Grease 3 4-cup molds with the butter. Line with ladyfingers and refrigerate.

2. Sprinkle the gelatin over the cold water. Set aside to soften for a few minutes.

3. Place the egg yolks in the top of a double boiler. Beat them well.

4. Mix together the sugar and the cornstarch. Add them to the egg yolks and beat again.

5. Add the boiling milk to the yolks, a little at a time, stirring with a wooden spoon. Cook over moderate heat so that the water in the bottom of the double boiler just simmers. Keep on stirring until the sauce starts to coat the spoon. Do not let it boil, or it will curdle. Add the instant coffee and stir.

6. Add the softened gelatin to the coffee custard and mix well. Be sure it is completely dissolved. Set aside to cool, then refrigerate.

7. When the custard is cold, but not yet set, add the brandy and vanilla and set back in the refrigerator.

8. As soon as the mixture starts to set, beat the egg whites with the cream of tartar until stiff but not dry. When the whites are almost stiff, add the superfine sugar. Have the whipped cream ready.

9. Blend the whipped cream alternately with the beaten egg whites into the coffee-brandy custard until well incorporated. Pour into the buttered molds and refrigerate for 4 to 6 hours. Garnish with toasted slivered almonds.

Bavarois au Citron
Lemon Bavarian Cream

SERVES 10 TO 12.

2 *tablespoons sweet butter for molds*
24 *ladyfingers*
2 *envelopes unflavored gelatin*
⅓ *cup cold water*
6 *egg yolks*
¼ *teaspoon salt*
¾ *cup superfine sugar*
1½ *cups milk, scalded*
1 *tablespoon vanilla extract*
1 *5¾-ounce can frozen reconstituted lemon juice*
1 *teaspoon lemon extract*
6 *egg whites*
⅛ *teaspoon cream of tartar*
1½ *cups heavy cream, whipped*
Garnishes: fresh or frozen strawberry sauce or canned rasp-
    berries, flavored to taste with liqueur

1. Butter 3 4-cup molds. Line with ladyfingers and refrigerate.
2. Soften the gelatin in the cold water.
3. Combine the egg yolks, salt, 6 tablespoons of the sugar, and the milk in the top of a double boiler and cook over simmering water until the mixture thickens enough to coat a spoon. This is called English Custard. Stir constantly and do not let it boil.
4. Add the softened gelatin to the hot English Custard and stir until completely dissolved. Cool the custard.
5. When cool, stir in the vanilla, lemon juice, and lemon extract. Place the mixture in the refrigerator.

6. As soon as the lemon mixture begins to set, beat the egg whites stiff with the cream of tartar and 6 more tablespoons sugar. Have the whipped cream ready.

7. Very gently, fold the whipped cream and egg whites alternately into the custard. Turn into the prepared mold and chill until firm.

8. Unmold by dipping into hot water very quickly and turn out onto a chilled platter. Garnish with fresh or frozen strawberry sauce or with canned raspberries, flavored with liqueur.

Bavarois à l'Orange
Orange Bavarian Cream

SERVES 12 TO 14.

2 tablespoons sweet butter for molds
24 ladyfingers
2 envelopes unflavored gelatin
½ cup cold water
8 egg yolks
6 tablespoons superfine sugar
¼ teaspoon salt
2 cups milk, scalded
1 12-ounce can frozen concentrated orange juice
1 tablespoon vanilla extract
1 teaspoon orange extract
8 egg whites
¼ teaspoon cream of tartar
2 cups heavy cream, whipped
Garnish: canned Mandarin oranges or fresh oranges with
      Grand Marnier or other orange liqueur

1. Butter 4 4-cup molds. Line them with ladyfingers and place in the refrigerator.

2. Sprinkle the gelatin over the cold water to soften.

3. Combine the egg yolks, 2 tablespoons of the sugar, the salt, and the milk in the top of a double boiler and cook over simmering water until the mixture thickens enough to coat a spoon. This is called English Custard. Stir constantly and do not let it boil.

4. Add the softened gelatin to the hot custard, stirring to dissolve. Let cool.

5. When cool, add the defrosted orange juice, the vanilla, and the orange extract. Set in the refrigerator.

6. As soon as the gelatin mixture starts to set, beat the egg whites with the remaining 4 tablespoons of sugar and the cream of tartar until stiff, but not dry. Have the whipped cream ready.

7. Very gently, fold the whipped cream and egg whites into the orange mixture. Turn into prepared molds and chill until firm.

8. Unmold by dipping the molds quickly into hot water and turning out onto chilled platters. Garnish with a fruit sauce of canned Mandarin oranges or sliced fresh oranges, flavored with Grand Marnier or other orange liqueur.

Bavarois aux Fraises
Strawberry Bavarian Cream

SERVES 10 TO 12.

2 *tablespoons sweet butter for molds*
24 *ladyfingers*
1 *1-pound package frozen strawberries in syrup*
1 *envelope unflavored gelatin*
¼ *cup cold water*
¼ *cup boiling water*
1 *3-ounce package wild-strawberry-flavored gelatin*
6 *egg yolks*
¼ *teaspoon salt*
6 *tablespoons superfine sugar*
1½ *cups milk, scalded*
1 *tablespoon vanilla extract*
6 *egg whites*
⅛ *teaspoon cream of tartar*
1½ *cups heavy cream, whipped*
Garnish: frozen strawberries, defrosted in their syrup,
or in season, fresh sugared strawberries with orange
or strawberry liqueur

1. Butter 3 4-cup molds. Line with ladyfingers and refrigerate.

2. Defrost the strawberries. Puree them in the blender with their syrup.

3. Sprinkle the unflavored gelatin over the cold water and let it soften.

4. Pour the boiling water over the wild-strawberry-flavored gelatin and stir to dissolve.

5. Combine the egg yolks, salt, 2 tablespoons of the sugar, and the milk in the top of a double boiler and cook over simmering water until the mixture thickens enough to coat a spoon. This is called English Custard. Stir constantly and do not let it boil.

6. Add the softened unflavored gelatin to the custard and let it cool.

7. When cool, stir in the strawberry puree, the wild-strawberry mixture, and the vanilla. Refrigerate.

8. As soon as the strawberry mixture starts to set, beat the egg whites with the cream of tartar and the remaining 4 tablespoons of sugar until stiff but not dry. Have the whipped cream ready.

9. Very gently, fold the whipped cream and egg whites alternately into the strawberry custard. Turn into the prepared molds and chill until firm.

10. Unmold by dipping the molds quickly into hot water and turning out onto chilled serving platters. Garnish with frozen strawberries in syrup or fresh strawberries with liqueur.

Coeur à la Crème
Cream Heart

It is best to make this in a heart-shaped mold. Unmold it on a round platter with fresh strawberries around it. It is also delicious with a strawberry or raspberry sauce passed separately. It looks like a Valentine's Day special.

SERVES 8.

1 *cup heavy cream*
1¼ *envelopes unflavored gelatin*
⅓ *cup cold water*
8 *ounces small-curd cottage cheese*
1 *3-ounce package cream cheese*
¼ *cup light cream*
½ *cup superfine sugar*
½ *cup boiling milk*

1. Chill 2 3-cup heart-shaped molds in the refrigerator.

2. In a small mixing bowl whip the heavy cream until it is firm. Refrigerate.

3. In a small dish, sprinkle the gelatin over the cold water to soften it.

4. In a large mixing bowl, start beating together the cottage cheese, cream cheese, light cream, and sugar until well blended.

5. Add the boiling milk to the softened gelatin. Mix well to dissolve the gelatin completely. Heat the gelatin and the milk together for

COEUR À LA CRÈME.

1 to 2 minutes to be sure it is dissolved. Add to the cheese mixture and mix well.

6. Place in the refrigerator until it starts to set or jell. Then blend in the whipped cream. Pour into the molds and keep in the refrigerator several hours or until they are ready to unmold.

Crème Brûlée
Crème Brûlée

The baking of the custard for Crème Brûlée can be done the day before, and the dessert completed an hour or so before you need it.

When you serve it at the table, pour good French brandy over the top. It is very rich, but so delicious.

SERVES 4.

5 *egg yolks*
2 *cups heavy cream, scalded*
¼ *cup superfine sugar*
1 *tablespoon vanilla extract*
Dark brown sugar
½ *cup French brandy*

1. Beat the egg yolks together with the cream. Add the sugar and vanilla and beat until blended. Preheat the oven to 400°.
2. Pour the mixture into a shallow Pyrex baking dish. Place the dish in a large baking pan with enough hot water to come about ½ way up the sides of the dish.
3. Reduce the oven temperature to 300° and bake for about 1 hour or until a knife inserted into the center comes out clean. Refrigerate overnight.
4. About 1 to 2 hours before you wish to serve the Brûlée, take it out of the refrigerator and spread it evenly with a layer of dark brown sugar ⅛- to ¼-inch thick. Set the dish under a very hot broiler, but not so close that the sugar will readily burn. Watch the melting of the sugar very carefully, and as soon as it gets to be crusty and dark, remove it. It should be very slightly burned, but not too crisp. Return it to the refrigerator for about 1 hour.
5. When you are ready to serve it, bring it to the table and pour the brandy over it.

Crème Renversée au Caramel
Baked Caramel Custard

This easy-to-do French custard is a delicious dessert, light and not too rich. The secret of a good custard is to be certain the water in the pan never boils so the custard does not get overcooked.

SERVES 8.

1 *cup granulated sugar*
½ *cup water*

8 *eggs*
1 *quart milk*
10 *tablespoons sugar*
2 *tablespoons vanilla extract*

1. In a preheated 300° oven, place a 9- x 12- x 2½-inch baking pan filled with 1¼ inches of water.

2. Combine the cup of sugar and the water in a saucepan. Cook until it is syrupy and turns to a medium brown. Remove from stove.

3. Pour this caramel into a 2-quart Pyrex baking dish and coat the sides and bottom with it by rotating the dish. In cooling, the caramel will stick to the dish.

CRÈME RENVERSÉE
AU CARAMEL.

4. In a large mixing bowl, beat the eggs thoroughly.

5. In a pot bring the milk to a boil together with the 10 tablespoons of sugar. Be sure the sugar is completely melted.

6. Beat the milk into the eggs, a little at a time. Then add the vanilla.

7. Pour into the caramel-lined Pyrex dish. Place the dish in the pan of hot water already in the oven. Bake for approximately 1 hour, or until a knife inserted into the center comes out clean.

8. Chill until ready to serve and then run a knife around the edge of the dish to loosen. Unmold onto a large platter that has a rim to catch the caramel sauce.

Petits Pots de Crème au Chocolat
Chocolate Pots de Crème

SERVES 6 TO 8.

2 *cups plus* 2 *tablespoons light or medium cream*
4 *squares semi-sweet baking chocolate*
6 *egg yolks*
5 *tablespoons superfine sugar*
⅛ *teaspoon salt*
1 *tablespoon vanilla extract*
Garnish: whipped cream or toasted slivered almonds

1. Heat the 2 cups of cream in the top of a double boiler.
2. Add the chocolate and stir until the 2 ingredients are thoroughly blended.
3. In a mixing bowl, beat the egg yolks until light and lemon colored.
4. Gradually beat in the sugar and salt, plus the extra 2 tablespoons of cream and the vanilla extract.
5. Little by little, pour in the hot chocolate mixture, stirring until blended.
6. Pour the mixture into little pot de crème cups or regular custard cups and place them in a baking pan. Pour hot water around the cups to reach ½ way up the sides. Cover the pan with aluminum foil and place in a preheated 325° oven. The water in the pan should barely simmer while the little pots de crème are baking. Bake for 25 to 30 minutes, or until a knife inserted into the center comes out clean. Cool and then chill in the refrigerator.
7. Serve topped with whipped cream or toasted slivered almonds.

Pouding au Caramel et Tapioca
Caramel Tapioca Pudding

SERVES 6.

1 *cup granulated sugar*
½ *cup water*

2 *tablespoons instant tapioca*
2½ *cups milk, scalded*
½ *cup granulated sugar*
¼ *teaspoon salt*
1 *tablespoon vanilla extract*
3 *whole eggs, beaten well*

1. Cook the sugar and water until caramelized into a medium-brown color.

2. Pour into a baking dish and rotate the dish to spread the caramel on the sides and bottom.

3. Place the tapioca, milk, and sugar in the top of a double boiler and cook until the tapioca becomes transparent.

4. Add the salt and vanilla.

5. Add the mixture to the eggs and then pour into the baking dish.

6. Place the baking dish into a pan with hot water coming ½ way up the sides of the dish.

7. Bake in a preheated 300° oven until done, approximately 40 minutes.

8. Chill until ready to serve. Then run a knife along the outside of the dish to loosen the pudding and unmold onto a large platter with a rim to catch the caramel sauce.

Glaces
Ice Creams

The old-fashioned way of making homemade ice cream is practically obsolete since commercial ice creams have become so easy to get and keep due to the presence of freezers in nearly every kitchen. Making ice cream in the ice-cube trays of a freezer will never take the place of the old-fashioned crank freezer. It takes some churning to make a smooth and delicious ice cream. Perhaps you can find an old ice-cream pail in the attic.

Glace au Cognac, Rhum, ou Kirsch
Brandy, Rum, or Kirsch Ice Cream

MAKES 3 QUARTS.

10 *egg yolks*
1½ *cups granulated sugar*
1 *quart light cream, scalded*
¼ *teaspoon salt*
½ *cup or more brandy, rum, or kirsch*
Rum-soaked raisins (*optional for rum ice cream*)

1. Beat the egg yolks with the sugar in the top of a double boiler. Add the cream and salt.

2. Cook over hot water, stirring constantly, until the mixture has slightly thickened and coats the spoon. Cool the mixture.

3. Stir in the brandy, rum, or kirsch, adding more to taste if desired. If you are making rum ice cream, you might wish to add some rum-soaked raisins.

4. Churn in an ice-cream pail according to directions. If you are using ice-cube trays in the freezer, whip the mixture several times during the freezing to keep it smooth.

Glace au Grand Marnier
Grand Marnier Ice Cream

Prepare as you do Brandy, Rum, or Kirsch Ice Cream but use ½ cup or more of Grand Marnier, and decrease the sugar to 1⅓ cups.

Glace au Thé Vert
Green Tea Ice Cream

When traveling through Japan in 1971, I tasted Green Tea Ice Cream for the first time. It was a delicious introduction to something new and different, and with the help of friends, this recipe was smuggled out of Japan for your pleasure.

MAKES 5 TO 6 PINTS.

8 *egg yolks*
1⅓ *cups granulated sugar*
1 *quart light cream, scalded, or 2 cups milk and 2 cups heavy cream, scalded*
¼ *teaspoon salt*
2 *teaspoons* Matcha *bright-colored, powdered tea,* dissolved in ½ cup hot water (stir well to get rid of all lumps)*

1. Beat the egg yolks with the sugar in the top of a double boiler. Add the cream, salt, and the dissolved green tea.
2. Cook, stirring constantly, until the mixture has slightly thickened and coats the spoon.
3. Freeze in an ice-cream churner according to directions. If you are using ice-cube trays in the refrigerator, stir the mixture a few times during the freezing process to help keep it smooth.

Mousse au Chocolat Monblason
Chocolate Mousse Monblason

SERVES 12.

2 *tablespoons sweet butter for molds*
24 *ladyfingers*
4 *squares semi-sweet baking chocolate*
1 *square unsweetened baking chocolate*
⅔ *cup plus 3 tablespoons superfine sugar*
2 *tablespoons powdered instant coffee*
⅓ *cup warm water*
2 *cups heavy cream*
¾ *cup sweet butter*
8 *egg yolks*

* This tea was used for the tea ceremony in Japan.

6 *egg whites*
Pinch cream of tartar
Garnish: ½ *cup toasted slivered almonds*

1. Butter 3 4-cup molds. Line them with the ladyfingers and place in the refrigerator.
2. Melt the chocolate in a double boiler. Add the ⅔ cup of sugar and blend in the instant coffee and the water. Cool.
3. Whip the cream and refrigerate.
4. Cream the butter with an electric mixer. Add the egg yolks, 1 at a time.
5. When the chocolate mixture cools and begins to stiffen, stir it into the egg yolk and butter combination.
6. Beat the egg whites with the cream of tartar. When they start to get stiff, add the 3 tablespoons of sugar and continue to beat until stiff but not dry.
7. Alternately blend the whipped cream and the stiffly beaten egg whites into the chocolate. Pour into the prepared refrigerated molds and either refrigerate or freeze. If you freeze the mousse, the mold has to be taken out of the freezer 6 hours before serving time and put into the refrigerator. Place your platter and plates in the refrigerator, especially in the summertime. When you unmold the mousse, garnish with toasted slivered almonds.

NOTE: To toast slivered almonds, place them in a 350° oven on a cookie sheet for about 10 minutes, stirring them around several times.

Oeufs à la Neige au Caramel
Snow Eggs with Caramel Sauce

SERVES 6.

2 *cups milk*
1 *tablespoon vanilla extract*
¼ *cup granulated sugar*
6 *egg whites*
3 *tablespoons granulated sugar*
6 *egg yolks*

⅓ *cup granulated sugar for caramel*
2 *tablespoons water*

Snow Eggs

1. Heat the milk in the top of a double boiler over hot water until it is scalded. Add the vanilla and the ¼ cup of sugar.

2. Beat the egg whites until they start forming peaks. Gradually add the 3 tablespoons of sugar and continue beating until the eggs are stiff, or of meringue consistency.

OEUFS A LA NEIGE
AU CARAMEL.

3. With a large spoon, take as much of the meringue mixture as the spoon will hold and drop spoonful by spoonful into the hot milk. Only do a few spoonfuls at a time. Cook the mounds of egg whites very gently for 2 minutes, not letting the milk boil. Turn them over and cook for 2 more minutes. Remove the meringues to a cake rack to drain and repeat the operation until all the meringue has been used.

4. Strain the milk and reserve it.

Custard Sauce

1. Beat the egg yolks well and put them in the top of a double boiler.

2. Add the leftover strained milk, adding enough fresh milk to make 2 full cups. Cook over simmering water, stirring constantly, until the mixture thickens enough to coat the spoon.

3. Cool rapidly by putting the top of the double boiler into ice water. Stir until the soft custard sauce is cool. Strain if the custard is at all lumpy. Set in the refrigerator.

Caramel Sauce

1. When you are almost ready to serve, make the caramel sauce. Put ⅓ cup granulated sugar into a saucepan with 2 tablespoons of water. Cook over moderately high heat, stirring until the sugar is melted.
2. Continue cooking until the water has evaporated and the sugar takes on a light brown color.
3. Fill a glass or crystal bowl with the Custard Sauce. Gently float the meringues on top of the Custard Sauce and trickle the caramel over the meringues.

Profiteroles à la Crème Chantilly
Cream Puffs with Crème Chantilly

MAKES 30 CREAM PUFFS.

1 *recipe Cream Puffs* (*p.* 38)
1 *cup heavy cream*
1½ *tablespoons superfine sugar*
2 *tablespoons Grand Marnier*
½ *cup Caramel Sauce* (*see above*)

1. Prepare the Cream Puffs according to the recipe on pp. 38–39, making them a little larger, so you will have approximately 30 instead of 50 tiny ones. Bake in a preheated 375° oven for 35 to 40 minutes, or until puffed and brown. Then slit the side of each with a sharp knife and let them stand in the turned-off oven for another 10 minutes to allow the insides to dry out.
2. Beat the cream until it stands in soft peaks. Add the sugar and Grand Marnier and beat ½ minute longer. Do not overbeat, or the cream will separate.
3. When the puffs are cool, make a small hole in the base of each one. Fill a pastry bag with the cream mixture and insert the tube into each puff. Fill the puffs.
4. Make a Caramel Sauce according to the recipe above. Dip the tops of the puffs lightly into the syrup. Let cool.
5. Arrange on a platter and keep cool in the refrigerator.

Meringues Glacées aux Fraises
Meringues with Ice Cream and Strawberry Sauce

This recipe is for meringue baskets to be filled with ice cream, fruit sauce, and whipped cream, or for oval or round meringues to be used for "sandwiches" of ice cream, garnished with fruit sauce and whipped cream. In addition to the classic vanilla ice cream and strawberry sauce, you can use a great many flavors of ice cream and sauces. These crispy meringues are different from the toppings we are used to seeing in this country on Lemon Meringue Pie and Baked Alaska.

MAKES 18 TO 24.

6 *egg whites*
¼ *teaspoon salt*
¼ *teaspoon cream of tartar*
1½ *cups superfine sugar*
1 *teaspoon vanilla extract*
Garnishes: vanilla ice cream, fresh or frozen whole straw-
berries, whipped cream

1. Let the egg whites stand at room temperature for a while in a mixing bowl.
2. Add the salt and cream of tartar and beat well with an electric mixer at high speed.
3. When the whites get frothy and are stiff enough to hold their shape, beat in the sugar gradually, 3 tablespoons at a time, beating continually while incorporating it.
4. Add the vanilla and continue the beating until the whites look glossy and stand in stiff but not dry peaks. This is extremely important.
5. Cover a baking sheet with lightly buttered waxed paper. Using a pastry bag or large spoon, shape the meringue into the desired form. If you use a pastry bag, it is easy to make the meringue into a basket. First, you make a circle of meringue about ⅜ inch thick and 3 inches in diameter. Then you pipe a border to a height of 1¼ to 1½ inches all around the circle. If you use a large spoon, shape the meringue into large round or oval mounds.
6. Bake in a preheated 225° oven until firm and dry, approximately 1 hour. Watch the meringues carefully during the baking to be sure they do not begin to take on a brown color. If the meringues look

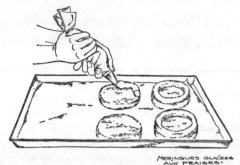

MERINGUES GLACÉES
AUX FRAISES

as if they are beginning to brown, open the oven door and turn down the heat a bit. When the meringues are done, turn off the heat and leave them in the oven for another 15 minutes.

7. When the meringues are cold, the baskets can be filled with vanilla ice cream and topped with strawberry sauce made from fresh or frozen whole or sliced berries, and whipped cream flavored with sugar and vanilla. The round or oval meringues can be used to "sandwich" a scoop of ice cream and can be garnished with a few tablespoons of sauce and some whipped cream.

NOTE: If you wish to keep the unfilled meringues for use at a later date, you can store them in a tightly covered container.

Desserts au Riz
Rice Desserts

Many delicious desserts can be made with rice. In making these desserts, the rice must be cooked properly so that each grain is separate and tender. I recommend using a long-grain converted rice which is parboiled but not precooked. It is not an instant rice preparation. It has been prepared by its processor to retain its natural vitamins and flavor, without your having to soak the rice or discard the cooking liquid. Using this type of rice, with slow cooking and the right amount of liquid, you will get the proper result—tender and separate grains with which to make a tempting dessert.

Gâteau de Riz au Caramel
Rice Cake with Caramel Sauce

SERVES 6 TO 8.

2 *cups granulated sugar*
¼ *cup water*
1½ *cups uncooked, converted, long-grain rice*
1½ *teaspoons salt*
3 *cups boiling water*
4 *tablespoons sweet butter*
6 *large eggs*
4 *cups light cream, scalded*
1 *cup granulated sugar*
1½ *tablespoons vanilla extract*

1. In a heavy saucepan, cook the 2 cups sugar with the ¼ cup water until you reach a candy consistency and the color starts to get light brown. Be careful not to let the sugar burn.

2. When the color reaches a medium brown, remove the pan from the stove and pour the caramel into a 2½-quart round Pyrex baking dish, rotating the dish around so that the sides and bottom are evenly coated with the caramel. In cooling, the caramel will stick to the dish. Set aside.

3. Add the converted rice and salt to the boiling water in a large saucepan. Cover and simmer over moderately low heat until all the water is absorbed, approximately 20 to 30 minutes. Remove from the stove and stir in the butter.

4. Beat the eggs in a large mixing bowl. A little at a time, add the cream, sugar, and vanilla.

5. Stop the beating. With a large spoon, incorporate the rice into the egg-cream mixture.

6. Transfer the mixture into the caramelized baking dish. Set into a shallow baking pan ½ filled with hot water and bake in a preheated 300° oven until the mixture is set, about 1 hour. When the cake is ready, a knife inserted into the center of the rice should come out clean.

7. Cool. When cold, unmold onto a round platter with a rim to catch the surplus caramel sauce.

Riz à la Neige
Snow Rice

SERVES 4 TO 6.

1 *cup uncooked, converted, long-grain rice*
1 *tablespoon salt*
2½ *cups boiling water*
3 *tablespoons sweet butter*
¼ *cup granulated sugar*
1½ *cups light cream*
1½ *teaspoons vanilla extract*
2 *cups heavy cream*
3 *teaspoons superfine sugar*

1. Add the rice and salt to the boiling water. Cover and simmer over moderately low heat until all the water is absorbed, approximately 20 to 30 minutes.

2. Transfer the rice to a 1½-quart baking dish. Stir in the butter. Add the sugar, light cream, and 1 teaspoon of the vanilla and mix well.

3. Cover the dish and set it into a shallow roasting pan with hot water coming ½ way up the sides of the dish.

4. Bake in a preheated 325° oven until all the cream has been absorbed, approximately 45 minutes. The rice grains should be tender and well separated. Let the rice cool in the baking dish with the cover on.

5. Meanwhile, whip the cream with the superfine sugar until it holds its shape but is not stiff. Add ½ teaspoon of the vanilla.

6. When the rice is cold, fold in the whipped cream and serve the pudding in individual glass bowls.

Soufflés
Soufflés

The mystique of the soufflé has discouraged many amateur cooks from attempting one. Actually, the making of a good soufflé is really quite easy, and with a little experimentation, almost everyone can be successful at it. The base for any soufflé can be prepared about 2 hours before serving. Then, the beaten egg whites can be added just before putting the soufflé into the oven. The most important factor is to use an oven that has a constant, reliable temperature. The ingredients will do the rest. The whites of egg beaten stiffly make the soufflé rise to glorious heights, and the flour keeps the whole thing in place until it is eaten.

The French do not bake their soufflés as long as the Americans do. They prefer a softer center. I always bake my soufflés using the French method: 375 to 400° for the first five minutes, then down to 325 to 350° for the remainder of the baking. It is hard to pinpoint the exact time that the soufflé is ready to be taken out of the oven. One look at it and I know whether it is done or not. That intuition will come after you make soufflés for a while. The general guideline for a two-quart mold is approximately 25 to 35 minutes, and for a three-quart, 35 to 40 minutes, depending on how soft or firm you prefer your soufflé to be.

Some chefs place the soufflé dish in a pan of hot water and bake it at a constant 325° for approximately an hour. It bakes like a pudding

. SOUFFLÉ .

and comes out quite firm. You can test it by inserting a knife into the center, and if it comes out clean, then the soufflé is done.

If you are able to buy organic eggs, I think you will find that your egg whites mount so high that your soufflés will rise at least two inches above the rim of the dish.

Soufflé Simple à la Vanille
Basic Vanilla Soufflé

This is the basic recipe for all dessert soufflés. It can be served just as it is with a sauce of strawberries, raspberries, or chocolate. With a little practice, you can add your own flavors to make chocolate, coffee, lemon, strawberry, or liqueur-based soufflés. The flavorings are added before the egg whites are folded in.

SERVES 6 TO 8.

4 *tablespoons sweet butter*
4 *tablespoons flour*
1½ *cups milk, scalded*
½ *cup superfine sugar*
5 *egg yolks*
2½ *tablespoons vanilla extract*
8 *egg whites*
3 *tablespoons superfine sugar*

1. In a saucepan, melt the butter. Add the flour and cook together for a few minutes, making sure not to let the mixture get brown.
2. Gradually add the scalded milk, cooking and stirring until you have a smooth white sauce.
3. Add the ½ cup of sugar and stir until dissolved in the sauce. Cool the sauce.
4. When the mixture is fairly cool, add the egg yolks, stirring well, and then add the vanilla.
5. Beat the egg whites stiff, but not dry, with an electric mixer. Add the 3 tablespoons of sugar and beat for 1 minute more.
6. Fold the egg whites gently into the vanilla sauce. Pour the mixture into a well-buttered 2½- to 3-quart soufflé dish or Pyrex baking dish.
7. Bake in a preheated 375° oven for 5 minutes. Reduce the heat to 350° and bake approximately 20 minutes longer, or until done. The outside should be crusty and brown, and the inside fluffy and still slightly soft and runny in the center. Serve immediately with strawberry sauce, raspberry sauce, or Chocolate Sauce (p. 24).

Soufflé au Chocolat Monblason
Chocolate Soufflé Monblason

SERVES 6.

2 *squares unsweetened baking chocolate*
⅓ *cup superfine sugar*
2 *teaspoons instant coffee dissolved in ⅓ cup hot water*
4 *tablespoons sweet butter*
2 *tablespoons flour*
1 *cup milk, scalded*
4 *egg yolks*
1 *tablespoon vanilla extract*
7 *egg whites*
⅛ *teaspoon cream of tartar*
3 *tablespoons superfine sugar*
1 *cup Crème Chantilly (p. 22)*

1. Melt the chocolate over hot water in a double boiler. Add the ⅓ cup sugar and stir. Then add the coffee which has been dissolved in the hot water.

2. In a saucepan, melt the butter. Add the flour and cook together for a few minutes, making sure not to let the mixture get brown. Gradually add the milk, cooking and stirring until you have a smooth white sauce. Then add the chocolate mixture. Set aside to cool.

3. When the mixture is fairly cool, add the egg yolks, stirring well, and then the vanilla.

4. Beat the egg whites with the cream of tartar until stiff, but not dry, with an electric mixer. Add the 3 tablespoons of sugar and beat for 1 minute more.

5. Fold the beaten egg whites gently into the chocolate sauce. Pour the mixture into a buttered 2- to 2½-quart Pyrex dish.

6. Bake at 375° for 5 minutes. Then reduce the heat to 350° and bake approximately 20 minutes longer, or until done. The outside should be crusty and brown, the inside fluffy and still slightly soft and runny in the center. Serve immediately with the Crème Chantilly.

Soufflé au Café
Coffee Soufflé

SERVES 6 TO 8.

4 *tablespoons sweet butter*
4 *tablespoons flour*
1½ *tablespoons powdered instant coffee*
½ *cup superfine sugar*
1½ *cups milk, scalded*
5 *egg yolks*
1 *tablespoon vanilla extract*
8 *egg whites*
⅛ *teaspoon cream of tartar*
4 *tablespoons superfine sugar*
1 *cup Crème Chantilly (p. 22)*

1. In a saucepan, melt the butter. Add the flour and cook together for a few minutes, making sure not to let the mixture get brown.

2. Dissolve the coffee and the ½ cup of sugar in the milk.

3. Gradually add the milk to the butter and flour, cooking and stirring until you get a smooth thick sauce. Cool the sauce.

4. When the mixture is fairly cool, add the egg yolks, stirring well, and then the vanilla.

5. Beat the egg whites with the cream of tartar until stiff, but not dry, with an electric mixer. Add the 4 tablespoons of sugar and beat for 1 minute more.

6. Fold the egg whites gently into the coffee sauce. Pour the mixture into a well-buttered 2½- to 3-quart soufflé dish or Pyrex baking dish.

7. Bake at 375° for 5 minutes. Reduce the heat to 350° and bake approximately 20 minutes longer, or until done. The outside should be crusty and brown, and the inside fluffy and still slightly soft and runny in the center. Serve immediately with the Crème Chantilly.

Soufflé au Citron
Lemon Soufflé

SERVES 8.

2 *tablespoons sweet butter*
2 *tablespoons flour*

¾ *cup milk*
¾ *cup granulated sugar*
Rind of 1 *lemon, finely grated*
⅓ *cup lemon juice*
5 *egg yolks*
1 *teaspoon vanilla extract*
½ *teaspoon lemon extract*
8 *egg whites*
¼ *teaspoon cream of tartar*
*Garnishes: whipped cream, Mandarin oranges with Cointreau
or Grand Marnier, or strawberry sauce*

1. In a saucepan, melt the butter and stir in the flour. Cook over low heat for a few minutes, making sure not to let the mixture brown.

2. In another saucepan, scald the milk and add all but 2 table-spoons of the sugar.

3. Gradually add the scalded milk and sugar to the butter-flour mixture, stirring and cooking over low heat until you have a smooth, thick white sauce.

4. Add the lemon rind and stir. Remove from the heat and cool slightly.

5. Stir in the lemon juice and egg yolks. Mix well.

6. Add the vanilla and the lemon extract.

7. Beat the egg whites until they stand in soft peaks. Add the cream of tartar and the 2 tablespoons of sugar gradually. Continue beating until the whites stand in stiff peaks, but are not dry.

8. Stir a little of the whites into the cooked mixture and very carefully fold in the rest of the egg whites. If the saucepan you cooked the sauce in is too small to hold the entire soufflé mixture, as is often the case, you can reverse the operation and gently pour the sauce onto the egg whites in a large bowl. This folding operation must be done quickly but gently. The secret of a light soufflé is the amount of air that is incorporated into the whites during the beating and kept inside of the soufflé mixture during the folding. You can also pour the sauce into a large bowl, and then add ¼ of the egg whites, folding gently, and then the remaining egg whites, folding quickly but gently.

9. Pour the mixture into a well-buttered 2½- to 3-quart soufflé dish or Pyrex baking dish.

10. Bake in a preheated 375° oven for 10 minutes. Reduce the heat to 325° for 15 to 20 minutes longer, or until the soufflé is puffed and brown on top. Lemon Soufflé can be served with whipped cream,

Mandarin oranges to which some Cointreau or Grand Marnier has been added, or a strawberry sauce.

Soufflé aux Fruits Confits Monblason
Soufflé with Candied Fruits Monblason

SERVES 8.

1 *cup candied fruits Nesselrode*
¼ *cup brandy*
5 *tablespoons sweet butter*
3½ *tablespoons flour*
7 *tablespoons superfine sugar*
1 *cup boiling milk*
5 *egg yolks*
⅓ *cup Grand Marnier or other orange liqueur*
8 *egg whites*
¼ *teaspoon cream of tartar*
6 *ladyfingers, cut into small pieces*
1½ *cups Crème Chantilly (p. 22)*

1. Marinate the candied fruits in the brandy for 2 hours.
2. Melt the butter and add the flour, stirring to blend well. Add ¼ cup of the sugar to the boiled milk and gradually add the milk to the butter-flour mixture, stirring until you have a smooth white sauce.
3. Cool the sauce to lukewarm. Add the egg yolks, mixing well, and set aside.
4. Stir in the fruits and brandy and the Grand Marnier.
5. Approximately 45 minutes before serving, beat the egg whites with the cream of tartar until stiff, using the electric mixer at full speed. When the whites begin to stiffen, add 3 tablespoons of the sugar, 1 tablespoon at a time, until the eggs are meringue-like, but not dry.
6. Mix a small portion of the beaten whites with the sauce in a double boiler and pour the entire mixture over the rest of the whites in the bowl and fold gently together. The more air you can keep in the batter by folding gently, the higher your soufflé will rise.
7. Pour ⅓ of the batter into a buttered 3-quart soufflé dish or Pyrex bowl. Spread ½ of the ladyfingers on top. Add another ⅓ of the batter, the other ½ of the ladyfingers, and then the rest of the batter. You should have about ¾ inch left at the top. Sprinkle the top lightly with some superfine sugar.

8. Place soufflé in 375° oven and bake for 5 minutes. Then reduce heat to 325° and bake 20 to 30 minutes longer, depending on how soft or well done you want the center. As soon as it is done, it must be served, or it will begin to fall. Each portion should be spooned lightly from the dish to the plate and topped by a spoonful of Crème Chantilly.

Soufflé aux Prunes Mirabelles
Mirabelle Plum Soufflé

This is an expensive soufflé to make, but an elegant one to serve at the end of a small dinner party. Follow the directions for Basic Vanilla Soufflé (p. 352), adding ½ cup imported canned Mirabelle plums, sliced in tiny pieces, plus ¼ cup Mirabelle liqueur. Decrease the amount of vanilla to 1 tablespoon of extract.

Soufflé de Pruneaux à la Georges Balanchine
Prune Soufflé à la George Balanchine

One day, while I was working in Sarasota, Florida, as chef to John Ringling North, the boss asked me if I would be willing to let George Balanchine, the celebrated choreographer, use my kitchen on a certain day. George wanted to show to the guests that he too had talent as a cook. He wanted to prepare a Russian culinary dinner for them. I told Mr. North that it would be fine, and that I would be glad to vacate the kitchen and go fishing. "Oh, no," he retorted. "I don't mean that. I just want you to stand by and watch in case of emergency. You may have to save us from starvation."

George started out beautifully by making a ring of good-looking Russian pastry, the center filled with delicious cooked cabbage mixed in a tasty sauce. So far so good.

While the guests were eating the Russian delicacy, our talented choreographer began to prepare a prune soufflé. Everything to me seemed to be all right, except for one thing. The soufflé had no base to hold it together. Prunes, yes. Whites of egg, yes. But no flour, no egg yolks, no flavoring. George did not feel disturbed by my presence, but he didn't ask me any questions and gave me the impression that he wanted to be left alone.

With apprehension, I waited for the moment when the soufflé

would be ready. At first, the soufflé rose majestically, and the butler prepared himself to take it into the dining room to be served. The butler did not run fast enough, however. The soufflé refused to cooperate and fell in a layer of prunes and egg whites only two inches high.

The roof came down. The dozen or so show business celebrities who were in the dining room exploded laughing and gave Mr. Balanchine the worst ribbing of his life—all in fun, of course.

Knowing that even the greatest chef can have a failure in the kitchen, the boss had asked me beforehand to have another dish ready to serve just in case. It took me only a couple of minutes to unmold a "Bombe Glacée," a combination of three different-flavored ice creams that I had made the day before.

I know that George could teach me a great deal about how to dance. As a fond remembrance of that day in the kitchen, I dedicate to him this version of Prune Soufflé.

SERVES 8.

2 cups dried prunes
½ cup granulated sugar
4 tablespoons sweet butter
2½ tablespoons flour
1 cup milk, scalded
4 egg yolks
¼ cup Grand Marnier or other orange liqueur
8 egg whites
⅛ tablespoon cream of tartar
2 tablespoons superfine sugar
2 cups Vanilla Sauce (p. 23)

1. Stew the prunes in just enough water to cover them, adding ¼ cup of the sugar. Simmer until tender. Drain. Remove the pits and put the prunes through a blender to make a smooth puree.

2. In a double boiler, melt the butter. Stir in the flour and cook together for a few minutes until golden but not browned. Gradually add the milk mixed with ¼ cup of the sugar. Continue cooking and stirring over low heat until you have a smooth white sauce. Add the prune pulp and cool.

3. When cooled to lukewarm, add the egg yolks and the Grand Marnier or other orange liqueur. Set aside.

4. Approximately 45 minutes before the soufflé is to be served, beat the egg whites with the cream of tartar. When they start to stiffen,

add the 2 tablespoons of sugar, 1 tablespoon at a time, and continue beating until they are stiff but not dry. Make sure to use the electric mixer at high speed when beating the egg whites.

5. Stir a little of the whites into the cooked mixture and very carefully fold in the rest of the egg whites.

6. Pour the batter into a well-buttered 2½-quart soufflé dish or Pyrex bowl. Sprinkle the top with additional superfine sugar and bake on the center rack of a preheated 375° oven for 8 minutes. Reduce the heat to 325° and bake about 20 minutes more, or until the soufflé is done—crusty on the outside and soft in the middle. Do not overcook. Serve with Vanilla Sauce.

Gâteau de Crème au Chocolat
Cream Cake with Chocolate Frosting

SERVES 8.

3 *eggs*
1 *cup superfine sugar*
2 *cups cake flour*
½ *teaspoon salt*
2 *teaspoons baking powder*
1¼ *cups heavy cream*
1½ *teaspoons vanilla extract*
Butter for greasing cake pans
2 *cups Chocolate Frosting* (*p.* 360)

1. In a small mixing bowl, beat the eggs thoroughly with the sugar.

2. Into a large mixing bowl sift the flour, salt, and baking powder.

3. Add the eggs, beating well. Then add the cream, continuing to beat until the cake mixture is smooth. Add the vanilla.

4. Pour the mixture either into 2 9-inch layer pans, or into an 8- x 8- x 2-inch cake pan. Butter the cake pans well. Bake in a preheated 350° oven until the cake shrinks from the sides of the pan and a toothpick inserted into the center comes out clean. This will take about 30 minutes if you are using layer pans, and between 40 to 50 minutes in

the square pan. Cool. Remove from pans and cover with Chocolate Frosting.

Chocolate Frosting

MAKES 3 CUPS.

5 *squares unsweetened baking chocolate*
¾ *cup sweet butter, softened*
1 *whole egg*
2 *egg yolks*
1 *cup superfine sugar*
2 *tablespoons powdered instant coffee*
⅓ *cup heavy cream*

1. Melt the chocolate in the top of a double boiler over simmering water.
2. In an electric mixer bowl, cream the butter with the egg and egg yolks.
3. Add the sugar and mix well.
4. Pour the melted chocolate into the mixture, then the instant coffee, and beat until well blended.
5. Pour in the cream and continue beating until smooth. If the frosting is too soft to spread, refrigerate it until it is of good spreading consistency. Spread evenly on the top, sides, and between the layers of the cake.

Gâteau de Fruits de l'Anniversaire
Birthday Fruit Cake

SERVES 8.

3¼ *cups flour*
1 *teaspoon baking powder*
1 *cup sweet butter*
4 *eggs*
¼ *teaspoon salt*
1 *cup superfine sugar*
⅓ *cup light corn syrup*
⅓ *cup light cream*

¼ *cup light rum*
2 *teaspoons vanilla extract*
1½ *cups candied fruits, diced*
1 *cup chopped walnuts or mixed nuts* (*no peanuts*)
¾ *cup dark raisins*
½ *cup white raisins*
¾ *cup currants*
Butter for greasing cake pans

1. Sift 3 cups of the flour together with the baking powder in a large mixing bowl.

2. Add the butter which has been cut into small pieces and cream together with an electric mixer until thoroughly blended.

3. Beat the eggs with the salt and sugar until light and thick.

4. Add the egg mixture to the flour mixture and mix until well blended.

5. Add the syrup, cream, rum, and vanilla.

6. In a bowl, mix the candied fruits, nuts, raisins, and currants with the remaining ¼ cup of flour.

7. Stir all these ingredients into the batter.

8. Place the batter into two well-buttered 9- x 5- x 3-inch loaf pans and bake in a preheated 350° oven for 10 minutes.

9. Reduce the oven temperature to 325° and continue the baking for 1½ hours, or until the cakes are done. To keep the cakes from burning on top, after 20 minutes of baking, place a piece of aluminum foil on top of each. When the cakes are cold, wrap them tightly in aluminum foil. They can be kept for a few days to improve the flavor and texture.

Gâteau Génois au Moka
French Butter Cake with Mocha Frosting

This cake is made without baking powder, and all the instructions must be followed very carefully. The most important things are to have all the ingredients at room temperature and to bake the cake in a preheated 350° oven.

SERVES 8.

Butter for greasing pans
½ *cup sweet butter*

6 *large eggs*
1 *cup superfine sugar*
1½ *teaspoons pure vanilla extract*
1½ *teaspoons lemon rind, finely grated*
1 *cup sifted cake flour*
3 *cups Mocha Frosting* (*see below*)
Garnish: chopped walnuts or toasted almonds

1. Prepare 3 9-inch layer pans by buttering them, then lining the bottoms with wax paper and buttering the wax paper. Set aside.

2. Clarify the butter by melting it. Pour off the yellow liquid and discard the milky residue. Set aside and keep warm.

3. Break the eggs into a lukewarm mixing bowl and beat until they are foamy.

4. Gradually, beat in the sugar at high speed until light and the volume has doubled. Be sure the sugar is well incorporated into the eggs.

5. Add the vanilla and lemon rind.

6. Stir in the flour, 2 tablespoons at a time, then the clarified butter, 1 tablespoon at a time.

7. Pour the batter into the 3 prepared cake pans. Bake at 350° for 25 to 35 minutes, or until done.

Mocha Frosting

MAKES 3 CUPS.

5 *squares unsweetened baking chocolate*
1 *cup sweet butter, softened*
5 *egg yolks*
1 *cup superfine sugar*
2 *tablespoons powdered instant coffee*
1 *teaspoon vanilla extract*
1 *tablespoon rum, or brandy*

1. Melt the chocolate in the top of a double boiler and set aside to cool.

2. Beat the softened butter in an electric mixer until creamy.

3. Alternately add 1 of the egg yolks and a little of the sugar, beating well until it is all well-blended and creamy.

4. Pour in the cooked melted chocolate and continue beating until mixed.

5. Beat in the coffee, vanilla, and rum or brandy.

6. Spread the frosting between the layers and over the top and sides of the cake and cover with chopped walnuts or toasted almonds.

Pâte Ordinaire
Basic Short Paste

I always use partially baked pastry crusts for open pies and quiches, and fully baked crusts for tarts filled with pastry cream and fresh fruit or berries. When baking the pastry, I always have a smaller pie dish to set inside the pastry-filled pie dish which holds it in place during the baking and keeps it from rising. When the crust starts to brown slightly, I remove the smaller dish. Then I either use the crust as is (for quiches) or finish the baking (for open fruit tarts).

1 *cup cake flour*
⅛ *teaspoon salt*
1 *tablespoon superfine sugar*
5 *tablespoons sweet butter*
1 *tablespoon vegetable shortening*
2½ *tablespoons ice water*

1. Sift the flour together with the salt and sugar and mix well.

2. Add the butter and shortening and blend thoroughly with your fingers or a pastry blender. Stir in the water and rapidly work the dough into a ball.

3. Refrigerate for 2 to 3 hours. When the dough is cold, it will roll out more easily.

4. Place the dough on a floured board; then press it into a fairly flat circle. Work fast, because if the dough gets soft, it will be difficult to handle. While it is still cold, roll it out thinly approximately ⅛-inch thick.

Pâte Sucrée
Delicate Short Paste

This pastry is more delicate than the Basic Short Paste (above). I often use this recipe for fresh fruit tarts, like strawberry and raspberry, made with pastry cream, and also for baked fruit tarts, such as apple and plum. For fresh fruit tarts, the pastry must be fully baked. For a baked apple tart, for example, I bake it until it is just lightly colored, and finish the baking when the parcooked apple filling is added.

1½ *cups cake flour*
4 *tablespoons superfine sugar*
⅛ *teaspoon baking powder*
6 *tablespoons sweet butter*
1 *egg, beaten*
1 *teaspoon cold water*
1 *teaspoon vanilla extract*

1. Sift together the flour, sugar, and baking powder.
2. Add the butter and blend with your fingers or a pastry blender.
3. Stir in the egg, water, and vanilla. Form the dough into a ball.
4. Wrap in wax paper and refrigerate for about 2 hours. When the dough is cold enough for easy handling, quickly roll it out on a floured pastry board. Do not let the pastry get warm. Working quickly is essential. When rolled to approximately ⅛ inch thick it is ready for use.

Tarte aux Pommes à l'Abricot
Apple Pie with Apricot Sauce

SERVES 8.

8 *medium-sized cooking apples*
8 *tablespoons sweet butter*
⅓ *cup granulated sugar*
Grated rind of 1 *lemon*
1 *recipe Delicate Short Paste* (*p.* 363) *or Basic Short Paste*
    (*p.* 363)
1 *cup Apricot Sauce* (*below*)
½ *cup toasted slivered almonds*

Apricot Sauce:
¾ *cup apricot jam*
⅓ *cup brandy, rum, or orange liqueur*

1. Peel, core, and slice the apples and simmer them in 4 tablespoons of the butter and the sugar until slightly tender.

2. Add the lemon rind and stir. Set aside.

3. Prepare the dough for your pie according to the directions on pp. 363–364.

4. Grease a round 9-inch pie plate or a rectangular 1½- x 7- x 11-inch tart pan very generously with the remaining 4 tablespoons of butter.

5. Line the pan to the rim with the pastry dough. Arrange the apples evenly in the pan. Fold the dough down to the level of the apples and with a fork make ridges along the top of the dough.

6. Bake in a preheated 400° oven for 20 minutes. Reduce the heat to 325° and bake for another 20 minutes. Do not refrigerate.

7. Combine the apricot jam with the brandy, rum, or liqueur. Place a portion of the pie on each plate and spread with 2 tablespoons of the sauce. Sprinkle some almonds on each portion. Serve warm.

Tarte aux Pommes à la Vosgienne
Apple Pie à la Vosgienne

---

1 *recipe Basic Short Paste* (*p.* 363)
6 *medium-sized cooking apples, peeled, cored, and*
   cut into segments
3 *to 4 tablespoons sweet butter*
3 *to 4 tablespoons granulated sugar*
1½ *cups light cream*
6 *tablespoons superfine sugar*
2 *eggs*
1 *teaspoon vanilla extract*

1. Follow the instructions for making a bottom pie shell on p. 363, baking at 350° in a 9-inch pie plate for 15 to 20 minutes or until slightly brown. Use an empty pie plate to weigh down unfilled crust while baking to prevent buckling. Set aside to cool slightly.

2. Place the apple segments into a baking dish with the butter and granulated sugar depending on the sweetness or tartness of the apples. Bake in a preheated 300° oven for about 1 hour, or until the moisture from the apples has almost evaporated and the sugar is slightly caramelized. Set aside. Raise the oven temperature to 400°.

3. Heat the cream and 4 tablespoons of the superfine sugar together over moderate heat.

4. In a mixing bowl, beat the eggs thoroughly. Then gradually add the heated cream and sugar, beating until well blended. Add the vanilla.

5. Pour a thin layer of the egg-cream mixture into the bottom of the partially baked pie shell.

6. Place the cooked apples in the shell and pour over them the rest of the egg-cream mixture.

7. Bake the pie in a 400° oven for 10 minutes. Then lower the oven temperature to 300° for 20 to 25 minutes, or until the custard is set. A knife inserted into the center of the custard should come out clean.

8. Sprinkle the remaining 2 tablespoons of sugar evenly over the top of the pie. Put it under the broiler until the top of the pie is glazed, but not burned. Remove and cool. Serve warm or at room temperature.

Tarte au Citron avec Amandes
Lemon Pie with Almonds

SERVES 8.

1 *recipe Basic Short Paste* (*p.* 363)
6 *ounces almond paste*
½ *cup light cream*
1 *large apple, peeled and cut fine*
4 *large lemons, peeled and segmented*
½ *cup powdered sugar*
2 *eggs*
1 *cup heavy cream*
3 *tablespoons superfine sugar, plus a little more*

1. Follow the instructions for making a bottom pie crust on p. 363, baking at 350° in a 9-inch pie plate for 15 to 20 minutes, or until slightly browned. Make sure the unfilled crust is weighted down by another pie plate while baking to prevent buckling. Set aside to cool.

2. Combine the almond paste and the light cream in the top of a double boiler over simmering water. Mix together into a smooth warm paste.

3. Add the apple pieces. Arrange the paste on the bottom of the pie crust.

4. On top of the almond paste, arrange the peeled lemon segments in a pattern to cover the paste. Spread with ¼ cup of the powdered sugar.

5. In a small bowl, combine and heat the eggs and the heavy cream. Add to that the other ¼ cup of powdered sugar.

6. Pour this mixture into the pie shell over the almond paste and lemons. Sprinkle with the superfine sugar and bake in a preheated 400° oven for 5 minutes. Then reduce the heat to 300° and bake for an additional 20 to 30 minutes, or until the custard is set. It is ready when you insert a knife into the center and it comes out clean. Serve lukewarm or at room temperature.

NOTE: During the baking, you can sprinkle a little more superfine sugar on top. It will give the pie a nice brown color.

Tarte aux Pêches à l'Abricot
Peach Pie with Apricot Sauce

SERVES 8.

2 *large cans peach halves, Elberta-type*
8 *tablespoons sweet butter*
¼ *cup granulated sugar*
Grated rind of 1 *lemon*
1 *recipe Delicate Short Paste* (*p.* 363) *or Basic Short Paste*
      (*p.* 363)
4 *tablespoons sweet butter for tart pan*
1 *recipe Apricot Sauce* (*p.* 364)
½ *cup slivered toasted almonds*

1. Drain the syrup from the peaches. In a large skillet, simmer the peaches in the butter and sugar, turning them 1 or 2 times until they are slightly browned. Do not let them burn.

2. Spread a little of the lemon rind on each peach half.

3. Prepare the dough as indicated on pp. 363–364 and fill with the fruit as described in the recipe for Apple Pie with Apricot Sauce on p. 364.

4. Bake in a preheated 400° oven for 20 minutes. Reduce the heat to 325° and bake for another 20 minutes. Do not refrigerate.

5. Prepare the Apricot Sauce as on p. 364, using the liqueur of your choice. Place a portion of peach pie on each plate and spread with 2 tablespoons of the sauce. Sprinkle with some toasted almonds. Serve warm.

Tarte aux Prunes à l'Abricot
Plum Pie with Apricot Sauce

SERVES 8.

2 *pounds fresh plums*
4 *tablespoons sweet butter*
⅓ *to* ½ *cup granulated sugar*
1 *recipe Delicate Short Paste* (*p.* 363) *or Basic Short Paste*
    (*p.* 363)
4 *tablespoons sweet butter for tart pan*
Apricot Sauce (*p.* 364), *made with brandy, kirsch, Grand*
    Marnier, or Mirabelle
½ *cup slivered toasted almonds*

1. Wash the plums. Slice each plum in half and remove the pit.
2. Sauté the plums in the butter with the sugar until tender.
3. Prepare the dough as indicated on pp. 363–364 and fill with the fruit as described in the recipe for Apple Pie with Apricot Sauce on p. 364.
4. Bake in a preheated 400° oven for 20 minutes. Reduce the heat to 325° and bake for another 20 minutes. Do not refrigerate.
5. Prepare the Apricot Sauce as described on p. 364, using the liqueur of your choice. Place a portion of plum pie on each plate and spread with 2 tablespoons of the sauce. Sprinkle with some toasted almonds. Serve warm.

Tarte au Fromage Frais
Fresh Cheese Pie

SERVES 6 TO 8.

1 *recipe Basic Short Paste* (*p.* 363)
1 *8-ounce package cream cheese*
7 *tablespoons sweet butter*
½ *cup superfine sugar*
¼ *teaspoon freshly grated or ground nutmeg*
2 *eggs*

1. Prepare pie pastry according to directions on p. 363.

2. Cream the cheese, butter, sugar, and nutmeg with an electric mixer until well blended.

3. Add the eggs and blend for another 2 minutes.

4. Pour the mixture into the partially baked pie crust and bake in a preheated 400° oven for 5 minutes.

5. Reduce the oven temperature to 325° and bake for approximately 20 to 25 minutes longer. The cheese pie is done when it is puffed and browned on top, or when you insert a knife into the center and it comes out clean. This pie can be served hot or cold.

Gâteau de Fromage à la Village
Country-Style Cheesecake

SERVES 10 TO 12.

4 *tablespoons sweet butter*
½ *cup graham cracker crumbs, or more if needed*
2 *pounds cream cheese, at room temperature*
¾ *cup heavy cream*
1½ *cups superfine sugar*
Grated rind of 1½ lemons and juice of same
6 *whole eggs, slightly beaten*
1½ *teaspoons vanilla extract*

1. Grease the inside of a soufflé dish or Pyrex dish measuring at least 9 inches in diameter and 3¼ inches deep generously with the butter. Sprinkle the butter with the graham cracker crumbs. Tap lightly with the tips of your fingers. Reserve the excess crumbs for the top.

2. Place the cream cheese in the bowl of an electric mixer. Start beating at low speed.

3. Add the cream and then the sugar and the rind of the lemons.

4. Continue beating, adding the eggs, lemon juice, and vanilla. Increase the beating speed until all the ingredients are well blended and smooth.

5. Pour the batter into the prepared dish and sprinkle the rest of the crumbs on top.

6. Place the baking dish into a large baking pan and fill the pan with boiling water to a depth of 1¼ inches. Bake in a preheated 325° oven for about 1½ hours. Turn off the oven and let the dish sit in the oven for another ½ hour. To prevent the top from burning, 10 minutes

after the baking time has begun, you can put a piece of wax paper over the top of the cake.

7. Let the cake pan stand on a rack until it cools off. Then put a large serving plate over the cake and carefully reverse it to unmold the cake.

NOTE: This cake should be served as it is without any garnish. It is smooth, delicate, and rich, and the addition of any sauce or fruits would actually detract from its flavor.

Crêpes Suzette
Crepes Suzette

MAKES APPROXIMATELY 24 CREPES.

Crepe Batter:
3 *eggs*
3 *egg yolks*
1 *cup milk*
½ *cup cold water*
⅓ *cup superfine sugar*
2 *cups flour*
½ *cup sweet butter, melted*
¼ *cup brandy*
1 *tablespoon vanilla extract*
Sweet butter for frying crepes

1. With an electric mixer, beat the eggs and egg yolks together with the milk and water for 1 minute.

2. Beat in the sugar and then the flour, a little at a time. When the flour is absorbed and not lumpy, beat at a higher speed until you have a smooth batter.

3. Add the melted butter, brandy, and vanilla. Cover and refrigerate overnight.

4. If you do not have a crepe pan, you can use a regular 5- or 6-inch frying pan. Melt a small piece of butter in the pan. Pour a small amount of batter in, just enough to cover the bottom in a thin layer. If the batter does not run freely and seems too thick, add a little more milk.

5. As soon as the crepe is lightly browned on one side, flip it over

and fry it quickly on the other side. The entire process should only take about 2 minutes if your frying pan is hot enough. Melt a small piece, approximately ¼ teaspoon, of butter in the pan before you fry each crepe.

Butter Sauce

½ *cup sweet butter*
¼ *cup granulated sugar*
Grated rind of 1 *orange*
1 *teaspoon vanilla extract*
Juice of 2 *oranges, strained*
2 *tablespoons superfine sugar*
⅓ *cup orange liqueur or Grand Marnier*
⅓ *cup cognac*

1. Fold the crepes in quarters and have them ready to put into the pan of a chafing dish.

2. In a small mixing bowl, blend together the butter, sugar, orange rind, and vanilla.

3. Place this seasoned butter in the chafing dish. When the butter is foaming, add the orange juice. Stir the mixture and be careful not to burn the butter.

4. Simmer and reduce the liquid by about a third. Carefully place the crepes in the pan. Move them about a little and after 1 or 2 minutes turn them over.

5. When the liquid has been absorbed by the crepes, sprinkle the crepes with the superfine sugar. Pour the liqueur or Grand Marnier and cognac all over them. Ignite and baste the crepes with the flaming liqueur. When the flames die down, start serving.

Crêpes aux Pêches Monblason
Peach Crepes Monblason

This dessert is my own creation. It is a sensational blending of flavors with the crepes, peaches, vanilla ice cream, Melba sauce, and cherry liqueur. If you add some sour cherries to the crepe batter as I do, you will really have a unique dessert.

SERVES 8.

8 *peach halves, canned Elberta or white peaches, or* 4 *fresh poached peaches in season, halved*

8 *crepes* (*p.* 370)
1 16-*ounce can pitted, sour cherries, drained and halved*
    (*optional*)
8 *scoops vanilla ice cream*
1 *cup prepared Melba sauce*
Half jigger cherry liqueur for each portion

1. Drain the peach halves of their syrup and set aside.
2. Make 8 crepes according to the directions on p. 370, using a skillet or crepe pan slightly smaller than your dessert plates. Keep the crepes warm until serving time. If you wish, you can add some split, pitted, canned sour cherries to the crepe batter.
3. Place a crepe on each serving plate and put a scoop of vanilla ice cream on top. Then place a peach half, flat side down, on each ice cream scoop. Pour the Melba sauce and cherry liqueur, equally divided, over all. Serve immediately.

Gaufres à la Française
French Dessert Waffles

I consider waffles a delicacy for Sunday breakfast, but in France it is considered a dessert. Try them hot with a scoop of vanilla ice cream, topped with fresh or frozen strawberry sauce. If you want to serve them for breakfast, the ideal accompaniments are maple syrup, bacon, or broiled sausages.

MAKES 12 WAFFLES.

1¾ *cups cake flour*
2 *teaspoons double-action baking powder*
1½ *teaspoons salt*
3 *egg yolks*
1 *cup milk*
1 *teaspoon vanilla extract*
5 *tablespoons sweet butter, melted*
3 *egg whites*

1. In the bowl of an electric mixer, combine the cake flour, baking powder, and salt.
2. Then add the egg yolks and milk, beating until smooth.

3. Add the vanilla and blend.

4. Pour in the butter and mix well.

5. Beat the egg whites until stiff but not dry and fold them gently into the batter. Bake in a hot waffle iron.

Fruits
Fruits

The French never use fruits with a salad dressing, but rejoice in eating a mixture of fresh or canned fruits flavored with champagne, raspberry, kirsch, or Grand Marnier liqueurs. Maraschino liqueur is also delicious with fruit.

Macédoine de Fruits Rafraîchis au Kirsch
Fruit Salad with Kirsch

Fruit assortment of your choice:
  Oranges, peeled and sliced
  Raspberries, hulled and sliced
  Whole strawberries, hulled and sliced
  Apples
  Apricots
  Pears }*—peeled, cored, and sliced*
  Fresh pineapple
  Grapes
  Bananas, peeled and sliced
Juice of 2 oranges
Juice of 1 lemon
Superfine sugar
Kirsch or other liqueur

1. Prepare the fruit and put it all into a bowl.

2. In another bowl, combine the orange and lemon juice and super-fine sugar to taste.

3. Pour the juice over the fruit and chill in the refrigerator for three hours.

4. Just before serving, add kirsch or another liqueur of your choice, 1 tablespoon at a time, until you arrive at the flavor you like.

Macédoine de Fruits Rafraîchis au Champagne
Fruit Salad with Champagne

SERVES 6 TO 8.

2 *pears, peeled and sliced*
2 *peaches, peeled and sliced*
4 *apricots, peeled and sliced*
1½ *wedges fresh pineapple*
24 *white grapes*
24 *sweet cherries*
2 *cups orange juice*
Juice of 1 *lemon*
2 *teaspoons vanilla extract*
Superfine sugar to taste
1 *cup dry champagne, or liqueur of your choice*

1. Put the fruit into a deep bowl.
2. Mix together the orange and lemon juice and the vanilla.
3. Add superfine sugar to taste.
4. Pour over the fruit and chill in the refrigerator for 3 hours.
5. Just before serving, add 1 cup of dry champagne, or liqueur of your choice to taste.

Pommes Cuites au Miel
Baked Apples with Honey

Apples vary greatly in their tartness, so it is difficult to advise the exact quantity of sugar to use when preparing baked apples. Only by tasting can the correct amount of sugar be determined. Before basting the apples, you have to add sugar to the liquid in the pan and if some of the liquid evaporates during the baking, you will need to add a little more. Just keep tasting the liquid in the pan so that when the apples are done you will have a nice syrup to pour over them.

SERVES 6.

6 *large baking apples* (*Rome Beauty or Northern Spy*)
6 *teaspoons sweet butter*
6 *tablespoons of honey*
Freshly grated or ground nutmeg
Granulated sugar
Garnish: whipped cream or vanilla ice cream

1. Wash the apples thoroughly as they are usually coated with spray when you buy them in the market. Core them ⅔ of the way down, being careful not to break through to the bottom. Slice off about an ⅛ inch from the top of the apple in one flat piece. On the outside of the apple, make short incisions through the skin all around about a third of the way down. This helps to keep the skin from breaking during the baking.

2. Place the apples in a baking pan. In each cavity, put 1 teaspoon of butter, 1 tablespoon of honey, and a dash of nutmeg and cover the flat top of the apple with a thin layer of granulated sugar.

3. Pour 1 inch of hot water into the pan and simmer in a pre-heated 350° oven for 30 minutes.

4. Then start basting the apples with the liquid in the pan, tasting for sweetness and adding more sugar to the liquid if necessary. Continue baking for another 30 minutes, or until done.

5. Sprinkle more granulated sugar on top of each apple to cover it completely. Then turn on the broiler and leave the oven door open so you can watch the apples. The sugar will melt and cook to form a stiff, slightly caramelized crust. Watch the apples very carefully, as the sugar can burn very quickly.

6. Let the apples cool off before serving. About 1 or 2 tablespoons of whipped cream or vanilla ice cream can be added as a garnish on each apple.

Pommes Cuites à la Grand-mère
Baked Apples with White Wine

This recipe is almost exactly the same as Baked Apples with Honey, except that you substitute ½ cup dry white wine for the honey and divide it equally among the 6 cavities. Follow the rest of the instructions as indicated.

Pommes Cuites Monblason
Baked Apples Monblason

These are home-style baked apples with a filling of raisins, nuts, and spices which are served with heavy cream or a dollop of sweetened whipped cream.

SERVES 8.

8 *large baking apples*
½ *cup raisins*
½ *cup chopped walnuts*
½ *cup granulated sugar*
¼ *teaspoon freshly grated or ground nutmeg*
5 *tablespoons sweet butter*
1 *cup heavy cream or Crème Chantilly* (p. 22)

1. Core the baking apples without cutting through the bottom of the apples. Cut off the tops of the apples and make a few short lengthwise incisions around the tops of the apples.
2. Mix together the raisins, chopped walnuts, sugar, and nutmeg.
3. Cream the butter and blend together with the raisin-nut mixture. Make sure you have enough seasoned butter to fill the center of each apple.
4. Arrange the apples in a baking dish. Pour in 1½ cups water and bake in a preheated 350° oven, approximately 1 hour. Make sure the apples do not get overcooked, or they will fall apart.
5. Serve warm with some heavy cream or Crème Chantilly.

Charlotte de Pommes
Apple Charlotte

This dessert takes some time to prepare, but it is not difficult at all. The toasted bread, butter, apples, apricot, and rum give a most distinctive and delicious flavor. The best mold to use is a 2-quart, cylindrical, metal mold which is about 3½ to 4 inches high, often called a charlotte mold. You can substitute a 2-quart soufflé dish if you do not have a charlotte mold.

SERVES 8.

5 *pounds cooking apples*
5 *tablespoons sweet butter*
¾ *cup granulated sugar*
¾ *cup apricot preserves*
1 *tablespoon vanilla extract*
⅓ *cup rum*
12 *or more slices of white bread, depending on size and
     shape of mold*
1 *cup sweet butter, melted*
*Garnishes: Apricot Sauce with rum (p. 364), or whipped cream,
     flavored with sugar and rum*

1. Peel and core the apples and cut them into quarters. Then slice them into pieces no more than ¼ inch thick.

2. Sauté the apples with the butter and sugar in a large covered skillet over moderately low heat until tender. Uncover and continue simmering until the water content has evaporated.

3. Stir in the apricot preserves, vanilla, and rum and continue simmering until all the liquid has almost completely evaporated. You should have a thick puree, stiff enough to hold peaks.

4. Remove the crusts from the bread slices. Cut 8 or more pieces into the shape of triangles which will fit together to cover the bottom of the mold. Sauté these pieces first in butter until they are lightly browned. Then fit them into the bottom of the mold. Make sure the bottom of the mold is entirely covered by the sautéed bread.

5. Cut the rest of the slices of bread into strips 1 inch wide. Dip each strip into the melted butter and place around the inside of the mold to cover it entirely.

6. Pour the apple puree into the mold. Cover the top with more strips of bread dipped into butter and pour any remaining melted butter along the edge of the mold on top of the bread.

7. Set the mold on a baking sheet to catch any butter drippings in the center level of a preheated 400° oven. Bake from 40 to 50 minutes, or until the bread on top and sides is golden brown.

8. Remove from the oven and let it cool to firm it up. Slip a knife between the mold and the toasted bread pieces. Unmold onto a platter.

APPLE CHARLOTTE.

If done according to directions, this dessert should stand up and hold its shape nicely. Serve hot or cold with either the Apricot Sauce made with rum, or with whipped cream flavored with sugar and rum.

Melon au Porto
Melon with Port

SERVES 6.

2 *medium-sized cantaloupes*
1 *cup tawny port*
Superfine sugar
Fresh mint leaves

1. Cut the cantaloupes in half. Remove the seeds and cut the melon into balls with a melon ball cutter. You can use the leftover melon that remains in the shell for fruit salad.
2. Let the melon balls stand in the port wine with some superfine sugar to taste for about 2 hours in the refrigerator, tightly covered. The amount of sugar to be used depends on the sweetness of the melons.
3. Serve the melon and port in champagne glasses and decorate with a green mint leaf.

Poires Belle Hélène
Pears Belle Hélène

This is an impressive-looking dessert, yet quite easy to make. If you cannot select perfect pears in the fruit market, then use an excellent brand of canned pears in heavy syrup.

SERVES 8.

4 *ripe but not soft fresh pears or* 8 *high-quality canned*
        pear halves in heavy syrup
2 *cups water and ¾ cup granulated sugar, if using fresh pears*
1½ *teaspoons vanilla extract*
8 *round pieces of sponge cake*
8 *large scoops of vanilla ice cream*
   Crystallized violets, found in gourmet food stores (*optional*)
   Chocolate Sauce (*p.* 24), *hot*

1. If you use fresh pears, peel them, cut them in halves, and remove the cores. In a pan, combine the water and sugar and bring to a boil. Add the pears and simmer, covered, for about 15 to 20 minutes, or until the pears can easily be pierced with a fork. Add the vanilla, and cool in the syrup.

2. If using canned pears, add the vanilla to the syrup, and let the pears stand in the syrup for 2 hours before serving.

3. When ready to serve, drain the syrup, place a piece of cake on each plate, a scoop of vanilla ice cream on it, and half of a pear flat side down on the ice cream. Garnish with the crystallized violets if desired. Serve the hot Chocolate Sauce separately.

Index